Prentice Hall Series in Innovative Technology

Dennis R. Allison, David J. Farber, and Bruce D. Shriver   *Series Advisors*

Bhasker	*A VHDL Primer*
Blachman	*Mathematica: A Practical Approach*
Johnson	*Superscalar Microprocessor Design*
Kane and Heinrich	*MIPS RISC Architecture, Second Edition*
Lawson	*Parallel Processing in Industrial Real-Time Applications*
Nelson, ed.	*Systems Programming with Modula-3*
Nutt	*Open Systems*
Rose	*The Little Black Book: Mail-Bonding with OSI Directory Services*
Rose	*The Open Book: A Practical Perspective on OSI*
Rose	*The Simple Book: An Introduction to Management of TCP/IP-Based Internets*
Shapiro	*A C + + Toolkit*
Slater	*Microprocessor-Based Design*
SPARC International Inc.	*The SPARC Architecture Manual, Version 8*
Strom, et al.	*Hermes: A Language for Distributed Computing*
Treseler	*Designing State Machine Controllers Using Programmable Logic*
Wirfs-Brock, Wilkerson, and Weiner	*Designing Object-Oriented Software*

AT&T

A VHDL Primer

Jayaram Bhasker

American Telephone and Telegraph Company
Bell Laboratories Division

Prentice Hall
Englewood Cliffs, NJ 07632

Editorial/production supervision: *Brendan M. Stewart*
Prepress buyer: *Mary E. McCartney*
Manufacturing buyer: *Susan Brunke*
Acquisitions editor: *Karen Gettman*

 Published by Prentice-Hall, Inc.
A Simon & Schuster Company
Englewood Cliffs, New Jersey 07632

The publisher offers discounts on this book when ordered in bulk quantities. For more information, write: Special Sales/Professional Marketing, Prentice-Hall, Professional & Technical Reference Division, Englewood Cliffs, NJ 07632.

Printed in the United States of America
10   9   8   7   6   5   4   3   2

ISBN 0-13-952987-X

Prentice-Hall International (UK) Limited, *London*
Prentice-Hall of Australia Pty. Limited, *Sydney*
Prentice-Hall Canada Inc., *Toronto*
Prentice-Hall Hispanoamericana, S.A., *Mexico*
Prentice-Hall of India Private Limited, *New Delhi*
Prentice-Hall of Japan, Inc., *Tokyo*
Simon & Schuster Asia Pte. Ltd., *Singapore*
Editora Prentice-Hall do Brasil, Ltda., *Rio de Janeiro*

Dedicated to

my parents, Nagamma and Appiah Jayaram

Contents

Preface

VHDL is a hardware description language that can be used to model a digital system. It contains elements that can be used to describe the behavior or structure of the digital system, with the provision for specifying its timing explicitly. The language provides support for modeling the system hierarchically and also supports top-down and bottom-up design methodologies. The system and its subsystems can be described at any level of abstraction ranging from the architecture level to gate level. Precise simulation semantics are associated with all the language constructs, and therefore, models written in this language can be verified using a VHDL simulator.

The aim of this book is to introduce the VHDL language to the reader at the beginner's level. No prior knowledge of the language is required. The reader is, however, assumed to have some knowledge of a high-level programming language, like C or Pascal, and a basic understanding of hardware design. This text is intended for both software and hardware designers interested in learning VHDL with no specific emphasis being placed on either discipline.

VHDL is a large and verbose language with many complex constructs that have complex semantic meanings and is difficult to understand initially (VHDL is often quoted to be an acronym for Very Hard Description Language). However, it is possible to quickly understand a subset of VHDL which is both simple and easy to use. The emphasis of this text is on presenting this set of simple and commonly used features of the language so that the reader can start writing models in VHDL. These features are powerful enough to be able to model designs of large degrees of complexity.

This book is not intended to replace the IEEE Standard VHDL Language Reference Manual, the official language guide, but to complement it by explaining the complex constructs of the language using an example-based approach. Emphasis is placed on providing illustrative examples that explain the different formulations of the language constructs and their semantics. The complete syntax of language constructs is often not described, instead, the most common usage of these constructs are presented. Syntax for constructs is written in a self-explanatory fashion rather than through the use of formal terminology (the Backus-Naur Form) that is used in the Language Reference Manual. This text does not cover the entire language but concentrates on the most useful aspects.

Book organization

Chapter 1 gives a brief history of the development of the VHDL language and presents its major capabilities. Chapter 2 provides a quick tutorial to demonstrate the primary modeling features. The following chapters expand on the concepts presented in this tutorial. Chapter 3 describes the basic elements of the language such as types, subtypes, objects, and literals. It also presents the predefined operators of the language.

Chapter 4 presents the behavior style of modeling. It introduces the different sequential statements that are available and explains how they may be used to model the sequential behavior of a design. This modeling style is very similar in semantics to that of any high-level programming language. Chapter 5 describes the dataflow style of modeling. It describes concurrent signal assignment statements, and block statements, and provides examples to show how the concurrent behavior of a design may be modeled using these statements.

Chapter 6 presents the structural style of modeling. In this modeling style, a design is expressed as a set of interconnected components, possibly in a hierarchy. Component instantiation statements are explained in detail in this chapter. Chapter 7 explains the notion of an entity-architecture pair and describes how component instances can be bound to designs residing in different libraries. This chapter also explains how to pass static information into a design using generics.

Chapter 8 describes subprograms. A subprogram is a function or a procedure. The powerful concept of subprogram and operator overloading is also introduced. Chapter 9 describes packages and the design library environment as defined by the language. It also explains how items stored in one library may be accessed by a design residing in another library. Advanced features of the language such as entity statements, aliases, guarded signals, and attributes are described in Chap. 10.

Chapter 11 describes a methodology for simulating VHDL models and describes techniques for writing test benches. Examples for generating various types of clocks and waveforms and their application to the design under test are presented. Chapter 12 contains a comprehensive set of hardware modeling examples. These include among others, examples of modeling combinational logic, synchronous logic, and finite-state machines.

In all the VHDL descriptions that appear in this book, reserved words are in **boldface**. A complete list of reserved words also appears in Appendix A. Most of the language constructs are explained using easy-to-understand words, rather than through the use of formal terminology adopted in the Language Reference Manual. Also, some constructs are described only in part to explain specific features. The complete language grammar is provided in Appendix B. Appendix C contains a complete description of a package that is referred to in Chaps. 11 and 12.

In all the language constructs that appear in this book, names in *italics* indicate information to be supplied by the model writer. For example,

> **entity** *entity-name* **is**
>   [**port** (*list-of-interface-ports*)] . . .

Entity, **is**, and **port** are reserved words while *entity-name* and *list-of-interface-ports* represent information to be provided by the model writer. The square brackets, [. . .], indicate optional items. Occasionally, ellipsis (. . .) are used in VHDL source to indicate code that is not relevant to that discussion. All examples that are described in this book have been validated using a native VHDL system.

Throughout this text, we shall refer to the circuit, system, design, or whatever it is that we are trying to model as the *entity*.

This book was prepared using the FrameMaker[1] workstation publishing software.

Book usage

The first time reader of this book is strongly urged to read the tutorial presented in Chap. 2. The remaining chapters are organized such that they use information from the previous chapters. However, if the tutorial is well

---

1. FrameMaker is a registered trademark of Frame Technology Corporation.

understood, it is possible to go directly to the chapter of interest. A complete chapter has been devoted to examples on hardware modeling; this can be used as a future reference. A list of suggested readings and books on the language and the complete language syntax is provided at the end of the book. For further clarifications on the syntax and semantics of the language constructs, the reader can refer to the IEEE Standard VHDL Language Reference Manual (IEEE Std 1076-1987), published by the IEEE.

Acknowledgments

I gratefully acknowledge the efforts of several of my colleagues in making this book possible. I am especially thankful to Dinesh Bettadapur, Ray Voith, Joel Schoen, Sindhu Xirasagar, Gary Imken, Paul Harper, Oz Levia, Jeff Jones, and Guru Rao. Their constructive criticism and timely review on earlier versions of the text have resulted in several improvements in the book. A special thanks to Gary Imken for being patient enough in answering a number of questions on the idiosyncrasies of VHDL.

I would also like to thank my wife, Geetha, for reviewing the first version of this text and for providing the motivational guidance during the entire preparation of this book.

J. Bhasker

October, 1991

CHAPTER 1   *Introduction*

This chapter provides a brief history of the development of VHDL and describes the major capabilities that differentiate it from other hardware description languages. The chapter also explains the concept of an entity.

1.1   *What Is VHDL?*

VHDL is an acronym for VHSIC Hardware Description Language (VHSIC is an acronym for Very High Speed Integrated Circuits). It is a hardware description language that can be used to model a digital system at many levels of abstraction ranging from the algorithmic level to the gate level. The complexity of the digital system being modeled could vary from that of a simple gate to a complete digital electronic system, or anything in between. The digital system can also be described hierarchically. Timing can also be explicitly modeled in the same description.

The VHDL language can be regarded as an integrated amalgamation of the following languages:

> sequential language +
> concurrent language +

```
net-list language +
timing specifications +
waveform generation language       => VHDL
```

Therefore, the language has constructs that enable you to express the concurrent or sequential behavior of a digital system with or without timing. It also allows you to model the system as an interconnection of components. Test waveforms can also be generated using the same constructs. All the above constructs may be combined to provide a comprehensive description of the system in a single model.

The language not only defines the syntax but also defines very clear simulation semantics for each language construct. Therefore, models written in this language can be verified using a VHDL simulator. It is a strongly typed language and is often verbose to write. It inherits many of its features, especially the sequential language part, from the Ada[1] programming language. Because VHDL provides an extensive range of modeling capabilities, it is often difficult to understand. Fortunately, it is possible to quickly assimilate a core subset of the language that is both easy and simple to understand without learning the more complex features. This subset is usually sufficient to model most applications. The complete language, however, has sufficient power to capture the descriptions of the most complex chips to a complete electronic system.

1.2   History

The requirements for the language were first generated in 1981 under the VHSIC program. In this program, a number of U.S. companies were involved in designing VHSIC chips for the Department of Defense (DoD). At that time, most of the companies were using different hardware description languages to describe and develop their integrated circuits. As a result, different vendors could not effectively exchange designs with one another. Also, different vendors provided DoD with descriptions of their chips in different hardware description languages. Reprocurement and reuse was also a big issue. Thus, a need for a standardized hardware description language for design, documentation, and verification of digital systems was generated.

A team of three companies, IBM, Texas Instruments, and Intermetrics, were first awarded the contract by the DoD to develop a version of the language in 1983. Version 7.2 of VHDL was developed and released to the public in 1985. There was a strong industry participation throughout the VHDL lan-

---

1. Ada is a registered trademark of the U.S. Government, Ada Joint Program Office.

guage development process, especially from the companies that were developing VHSIC chips. After the release of version 7.2, there was an increasing need to make the language an industry-wide standard. Consequently, the language was transferred to the IEEE for standardization in 1986. After a substantial enhancement to the language, made by a team of industry, university, and DoD representatives, the language was standardized by the IEEE in December 1987; this version of the language is now known as the IEEE Std 1076-1987. The official language description appears in the IEEE Standard VHDL Language Reference Manual made available by the IEEE. The language described in this book is based on this standard. The language has since also been recognized as an American National Standards Institute (ANSI) standard.

The Department of Defense, since September 1988, requires all its digital Application-Specific Integrated Circuit (ASIC) suppliers to deliver VHDL descriptions of the ASICs and their subcomponents, at both the behavioral and structural levels. Test benches that are used to validate the ASIC chip at all levels in its hierarchy must also be delivered in VHDL. This set of government requirements is described in military standard 454.

1.3   Capabilities

The following are the major capabilities that the language provides along with the features that differentiate it from other hardware description languages.

- The language can be *used as an exchange medium between chip vendors and CAD tool users*. Different chip vendors can provide VHDL descriptions of their components to system designers. CAD tool users can use it to capture the behavior of the design at a high level of abstraction for functional simulation.

- The language can also be *used as a communication medium between different CAD and CAE tools*, for example, a schematic capture program may be used to generate a VHDL description for the design which can be used as an input to a simulation program.

- The language supports *hierarchy*, that is, a digital system can be modeled as a set of interconnected components; each component, in turn, can be modeled as a set of interconnected subcomponents.

- The language supports *flexible design methodologies*: top-down, bottom-up, or mixed.

- The language is *not technology-specific*, but is capable of supporting technology-specific features. It can also support various hardware technologies, for example, you may define new logic types and new components, you may also specify technology-specific attributes. By being technology independent, the same behavior model can be synthesized into different vendor libraries.

- It supports both *synchronous and asynchronous timing* models.

- Various digital modeling techniques such as finite-state machine descriptions, algorithmic descriptions, and boolean equations can be modeled using the language.

- The language is publicly available, human readable, machine readable, and above all, it is *not proprietary.*

- It is an *IEEE and ANSI standard*, and therefore, models described using this language are portable. The government also has a strong interest in maintaining this as a standard so that re-procurement and second-sourcing may become easier.

- The language supports *three basic different description styles*: structural, dataflow, and behavioral. A design may also be expressed in any combination of these three descriptive styles.

- It supports a wide *range of abstraction levels* ranging from abstract behavioral descriptions to very precise gate-level descriptions. It does not, however, support modeling at or below the transistor level. It allows a design to be captured at a mixed level using a single coherent language.

- *Arbitrarily large designs can be modeled* using the language and there are no limitations that are imposed by the language on the size of a design.

- The language has elements that make *large scale design modeling easier*, for example, components, functions, procedures, and packages.

- There is no need to learn a different language for simulation control. *Test benches can be written* using the same language to test other VHDL models.

- Nominal propagation delays, min-max delays, setup and hold timing, timing constraints, and spike detection can all be described very naturally in this language.

- The use of generics and attributes in the models *facilitate back-annotation* of static information such as timing or placement information.

- Generics and attributes are also useful in describing *parameterized designs*.

- A model can not only describe the functionality of a design, but can also contain *information about the design itself* in terms of user-defined attributes, for example, total area and speed.

- A common language can be used to describe library components from different vendors. Tools that understand VHDL models will have no difficulty in reading models from a variety of vendors since the language is a standard.

- Models written in this language can be verified by simulation since *precise simulation semantics are defined* for each language construct.

- Behavioral models that conform to a certain synthesis description style are *capable of being synthesized* to gate-level descriptions.

- The *capability of defining new data types* provides the power to describe and simulate a new design technique at a very high level of abstraction without any concern about the implementation details.

1.4   Hardware Abstraction

VHDL is used to describe a model for a digital hardware device. This model specifies the external view of the device and one or more internal views. The internal view of the device specifies the functionality or structure, while the external view specifies the interface of the device through which it communicates with the other models in its environment. Figure 1.1 shows the hardware device and the corresponding software model.

The device to device model mapping is strictly a one to many. That is, a hardware device may have many device models. For example, a device modeled at a high level of abstraction may not have a clock as one of its inputs, since the clock may not have been used in the description. Also the data transfer at the interface may be treated in terms of say, integer values, instead of logical values. In VHDL, each device model is treated as a distinct representation of a unique device, called an *entity* in this text. Figure 1.2 shows the VHDL view of a hardware device that has multiple device models, with each device model representing one entity. Even though entity 1 through N repre-

sent N different entities from the VHDL point of view, in reality they represent the same hardware device.

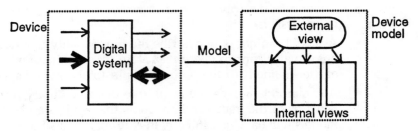

Figure 1.1 Device versus device model.

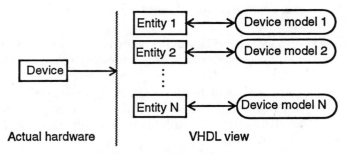

Figure 1.2 A VHDL view of a device.

The entity is thus a hardware abstraction of the actual hardware device.
Each entity is described using one model that contains one external view and
one or more internal views. At the same time, a hardware device may be represented by one or more entities.

❑

CHAPTER 2   *A Tutorial*

This chapter provides a quick introduction to the language. It describes the major modeling features of the language. At the conclusion of this chapter, you will be able to write simple VHDL models.

2.1   *Basic Terminology*

VHDL is a hardware description language that can be used to model a digital system. The digital system can be as simple as a logic gate or as complex as a complete electronic system. A hardware abstraction of this digital system is called an *entity* in this text. An entity X, when used in another entity Y, becomes a *component* for the entity Y. Therefore, a component is also an entity, depending on the level at which you are trying to model.

To describe an entity, VHDL provides five different types of primary constructs, called *design units*. They are

1. Entity declaration
2. Architecture body
3. Configuration declaration

4. Package declaration
5. Package body

An entity is modeled using an entity declaration and at least one architecture body. The entity declaration describes the external view of the entity, for example, the input and output signal names. The architecture body contains the internal description of the entity, for example, as a set of interconnected components that represents the structure of the entity, or as a set of concurrent or sequential statements that represents the behavior of the entity. Each style of representation can be specified in a different architecture body or mixed within a single architecture body. Figure 2.1 shows an entity and its model.

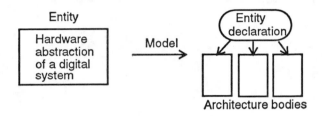

Figure 2.1 An entity and its model.

A configuration declaration is used to create a configuration for an entity. It specifies the binding of one architecture body from the many architecture bodies that may be associated with the entity. It may also specify the bindings of components used in the selected architecture body to other entities. An entity may have any number of different configurations.

A package declaration encapsulates a set of related declarations such as type declarations, subtype declarations, and subprogram declarations that can be shared across two or more design units. A package body contains the definitions of subprograms declared in a package declaration.

Figure 2.2 shows three entities called E1, E2, and E3. Entity E1 has three architecture bodies, E1_A1, E1_A2, and E1_A3. Architecture body E1_A1 is a purely behavioral model without any hierarchy. Architecture body E1_A2 uses a component called BX, while architecture body E1_A3 uses a component called CX. Entity E2 has two architecture bodies, E2_A1 and E2_A2, and architecture body E2_A1 uses a component called M1. Entity E3 has three architecture bodies, E3_A1, E3_A2, and E3_A3. Notice that each entity has a single entity declaration but more than one architecture body.

The dashed lines represent the binding that may be specified in a configuration for entity E1. There are two types of binding shown: binding of an architecture body to its entity and the binding of components used in the architecture body with other entities. For example, architecture body, E1_A3, is bound to entity E1, while architecture body, E2_A1, is bound to entity E2. Component M1 in architecture body, E2_A1, is bound to entity E3. Component CX in the architecture body, E1_A3, is bound to entity E2. However, one may choose a different configuration for entity E1 with the following bindings:

- Architecture E1_A2 is bound to its entity E1
- Component BX to entity E3
- Architecture E3_A1 is bound to its entity E3

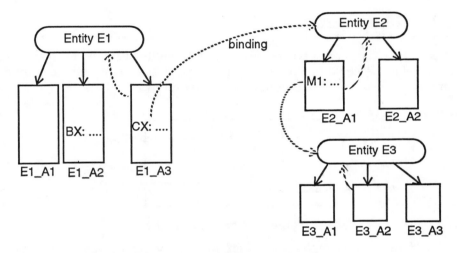

Figure 2.2 A configuration for entity E1.

Once an entity has been modeled, it needs to be validated by a VHDL system. A typical VHDL system consists of an analyzer and a simulator. The analyzer reads in one or more design units contained in a single file and compiles them into a design library after validating the syntax and performing some static semantic checks. The design library is a place in the host environment (that is, the environment that supports the VHDL system) where compiled design units are stored.

The simulator simulates an entity, represented by an entity-architecture pair or by a configuration, by reading in its compiled description from the design library and then performing the following steps:

1. Elaboration
2. Initialization
3. Simulation

A note on the language syntax. The language is case-insensitive, that is, lower-case and upper-case characters are treated alike. For example, CARRY, CarrY, or carrY, all refer to the same name. The language is also free-format, very much like in Ada and Pascal programming languages. Comments are specified in the language by preceding the text with two consecutive dashes (--). All text between the two dashes and the end of that line is treated as a comment.

The terms introduced in this section are described in greater detail in the following sections.

2.2   Entity Declaration

The entity declaration specifies the name of the entity being modeled and lists the set of interface ports. *Ports* are signals through which the entity communicates with the other models in its external environment.

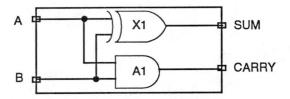

Figure 2.3 A half-adder circuit.

Here is an example of an entity declaration for the half-adder circuit shown in Fig. 2.3.

```
entity HALF_ADDER is
    port (A, B: in BIT; SUM, CARRY: out BIT);
end HALF_ADDER;
-- This is a comment line.
```

The entity, called HALF_ADDER, has two input ports, A and B (the mode **in** specifies input port), and two output ports, SUM and CARRY (the mode **out** specifies output port). BIT is a predefined type of the language; it is an enumeration type containing the character literals '0' and '1'. The port types for this entity have been specified to be of type BIT, which means that the ports can take the values, '0' or '1'.

The following is another example of an entity declaration for a 2-to-4 decoder circuit shown in Fig. 2.4.

entity DECODER2x4 **is**
    port (A, B, ENABLE: **in** BIT; Z: **out** BIT_VECTOR(0 **to** 3));
end DECODER2x4;

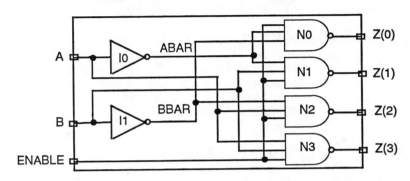

Figure 2.4 A 2-to-4 decoder circuit.

This entity, called DECODER2x4, has three input ports and four output ports. BIT_VECTOR is a predefined unconstrained array type of BIT. An unconstrained array type is a type in which the size of the array is not specified. The range "0 **to** 3" for port Z specifies the array size.

From the last two examples of entity declarations, we see that the entity declaration does not specify anything about the internals of the entity. It only specifies the name of the entity and the interface ports.

2.3   *Architecture Body*

The internal details of an entity are specified by an architecture body using any of the following modeling styles:

1. As a set of interconnected components (to represent structure),

2. As a set of concurrent assignment statements (to represent dataflow),

3. As a set of sequential assignment statements (to represent behavior),

4. Any combination of the above three.

2.3.1   Structural Style of Modeling

In the structural style of modeling, an entity is described as a set of interconnected components. Such a model for the HALF_ADDER entity, shown in
Fig. 2.3, is described in an architecture body as shown below.

```
architecture HA_STRUCTURE of HALF_ADDER is
    component XOR2
        port (X, Y: in BIT; Z: out BIT);
    end component;
    component AND2
        port (L, M: in BIT; N: out BIT);
    end component;
begin
    X1: XOR2 port map (A, B, SUM);
    A1: AND2 port map (A, B, CARRY);
end HA_STRUCTURE;
```

The name of the architecture body is HA_STRUCTURE. The entity declaration for HALF_ADDER (presented in the previous section) specifies the
interface ports for this architecture body. The architecture body is composed
of two parts: the declarative part (before the keyword **begin**) and the statement part (after the keyword **begin**). Two component declarations are present
in the declarative part of the architecture body. These declarations specify the
interface of components that are used in the architecture body. The components XOR2 and AND2 may either be predefined components in a library, or
if they do not exist, they may later be bound to other components in a library.

The declared components are instantiated in the statement part of the
architecture body using component instantiation statements. X1 and A1 are
the component labels for these component instantiations. The first component
instantiation statement, labeled X1, shows that signals A and B (the input
ports of the HALF_ADDER), are connected to the X and Y input ports of a
XOR2 component, while output port Z of this component is connected to output port SUM of the HALF_ADDER entity.

Similarly, in the second component instantiation statement, signals A
and B are connected to ports L and M of the AND2 component, while port N
is connected to the CARRY port of the HALF_ADDER. Note that in this case,
the signals in the port map of a component instantiation and the port signals
in the component declaration are associated by position (called *positional association*). The structural representation for the HALF_ADDER does not say
anything about its functionality. Separate entity models would be described
for the components XOR2 and AND2, each having its own entity declaration
and architecture body.

A structural representation for the DECODER2x4 entity, shown in Fig. 2.4, is shown next.

```
architecture DEC_STR of DECODER2x4 is
    component INV
        port (A: in BIT; Z: out BIT);
    end component;
    component NAND3
        port (A, B, C: in BIT; Z: out BIT);
    end component;
    signal ABAR, BBAR: BIT;
begin
    I0: INV port map (A, ABAR);
    I1: INV port map (B, BBAR);
    N0: NAND3 port map (ABAR, BBAR, ENABLE, Z(0));
    N1: NAND3 port map (ABAR, B, ENABLE, Z(1));
    N2: NAND3 port map (A, BBAR, ENABLE, Z(2));
    N3: NAND3 port map (A, B, ENABLE, Z(3));
end DEC_STR;
```

In this example, the name of the architecture body is DEC_STR, and it is associated with the entity declaration with the name DECODER2x4; therefore, it inherits the list of interface ports from that entity declaration. In addition to the two component declarations (for INV and NAND3), the architecture body contains a signal declaration that declares two signals, ABAR and BBAR, of type BIT. These signals, that represent wires, are used to connect the various components that form the decoder. The scope of these signals is restricted to the architecture body, and therefore, these signals are not visible outside the architecture body. Contrast these signals with the ports of an entity declaration that are available for use within any architecture body associated with the entity declaration.

A component instantiation statement is a concurrent statement, as defined by the language. Therefore, the order of these statements is not important. The structural style of modeling describes only an interconnection of components (viewed as black boxes) without implying any behavior of the components themselves, nor of the entity that they collectively represent. In the architecture body DEC_STR, the signals A, B, and ENABLE, used in the component instantiation statements are the input ports declared in the DECODER2x4 entity declaration. For example, in the component instantiation labeled N3, port A is connected to input A of component NAND3, port B is connected to input port B of component NAND3, port ENABLE is connected to input port C, and the output port Z of component NAND3 is connected to port Z(3) of the DECODER2x4 entity. Again positional association is used to map signals in a port map of a component instantiation with the ports of a component specified in its declaration. The behavior of the components

NAND3 and INV are not apparent, nor is the behavior of the decoder entity that the structural model represents.

2.3.2   Dataflow Style of Modeling

In this modeling style, the flow of data through the entity is expressed primarily using concurrent signal assignment statements. The structure of the entity is not explicitly specified in this modeling style, but it can be implicitly deduced. Consider the following alternate architecture body for the HALF_ADDER entity that uses this style.

```
architecture HA_CONCURRENT of HALF_ADDER is
begin
    SUM <= A xor B after 8 ns;
    CARRY <= A and B after 4 ns;
end HA_CONCURRENT;
```

The dataflow model for the HALF_ADDER is described using two concurrent signal assignment statements (sequential signal assignment statements are described in the next section). In a signal assignment statement, the symbol <= implies an assignment of a value to a signal. The value of the expression on the right-hand-side of the statement is computed and is assigned to the signal on the left-hand-side, called the *target signal*. A concurrent signal assignment statement is executed only when any signal used in the expression on the right-hand-side has an event on it, that is, the value for the signal changes.

Delay information is included in the signal assignment statements using **after** clauses. If either signal A or B, which are input port signals of HALF_ADDER entity, has an event, say at time T, the right-hand-side expressions of both signal assignment statements are evaluated. Signal SUM is scheduled to get the new value after 8 ns while signal CARRY is scheduled to get the new value after 4 ns. When simulation time advances to $(T+4)$ ns, CARRY will get its new value and when simulation time advances to $(T+8)$ ns, SUM will get its new value. Thus, both signal assignment statements execute concurrently.

Concurrent signal assignment statements are concurrent statements, and therefore, the ordering of these statements in an architecture body is not important. Note again that this architecture body, with name HA_CONCURRENT, is also associated with the same HALF_ADDER entity declaration.

Here is a dataflow model for the DECODER2x4 entity.

```
architecture DEC_DATAFLOW of DECODER2x4 is
    signal ABAR, BBAR: BIT;
begin
    Z(3) <= not (A and B and ENABLE);          -- statement 1
    Z(0) <= not (ABAR and BBAR and ENABLE);    -- statement 2
    BBAR <= not B;                             -- statement 3
    Z(2) <= not (A and BBAR and ENABLE);       -- statement 4
    ABAR <= not A;                             -- statement 5
    Z(1) <= not (ABAR and B and ENABLE);       -- statement 6
end DEC_DATAFLOW;
```

The architecture body consists of one signal declaration and six concurrent signal assignment statements. The signal declaration declares signals ABAR and BBAR to be used locally within the architecture body. In each of the signal assignment statements, no **after** clause was used to specify delay. In all such cases, a default delay of 0 ns is assumed. This delay of 0 ns is also known as delta delay, and it represents an infinitesimally small delay. This small delay corresponds to a zero delay with respect to simulation time and does not correspond to any real simulation time.

To understand the behavior of this architecture body, consider an event happening on one of the input signals, say input port B at time T. This would cause the concurrent signal assignment statements 1, 3, and 6, to be triggered. Their right-hand-side expressions would be evaluated and the corresponding values would be scheduled to be assigned to the target signals at time $(T+\Delta)$. When simulation time advances to $(T+\Delta)$, new values to signals Z(3), BBAR, and Z(1), are assigned. Since the value of BBAR changes, this will in turn trigger signal assignment statements, 2 and 4. Eventually, at time $(T+2\Delta)$, signals Z(0) and Z(2) will be assigned their new values.

The semantics of this concurrent behavior indicate that the simulation, as defined by the language, is event-triggered and that simulation time advances to the next time unit when an event is scheduled to occur. Simulation time could also advance a multiple of delta time units. For example, events may have been scheduled to occur at times 1, 3, 4, $4+\Delta$, 5, 6, $6+\Delta$, $6+2\Delta$, $6+3\Delta$, 10, $10+\Delta$, 15, $15+\Delta$ time units.

The **after** clause may be used to generate a clock signal as shown in the following concurrent signal assignment statement.

```
CLK <= not CLK after 10 ns;
```

This statement creates a periodic waveform on the signal CLK with a time period of 20 ns as shown in Fig. 2.5.

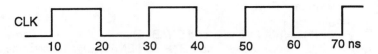

CLK

10   20   30   40   50   60   70 ns

Figure 2.5 A clock waveform with constant on-off period.

2.3.3   Behavioral Style of Modeling

In contrast to the styles of modeling described earlier, the behavioral style of modeling specifies the behavior of an entity as a set of statements that are executed sequentially in the specified order. This set of sequential statements, that are specified inside a process statement, do not explicitly specify the structure of the entity but merely specifies its functionality. A process statement is a concurrent statement that can appear within an architecture body. For example, consider the following behavioral model for the DECODER2x4 entity.

```
architecture DEC_SEQUENTIAL of DECODER2x4 is
begin
    process (A, B, ENABLE)
        variable ABAR, BBAR: BIT;
    begin
        ABAR := not A;                          -- statement 1
        BBAR := not B;                          -- statement 2
        if (ENABLE = '1') then                  -- statement 3
            Z(3) <= not (A and B);              -- statement 4
            Z(0) <= not (ABAR and BBAR);        -- statement 5
            Z(2) <= not (A and BBAR);           -- statement 6
            Z(1) <= not (ABAR and B);           -- statement 7
        else
            Z <= "1111";                        -- statement 8
        end if;
    end process;
end;
```

A process statement, too, has a declarative part (between the keywords **process** and **begin**), and a statement part (between the keywords **begin** and **end process**). The statements appearing within the statement part are sequential statements and are executed sequentially. The list of signals specified within the parenthesis after the keyword **process** constitutes a sensitivity list and the process statement is invoked whenever there is an event on any signal in this list. In the previous example, when an event occurs on signals A, B, or ENABLE, the statements appearing within the process statement are executed sequentially.

The variable declaration (starts with the keyword **variable**) declares two variables called ABAR and BBAR. A variable is different from a signal in that it is always assigned a value instantaneously and the assignment operator used is the := compound symbol; contrast this with a signal that is assigned a value always after a certain delay (user-specified or the default delta delay), and the assignment operator used to assign a value to a signal is the <= compound symbol. Also, variables can only be declared within a process and their scope is limited to that process (variables can also be declared in subprograms; subprograms are discussed in Chap. 8). Note, however, that signals cannot be declared within a process.

Signal assignment statements appearing within a process are called *sequential signal assignment statements*. Sequential signal assignment statements, including variable assignment statements, are executed sequentially independent of whether an event occurs on any signals in its right-hand-side expression or not; contrast this with the execution of concurrent signal assignment statements in the dataflow modeling style. In the previous architecture body, if an event occurs on any signal, A, B, or ENABLE, statement 1 which is a variable assignment statement, is executed, then statement 2 is executed, and so on. Execution of the third statement, an **if** statement, causes control to jump to the appropriate branch based on the value of the signal, ENABLE. If the value of ENABLE is '1', the next four signal assignment statements, 4 through 7, are executed independent of whether A, B, ABAR, or BBAR changed values, and the target signals are scheduled to get their respective values after delta delay. If ENABLE has a value '0', a value of '1' is assigned to each of the elements of the output array, Z. When execution reaches the end of the process, the process suspends itself, and waits for another event to occur on a signal in its sensitivity list.

It is possible to use **case** or **loop** statements within a process. The semantics and structure of these statements are very similar to those in other high-level programming languages like C or Pascal. An explicit **wait** statement can also be used to suspend a process. It can be used to wait for a certain amount of time or to wait until a certain condition becomes true, or to wait until an event occurs on one or more signals. Here is an example of a process statement that generates a clock with a different on-off period. Figure 2.6 shows the generated waveform.

```
process
begin
    CLK <= '0';
    wait for 20 ns;
    CLK <= '1';
    wait for 12 ns;
end process;
```

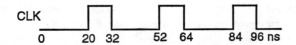

Figure 2.6 A clock waveform with varying on-off period.

This process does not have a sensitivity list since explicit **wait** statements are present inside the process. It is important to remember that a process never terminates. It is always either being executed or in a suspended state. All processes are executed once during the initialization phase of simulation until they get suspended. Therefore, a process with no sensitivity list and with no explicit **wait** statements will never suspend itself.

A signal can represent not only a wire but also a place holder for a value, that is, it can be used to model a flip-flop. Here is such an example. Port signal Q models a level-sensitive flip-flop.

```
entity LS_DFF is
    port (Q: out BIT; D, CLK: in BIT);
end LS_DFF;

architecture LS_DFF_BEH of LS_DFF is
begin
    process (D, CLK)
    begin
        if (CLK = '1') then
            Q <= D;
        end if;
    end process;
end LS_DFF_BEH;
```

2.3.4   Mixed Style of Modeling

It is possible to mix the three modeling styles that we have seen so far in a single architecture body. That is, within an architecture body, we could use component instantiation statements (that represent structure), concurrent signal assignment statements (that represent dataflow), and process statements (that represent behavior). Here is an example of a mixed style model for a one-bit full-adder shown in Fig. 2.7.

```
entity FULL_ADDER is
    port (A, B, CIN: in BIT; SUM, COUT: out BIT);
end FULL_ADDER;

architecture FA_MIXED of FULL_ADDER is
    component XOR2
```

```
                    port (A, B: in BIT; Z: out BIT);
                end component;
                signal S1: BIT;
        begin
                X1: XOR2 port map (A, B, S1);                    -- structure.
                process (A, B, CIN)                              -- behavior.
                    variable T1, T2, T3: BIT;
                begin
                    T1 := A and B;
                    T2 := B and CIN;
                    T3 := A and CIN;
                    COUT <= T1 or T2 or T3;
                end process;
                SUM <= S1 xor CIN;                               -- dataflow.
        end FA_MIXED;
```

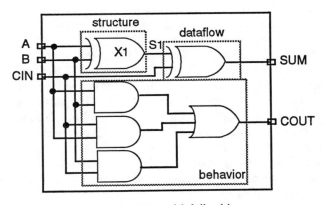

Figure 2.7 A 1-bit full-adder.

The full-adder is represented using one component instantiation statement, one process statement and one concurrent signal assignment statement. All of these statements are concurrent statements, and therefore, their order of appearance within the architecture body is not important. Note that a process statement itself is a concurrent statement; however, statements within a process statement are always executed sequentially. S1 is a signal locally declared within the architecture body and is used to pass the value from the output of the component X1 to the expression for signal SUM.

2.4   Configuration Declaration

A configuration declaration is used to select one of the possibly many architecture bodies that an entity may have, and to bind components, used to represent structure in that architecture body, to entities represented by an entity-architecture pair or by a configuration, that reside in a design library. Consider the following configuration declaration for the HALF_ADDER entity.

```
library CMOS_LIB, MY_LIB;
configuration HA_BINDING of HALF_ADDER is
    for HA_STRUCTURE
        for X1: XOR2
            use entity CMOS_LIB.XOR_GATE(DATAFLOW);
        end for;
        for A1: AND2
            use configuration MY_LIB.AND_CONFIG;
        end for;
    end for;
end HA_BINDING;
```

The first statement is a **library** context clause that makes the library names CMOS_LIB and MY_LIB visible within the configuration declaration. The name of the configuration is HA_BINDING, and it specifies a configuration for the HALF_ADDER entity. The next statement specifies that the architecture body HA_STRUCTURE (described in Sec. 2.3.1) is selected for this configuration. Since this architecture body contains two component instantiations, two component bindings are required. The first statement (**for** X1: . . . **end for**) binds the component instantiation, with label X1, to an entity represented by the entity-architecture pair, XOR_GATE entity declaration and the DATAFLOW architecture body, that resides in the CMOS_LIB design library. Similarly, component instantiation A1 is bound to a configuration of an entity defined by the configuration declaration, with name AND_CONFIG, residing in the MY_LIB design library.

There are no behavioral or simulation semantics associated with a configuration declaration. It merely specifies a binding that is used to build a configuration for an entity. These bindings are performed during the elaboration phase of simulation when the entire design to be simulated is being assembled. Having defined a configuration for the entity, the configuration can then be simulated.

When an architecture body does not contain any component instantiations, for example, when dataflow style is used, such an architecture body can also be selected to create a configuration. For example, the DEC_DATAFLOW architecture body can be selected for the DECODER2x4 entity using the following configuration declaration.

```
configuration DEC_CONFIG of DECODER2x4 is
    for DEC_DATAFLOW
```

```
        end for;
    end DEC_CONFIG;
```

DEC_CONFIG defines a configuration that selects the DEC_DATA-FLOW architecture body for the DECODER2x4 entity. The configuration DEC_CONFIG, that represents one possible configuration for the DECODER2x4 entity, can now be simulated.

2.5   Package Declaration

A package declaration is used to store a set of common declarations like components, types, procedures, and functions. These declarations can then be imported into other design units using a context clause. Here is an example of a package declaration.

```
    package EXAMPLE_PACK is
        type SUMMER is (MAY, JUN, JUL, AUG, SEP);
        component D_FLIP_FLOP
            port (D, CK: in BIT; Q, QBAR: out BIT);
        end component;
        constant PIN2PIN_DELAY: TIME := 125 ns;
        function INT2BIT_VEC (INT_VALUE: INTEGER)
            return BIT_VECTOR;
    end EXAMPLE_PACK;
```

The name of the package declared is EXAMPLE_PACK. It contains type, component, constant, and function declarations. Notice that the behavior of the function INT2BIT_VEC does not appear in the package declaration; only the function interface appears. The definition or body of the function appears in a package body (see next section).

Assume that this package has been compiled into a design library called DESIGN_LIB. Consider the following context clauses associated with an entity declaration.

```
    library DESIGN_LIB;
    use DESIGN_LIB.EXAMPLE_PACK.all;
    entity RX is . . .
```

The library context clause makes the name of the design library DESIGN_LIB visible within this description, that is, the name DESIGN_LIB can be used within the description. This is followed by a use context clause that imports all declarations in package EXAMPLE_PACK into the entity declaration of RX.

It is also possible to selectively import declarations from a package declaration into other design units. For example,

```
library DESIGN_LIB;
use DESIGN_LIB.EXAMPLE_PACK.D_FLIP_FLOP;
use DESIGN_LIB.EXAMPLE_PACK.PIN2PIN_DELAY;
architecture RX_STRUCTURE of RX is . . .
```

The two **use** context clauses make the component declaration for D_FLIP_FLOP and the constant declaration for PIN2PIN_DELAY, visible within the architecture body.

Another approach to selectively import items declared in a package is by using selected names. For example,

```
library DESIGN_LIB;
package ANOTHER_PACKAGE is
    function POCKET_MONEY
        (MONTH: DESIGN_LIB.EXAMPLE_PACK.SUMMER)
        return INTEGER;
    constant TOTAL_ALU: INTEGER; -- A deferred constant.
end ANOTHER_PACKAGE;
```

The type SUMMER declared in package EXAMPLE_PACK is used in this new package by specifying a selected name. In this case, a **use** context clause was not necessary. Package ANOTHER_PACKAGE also contains a constant declaration with the value of the constant not specified; such a constant is referred to as a *deferred constant*. The value of this constant is supplied in a corresponding package body.

2.6   *Package Body*

A package body is primarily used to store the definitions of functions and procedures that were declared in the corresponding package declaration, and also the complete constant declarations for any deferred constants that appear in the package declaration. Therefore, a package body is always associated with a package declaration; furthermore, a package declaration can have at most one package body associated with it. Contrast this with an architecture body and an entity declaration where multiple architecture bodies may be associated with a single entity declaration. A package body may contain other declarations as well (see Chap. 9).

Here is the package body for the package EXAMPLE_PACK declared in the previous section.

```
package body EXAMPLE_PACK is
    function INT2BIT_VEC (INT_VALUE: INTEGER)
        return BIT_VECTOR is
    begin
        -- Behavior of function described here.
    end INT2BIT_VEC;
end EXAMPLE_PACK;
```

The name of the package body must be the same as that of the package declaration with which it is associated. It is important to note that a package body is not necessary if the corresponding package declaration has no function and procedure declarations and no deferred constant declarations. Here is the package body that is associated with the package ANOTHER_PACKAGE that was declared in the previous section.

```
package body ANOTHER_PACKAGE is
    constant TOTAL_ALU: INTEGER := 10; -- A complete constant
                                       -- declaration.
    function POCKET_MONEY    -- Function body.
        (MONTH: DESIGN_LIB.EXAMPLE_PACK.SUMMER)
        return INTEGER is
    begin
        case MONTH is
            when MAY => return 5;
            when JUL I SEP => return 6; -- When JUL or SEP.
            when others => return 2;
        end case;
    end POCKET_MONEY;
end ANOTHER_PACKAGE;
```

2.7   *Model Analysis*

Once an entity is described in VHDL, it can be validated using an analyzer and a simulator that are part of a VHDL system. The first step in the validation process is analysis. The analyzer takes a file that contains one or more design units (remember that a design unit is an entity declaration, an architecture body, a configuration declaration, a package declaration or a package body) and compiles them into an intermediate form. The format of this compiled intermediate representation is not defined by the language. During compilation, the analyzer validates the syntax and performs static semantic checks. The generated intermediate form is stored in a specific design library, that has been designated as the working library.

A design library is a location in the host environment (the environment that supports the VHDL system) where compiled descriptions are stored.

Each design library has a logical name that is used when referring to a library in a VHDL description. The mapping of the logical library name to a physical storage location is provided externally by the host environment and is not defined by the language. As an example, a design library can be implemented as a directory in the host environment with the compiled design units being stored as files within this directory. The mapping of physical names to logical names may be supplied in a special file that the VHDL system can interpret.

An arbitrary number of design libraries may exist simultaneously. Of all the design libraries that may coexist, one particular library is designated as the working library with the logical name, WORK. The language analyzer always compiles descriptions into this library; therefore, at any given time, only one library is updated. Figure 2.8 shows the compilation process and is a typical environment for analysis.

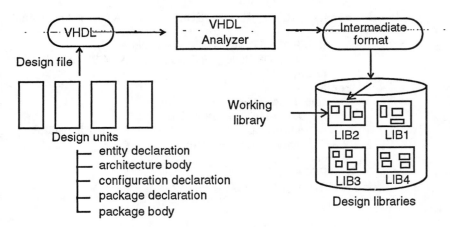

Figure 2.8 The compilation process.

If compiled descriptions need to be stored in a different design library, the reference to WORK is changed to point to this design library prior to analysis. The mapping of WORK to a design library is again provided by the host environment. Items compiled in one design library can be imported into design units compiled in a different design library by using the **library** and **use** context clauses, or by making items visible directly by selection.

There is a design library with the logical name STD that is predefined in the VHDL language environment. This library contains two packages: STANDARD and TEXTIO. The STANDARD package contains declarations for all the predefined types of the language, for example, BIT, TIME, INTEGER, and so forth, and the TEXTIO package contains procedures and functions that are necessary for supporting formatted ASCII read and write operations.

2.8   Simulation

Once the model description is successfully compiled into one or more design libraries, the next step in the validation process is simulation. For a hierarchical entity to be simulated, all of its lowest level components must be described at the behavioral level. A simulation can be performed on either one of the following:

- an entity declaration and an architecture body pair,
- a configuration.

Preceding the actual simulation are two major steps:

1. *Elaboration phase*: In this phase, the hierarchy of the entity is expanded and linked, components are bound to entities in a library and the top-level entity is built as a network of behavioral models that is ready to be simulated. Also, storage is allocated for all data objects (signals, variables, and constants) declared in the design units. Initial values are also assigned to these objects.

2. *Initialization phase*: The effective values for all explicitly declared signals are computed, implicit signals (discussed in later chapters) are assigned values, processes are executed once until they suspend, and simulation time is reset to 0 ns.

Simulation commences by advancing time to that of the next event. Values that are scheduled to be assigned to signals at this time are assigned. Each process that has a signal in its sensitivity list whose value just changed, is executed until it suspends. Simulation stops when a user-specified time limit is reached, or when an assertion violation occurs, depending on the implementation of the VHDL system (assertion statements are discussed in Chap. 4), or when the maximum time as defined by the language is reached.

What to Expect Next

This chapter provided a brief overview of the major aspects of the language. Some of the other important features like types, overloading, and resolution functions, were not discussed. The following chapters discuss these features and others in considerable detail.

❏

CHAPTER 3   *Basic Language Elements*

This chapter describes the basic elements of the language. These include data objects that store values of a given type, literals that represent constant values, and operators that operate on data objects. Every data object belongs to a specific type. The various categories of types and the syntax for specifying user-defined types are discussed here. The chapter also describes how to associate types with objects by using object declarations.

It is important to understand the notion of data types and objects since VHDL is a strongly-typed language. This means that operations and assignments are legal in the language only if the types of the operands and the result match according to a set of rules; it does not allow objects and literals of different types to be mixed freely in expressions. Examples of illegal operations are adding a real value to an integer value, and assigning a boolean value to an object of type BIT. It is, therefore, important to understand what types are and how they can be correctly used in the language.

A first-time reader may wish to skip the section on access types, incomplete types, and file types since this material is of a more advanced nature.

3.1   Identifiers

An identifier in VHDL is composed of a sequence of one or more characters. A legal character is an upper-case letter (A . . . Z), or a lower-case letter (a . . . z), or a digit (0 . . . 9) or the underscore (_) character. The first character in an identifier must be a letter and the last character may not be an underscore. Lower-case and upper-case letters are considered to be identical when used in an identifier; as an example, Count, COUNT, and CouNT, all refer to the same identifier. Also, two underscore characters cannot appear consecutively. Some more examples of identifiers are

```
DRIVE_BUS      SelectSignal     RAM_Address
SET_CK_HIGH    CONST32_59       r2d2
```

Comments in a description must be preceded by two consecutive hyphens (--); the comment extends to the end of the line. Comments can appear anywhere within a description. Examples are

```
-- This is a comment; it ends at the end of this line.
-- To continue a comment onto a second line, a separate
-- comment line must be started.
entity UART is end; -- This comment starts after the entity declaration.
```

The language defines a set of reserved words; these are listed in Appendix A.1. These words, also called *keywords*, have a specific meaning in the language, and therefore, cannot be used as identifiers.

3.2   Data Objects

A data object holds a value of a specified type. It is created by means of an object declaration. An example is

variable COUNT: INTEGER;

This results in the creation of a data object called COUNT which can hold integer values. The object COUNT is also declared to be of *variable* class.

Every data object belongs to one of the following three classes:

1. *Constant*: An object of constant class can hold a single value of a given type. This value is assigned to the object before simulation starts and the value cannot be changed during the course of the simulation.

2. *Variable*: An object of variable class can also hold a single value of a given type. However in this case, different values can be assigned to the object at different times using a variable assignment statement.

3. *Signal*: An object belonging to the signal class has a past history of values, a current value, and a set of future values. Future values can be assigned to a signal object using a signal assignment statement.

Signal objects can be regarded as wires in a circuit while variable and constant objects are analogous to their counterparts in a high-level programming language like C or Pascal. Signal objects are typically used to model wires and flip-flops while variable and constant objects are typically used to model the behavior of the circuit.

An *object declaration* is used to declare an object, its type, and its class, and optionally assign it a value. Some examples of object declarations of various types and classes follow.

Constant Declarations

Examples of constant declarations are

```
constant RISE_TIME: TIME := 10 ns;
constant BUS_WIDTH: INTEGER := 8;
```

The first declaration declares the object RISE_TIME that can hold a value of type TIME (a predefined type in the language) and the value assigned to the object at the start of simulation is 10 ns. The second constant declaration declares a constant BUS_WIDTH of type INTEGER with a value of 8.

An example of another form of constant declaration is

```
constant NO_OF_INPUTS: INTEGER;
```

The value of the constant has not been specified in this case. Such a constant is called a *deferred constant* and it can appear only inside a package declaration. The complete constant declaration with the associated value must appear in the corresponding package body.

Variable Declarations

Examples of variable declarations are

```
variable CTRL_STATUS: BIT_VECTOR(10 downto 0);
variable SUM: INTEGER range 0 to 100 := 10;
variable FOUND, DONE: BOOLEAN;
```

The first declaration specifies a variable object CTRL_STATUS as an array of 11 elements, with each array element of type BIT. In the second declaration, an explicit initial value has been assigned to the variable SUM. When simulation starts, SUM will have an initial value of 10. If no initial value is specified for a variable object, a default value is used as an initial value. This default value is T'LEFT, where T is the object type and LEFT is a predefined attribute of a type that gives the leftmost value in the set of values belonging to type T. In the third declaration, the initial values assigned to FOUND and DONE at start of simulation is FALSE (FALSE is the leftmost value of the predefined type, BOOLEAN). The initial value for all the array elements of CTRL_STATUS is '0'.

Signal Declarations

Here are some examples of signal declarations.

```
signal CLOCK: BIT;
signal DATA_BUS: BIT_VECTOR(0 to 7);
signal GATE_DELAY: TIME := 10 ns;
```

The interpretation for these signal declarations is very similar to that of the variable declarations. The first signal declaration declares the signal object CLOCK of type BIT and gives it an initial value of '0' ('0' being the leftmost value of type BIT). The third signal declaration declares a signal object GATE_DELAY of type TIME that has an initial value of 10 ns. Other forms of signal declarations are described in Chaps. 5 and 10.

Other Ways to Declare Objects

Not all objects in a VHDL description are created using object declarations. These other objects are declared as

1. ports of an entity. All ports are signal objects.
2. generics of an entity (discussed in Chap. 7). These are constant objects.
3. formal parameters of functions and procedures (discussed in Chap. 8). Function parameters are constant objects or signal objects while procedure parameters can belong to any object class.
4. a file declared by a file declaration (see file types in next section).

There are two other types of objects that are implicitly declared. These are the indices of a for . . . loop statement and the generate statement (generate statements are discussed in Chap. 10). An example of such an implicit declaration for the loop index in a **for . . . loop** statement is shown.

```
for COUNT in 1 to 10 loop
    SUM := SUM + COUNT;
end loop;
```

In this **for . . . loop** statement, object COUNT has an implicit declaration of type INTEGER with range 1 to 10, and therefore, need not be explicitly declared. The object COUNT is created when the loop is first entered and ceases to exist after the loop is exited.

In the rest of this text, we shall follow the standard practice of referring to signal objects as signals, variable objects as variables, and constant objects as constants.

3.3   Data Types

Every data object in VHDL can hold a value that belongs to a set of values. This set of values is specified by using a *type declaration*. A *type* is a name that has associated with it a set of values and a set of operations. Certain types, and operations that can be performed on objects of these types, are predefined in the language. For example, INTEGER is a predefined type with the set of values being integers in a specific range provided by the VHDL system. The minimum range that must be provided is $-(2^{31}-1)$ through $+(2^{31}-1)$. Some of the allowable and frequently used predefined operators are +, for addition, −, for subtraction, /, for division, and *, for multiplication. BOOLEAN is another predefined type that has the values FALSE and TRUE, and some of its predefined operators are **and, or, nor, nand**, and **not**. The declarations for the predefined types of the language are contained in package STANDARD (see Appendix A); the operators for these types are predefined in the language.

The language also provides the facility to define new types by using type declarations and also to define a set of operations on these types by writing functions that return values of this new type. All the possible types that can exist in the language can be categorized into the following four major categories:

1. *Scalar* types: Values belonging to these types appear in a sequential order.
2. *Composite* types: These are composed of elements of a single type (an array type) or elements of different types (a record type).

3. *Access* types: These provide access to objects of a given type (via pointers).

4. *File* types: These provides access to objects that contain a sequence of values of a given type.

It is possible to derive restricted types, called subtypes, from other pre-defined or user-defined types.

3.3.1   Subtypes

A *subtype* is a type with a constraint. The constraint specifies the subset of values for the type. The type is called the *base type* of the subtype. An object is said to belong to a subtype if it is of the base type and if it satisfies the constraint. *Subtype declarations* are used to declare subtypes. An object can be declared to either belong to a type or to a subtype.

The set of operations belonging to a subtype is the same as that associated with its base type. Subtypes are useful for range checking and for imposing additional constraints on types.

Examples of subtypes are

```
subtype MY_INTEGER is INTEGER range 48 to 156;
type DIGIT is ('0', '1', '2', '3', '4', '5', '6', '7', '8', '9');
subtype MIDDLE is DIGIT range '3' to '7';
```

In the first example, MY_INTEGER is a subtype of the INTEGER base type and has a range constraint with values ranging from 48 through 156. DIGIT is a user-defined enumeration type. The last subtype declaration declares a new subtype called MIDDLE whose base type is DIGIT and has the values '3', '4', '5', '6' and '7'.

A subtype need not impose a constraint. In such a case, the subtype simply gives another name to an already existing type. For example:

```
subtype NUMBER is DIGIT;
```

NUMBER is a subtype with no constraint. Therefore, its set of values are the same as that for type DIGIT.

3.3.2   Scalar Types

The values belonging to this type are ordered, that is, relational operators can be used on these values. For example, BIT is a scalar type and the expression '0' < '1' is valid and has the value TRUE. There are four different kinds of scalar types. These types are

1. enumeration,

    2. integer,

    3. physical,

    4. floating point.

Integer types, floating point types, and physical types are classified as *numeric* types since the values associated with these types are numeric. Further, enumeration and integer types are called *discrete* types since these types have discrete values associated with them. Every value belonging to an enumeration type, integer type, or a physical type has a *position number* associated with it. This number is the position of the value in the ordered list of values belonging to that type.

Enumeration Types

An enumeration type declaration defines a type that has a set of user-defined values consisting of identifiers and character literals. Examples are

```
type MVL is ('U', '0', '1', 'Z');
type MICRO_OP is (LOAD, STORE, ADD, SUB, MUL, DIV);
subtype ARITH_OP is MICRO_OP range ADD to DIV;
```

Examples of objects defined for these types are

```
signal CONTROL_A: MVL;
signal CLOCK: MVL range '0' to '1';-- Implicit subtype declaration.
variable IC: MICRO_OP := STORE; -- STORE is the initial value for IC.
variable ALU: ARITH_OP;
```

MVL is an enumeration type that has the set of ordered values, 'U', '0', '1', and 'Z'. ARITH_OP is a subtype of the base type MICRO_OP and has a range constraint specified to be from ADD to DIV, that is, the values ADD, SUB, MUL, and DIV belong to the subtype ARITH_OP. A range constraint can also be specified in an object declaration as shown in the signal declaration for CLOCK; here the value of signal CLOCK is restricted to '0' or '1'.

The order of values appearing in an enumeration type declaration defines the lexical order for the values. That is, when using relational operators, a value is always less than a value that appears to its right in the order. For instance, in the MICRO_OP type declaration, STORE < DIV is true, and SUB > MUL is false. Values of an enumeration type also have a position number associated with them. The position number of the leftmost element is 0. The position number of any particular element is one more than the position number of the element to its left.

The values of an enumeration type are called *enumeration literals*. For example, consider the following enumeration type declaration.

type CAR_STATE **is** (STOP, SLOW, MEDIUM, FAST);

The enumeration literals specified in this type declaration are STOP, SLOW, MEDIUM, and FAST; therefore, objects of type CAR_STATE may be assigned only these values.

If the same literal is used in two different enumeration type declarations, the literal is said to be *overloaded*. In such a case, whenever such a literal is used, the type of the literal is determined from its surrounding context. The following example clarifies this.

```
type MVL is ('U', '0', '1', 'Z');           -- line 1
type TWO_STATE is ('0', '1');               -- line 2
. . .
variable CLOCK: TWO_STATE;                  -- line 3
variable LATCH_CTRL: MVL;                   -- line 4
. . .
CLOCK := '0';                               -- line 5
LATCH_CTRL := LATCH_CTRL xor '0';           -- line 6
. . .
```

Here '0' and '1' are two literals that are overloaded since they appear in both the types, MVL and TWO_STATE. The value '0' being assigned to CLOCK in line 5 refers to the literal in the TWO_STATE type since variable CLOCK is of that type. The value '0' in the expression for LATCH_CTRL refers to the literal in type MVL since the first argument of the **xor** operator is of type MVL (this assumes that the **xor** operator is allowed for MVL type operands, which is achieved by overloading the operator; overloading is discussed in Chap. 8).

The predefined enumeration types of the language are CHARACTER, BIT, BOOLEAN, and SEVERITY_LEVEL. Values belonging to the type CHARACTER constitute the 128 characters of the ASCII character set. These values are called *character literals* and are always written between two single quotes (' '). Examples are

'A',   '_',   '''' (the single quote character itself),
'3' (the character literal 3)

The predefined type BIT has the literals '0' and '1', while type BOOLEAN has the literals FALSE and TRUE. Type SEVERITY_LEVEL has the values NOTE, WARNING, ERROR, and FAILURE; this type is typically used in assertion statements (assertion statements are described in Chap. 4).

Integer Types

An integer type defines a type whose set of values fall within a specified integer range. Examples of integer type declarations are

> **type** INDEX **is range** 0 **to** 15;
> **type** WORD_LENGTH **is range** 31 **downto** 0;
> **subtype** DATA_WORD **is** WORD_LENGTH **range** 15 **downto** 0;
> **type** MY_WORD **is range** 4 **to** 6;

Some object declarations using these types are

> **constant** MUX_ADDRESS: INDEX := 5;
> **signal** DATA_BUS: DATA_WORD;

INDEX is an integer type that includes the integer values from 0 through 15. DATA_WORD is a subtype of WORD_LENGTH that includes the integer values ranging from 15 through 0. The position of each value of an integer type is the value itself. For example, in the type declaration of WORD_LENGTH, value 31 is at position 31, value 14 is at position 14, and so on. In the declaration of MY_WORD, the position number of values 4, 5, and 6, is 4, 5, and 6, respectively. Contrast this with the position number of elements of an enumeration type; the position number in case of integer types does not refer to the index of the element in the range, but to its numeric value itself. The bounds of the range for an integer type must be constants or locally static expressions; a *locally static expression* is an expression that computes to a constant value at compile time (a *globally static expression* is an expression that computes to a constant value at elaboration time).

Values belonging to an integer type are called *integer literals*. Examples of integer literals are

> 56349   6E2   0   98_71_28

Literal 6E2 refers to the decimal value $6 * (10^2) = 600$. The underscore (_) character can be used freely in writing integer literals and has no impact on the value of the literal; 98_71_28 is same as 987128.

INTEGER is the only predefined integer type of the language. The range of the INTEGER type is implementation dependent but must at least cover the range $-(2^{31} - 1)$ to $+(2^{31} - 1)$.

Floating Point Types

A floating point type has a set of values in a given range of real numbers. Examples of floating point type declarations are

```
type TTL_VOLTAGE is range –5.5 to –1.4;
type REAL_DATA is range 0.0 to 31.9;
```

An example of an object declaration is

```
variable LENGTH: REAL_DATA range 0.0 to 15.9;
. . .
variable L1, L2, L3: REAL_DATA range 0.0 to 15.9;
```

LENGTH is a variable object of type REAL_DATA that has been constrained to take real values in the range 0.0 through 15.9 only. Notice that in this case, the range constraint was specified in the variable declaration itself. Alternately, it is possible to declare a subtype and then use this subtype in the variable declarations as shown.

```
subtype RD16 is REAL_DATA range 0.0 to 15.9;
. . .
variable LENGTH: RD16;
. . .
variable L1, L2, L3: RD16;
```

The range bounds specified in a floating point type declaration must be constants or locally static expressions.

Floating point literals are values of a floating point type. Examples of floating point literals are

```
16.26      0.0      0.002   3_1.4_2
```

Floating point literals differ from integer literals by the presence of the dot (.) character. Thus 0 is an integer literal while 0.0 is a floating point literal.

Floating point literals can also be expressed in an exponential form. The exponent represents a power of ten and the exponent value must be an integer. Examples are

```
62.3E–2      5.0E+2
```

Integer and floating point literals can also be written in a base other than 10 (decimal). The base can be any value between 2 and 16. Such literals are called *based literals*. In this case, the exponent represents a power of the specified base. The syntax for a based literal is

```
base # based-value #                 -- form 1
base # based-value # E exponent       -- form 2
```

Examples are

```
2#101_101_000#      represents (101101000)₂ = (360) in decimal,
16#FA#              represents (FA)₁₆ = (11111010)₂ = (250) in decimal,
16#E#E1             represents (E)₁₆ * (16¹) = 14 * 16 = (224) in decimal,
2#110.01#           represents (110.01)₂ = (6.25) in decimal.
```

The base and the exponent values in a based literal must be in decimal notation.

The only predefined floating point type is REAL. The range of REAL is again implementation dependent but it must at least cover the range $-1.0E38$ to $+1.0E38$ and it must allow for at least six decimal digits of precision.

Physical Types

A physical type contains values that represent measurement of some physical quantity, like time, length, voltage, and current. Values of this type are expressed as integer multiples of a base unit. An example of a physical type declaration is

```
type CURRENT is range 0 to 1E9
    units
        nA;                            -- (base unit) nano-ampere
        uA      = 1000 nA;             -- micro-ampere
        mA      = 1000 uA;             -- milli-ampere
        Amp     = 1000 mA;             -- ampere
    end units;

subtype FILTER_CURRENT is CURRENT range 10 uA to 5 mA;
```

CURRENT is defined to be a physical type that contains values from 0 nA to 10^9 nA. The base unit is a nano-ampere while all others are derived units. The position number of a value is the number of base units represented by that value. For example, 2 uA has a position of 2000 while 100 nA has a position of 100.

Values of a physical type are called *physical literals*. Physical literals are written as an integer literal followed by the unit name. For example, "10 nA" is a physical literal (note that a space between 10 and nA is essential) while "Amp" is also a literal that implies 1 Amp. Other examples are

```
100 ns        10 V       50 sec         Kohm (implies 1 Kohm)
```

The only predefined physical type is TIME and its range of base values, which again is implementation dependent, must at least be $-(2^{31}-1)$ to $+(2^{31}-1)$. The declaration of type TIME appears in package STANDARD (see Appendix A).

3.3.3   Composite Types

A composite type represents a collection of values. There are two composite types: an array type and a record type. An array type represents a collection of values all belonging to a single type; on the other hand, a record type represents a collection of values that may belong to same or different types. An object belonging to a composite type, therefore, represents a collection of subobjects, one for each element of the composite type. An element of a composite type could have a value belonging to either a scalar type, a composite type, or an access type. For example, a composite type may be defined to represent an array of an array of records. This provides the capability of defining arbitrarily complex composite types.

Array Types

An object of an array type consists of elements that have the same type. Examples of array type declarations are

```
type ADDRESS_WORD is array (0 to 63) of BIT;
type DATA_WORD is array (7 downto 0) of MVL;
type ROM is array (0 to 125) of DATA_WORD;
type DECODE_MATRIX is array (POSITIVE range 15 downto 1,
    NATURAL range 3 downto 0) of MVL;
-- POSITIVE and NATURAL are predefined subtypes; these are:
subtype NATURAL is INTEGER range 0 to INTEGER'HIGH;
subtype POSITIVE is INTEGER range 1 to INTEGER'HIGH;
-- The HIGH attribute gives the highest value belonging to the type.
```

Examples of object declarations using these types are

```
variable ROM_ADDR: ROM;
signal ADDRESS_BUS: ADDRESS_WORD;
constant DECODER: DECODE_MATRIX; -- A deferred constant.
variable DECODE_VALUE: DECODE_MATRIX;
```

ADDRESS_BUS is a one-dimensional array object that consists of 64 elements of type BIT. ROM_ADDR is a one-dimensional array object that consists of 126 elements, each element being another array object consisting of 8 elements of type MVL. We have thus created an array of arrays.

Elements of an array can be accessed by specifying the index values into the array. For example, ADDRESS_BUS(26) refers to the 27th element of ADDRESS_BUS array object; ROM_ADDR(10)(5) refers to the value (of type MVL) at index 5 of the ROM_ADDR(10) data object (of type DATA_WORD); DECODER(5, 2) refers to the value of the element at the 2nd column and 5th row of the two-dimensional object. Notice the difference in addressing for a two-dimensional array type and an array of a type which is an array of another type.

The language allows for an arbitrary number of dimensions to be associated with an array. It also allows an array object to be assigned to another array object of the same type using a single assignment statement. Assignment can be made to an entire array, or to an element of an array, or to a slice of an array. For example,

```
ROM_ADDR(5) := "0100_0100";    -- Assign to an element of an array.
DECODE_VALUE := DECODER;        -- An entire array is assigned.
ADDRESS_BUS (8 to 15) <= X"FF"; -- Assign to a slice of an array.
```

These examples of array types are constrained array declarations since the number of elements in the type is explicitly specified. The language also allows array types to be unconstrained, in this case, the number of elements in the array is not specified in the type declaration. Instead, the object declaration for that type declares the number of elements of the array. A subtype declaration may also specify the index constraint for an unconstrained array type. A subprogram parameter may be an object specified to be of an unconstrained type; in this case, the constraint is specified by the actual parameter passed in during the subprogram call. Subprograms are discussed in Chap. 8. Examples of unconstrained array declarations are

```
-- The "<>" symbol is called the "box" symbol in the language.
type STACK_TYPE is array (INTEGER range <>)
    of ADDRESS_WORD;
subtype STACK is STACK_TYPE(0 to 63);
type OP_TYPE is (ADD, SUB, MUL, DIV);
type TIMING is array (OP_TYPE range <>, OP_TYPE range <>)
    of TIME;
```

Examples of object declarations using these types are

```
variable FAST_STK: STACK_TYPE(-127 to 127);
constant ALU_TIMING: TIMING :=
    -- ADD, SUB, MUL
    ((10 ns, 20 ns, 45 ns), -- ADD
     (20 ns, 15 ns, 40 ns), -- SUB
     (45 ns, 40 ns, 30 ns)); -- MUL
```

STACK_TYPE is defined to be an unconstrained array type that specifies the index of the array as an integer type and the element types as type ADDRESS_WORD. STACK is a subtype of the base type STACK_TYPE with the specified index constraint. The variable declaration for FAST_STK, defined to be of type STACK_TYPE, also specifies an index constraint. The constant ALU_TIMING specifies the timing for a two-operator ALU, where the operators could be ADD, SUB, or MUL; for example, an ALU that performs ADD and SUB operations has a delay of 20 ns. The declaration for ALU_TIMING is a special case of a constant declaration where no constraint need be specified for the unconstrained array type, since the size of the constant object is determined from the number of values in the constant.

There are two predefined one-dimensional unconstrained array types in the language, STRING and BIT_VECTOR. STRING is an array of characters while BIT_VECTOR is an array of bits. Examples are

```
variable MESSAGE: STRING(1 to 17) := "Hello, VHDL world";
signal RX_BUS: BIT_VECTOR(0 to 5) := O"37";
-- O"37" is a bit-string literal representing the octal value 37.
constant ADD_CODE: BIT_VECTOR := ('0', '1', '1', '1', '0');
```

A value representing a one-dimensional array of characters is called a *string literal*. String literals are written by enclosing the sequence of characters within double quotes ("..."). Examples of string literals are

```
"THIS IS A TEST"
"SPIKE DETECTED!"
"State ""READY"" entered!"-- 2 double quote characters in a sequence
                          -- represents one double quote character.
```

A string literal can be assigned to different types of objects, for example, to a STRING type object or to a BIT_VECTOR type object. The type of a string literal is, therefore, determined from the context in which it appears. Here are some examples.

```
-- Example 1:
variable ERROR_MESSAGE: STRING(1 to 19);
ERROR_MESSAGE := "Fatal ERROR: abort!";

-- Example 2:
variable BUS_VALUE: BIT_VECTOR(0 to 3);
BUS_VALUE := "1101";
```

In the first example, the string literal is of type STRING while in the second example, the string literal is of type BIT_VECTOR. The type of a string literal can also be explicitly stated by using a qualified expression (qualified expressions are described in Chap. 10).

A string literal that represents a sequence of bits (values of type BIT) can also be represented as a *bit string literal*. This sequence of bits, called *bit strings*, can be represented either as a binary value, or as an octal value, or as a hexadecimal value. The underscore character can again be freely used in bit string literals for clarity. Examples are

```
X"FF0"                 .      -- X for hexadecimal.
B"00_0011_1101"              -- B for binary.
O"327"                       -- O for octal.
X"FF_F0_AB"
```

There are many different ways to assign values to an array object. Here are some examples.

```
variable OP_CODES : BIT_VECTOR(1 to 5);
OP_CODES := "01001";          -- A string literal is assigned.
OP_CODES := ('0', '1', '0', '0', '1'); -- Positional association is implicit;
    -- first value is assigned to OP_CODES(0), second value to
    -- OP_CODES(1), and so on.
OP_CODES := (2=>'1', 5=>'1', others=>'0'); -- Named association;
    -- second and fifth element of OP_CODES get the value '1', and
    -- the rest get a value of '0'.
OP_CODES := (others=>'0'); -- All values set to '0'.
```

Notice the use of the keyword others to mean all unassigned values; when used, it must be the last. The expressions used in the last three assignments to OP_CODES are examples of array aggregates. An *aggregate* is a set of comma separated elements enclosed within parenthesis.

Record Types

An object of a record type is composed of elements of same or different types. It is analogous to the record data type in Pascal and the struct declaration in C. An example of a record type declaration is

```
type PIN_TYPE is range 0 to 10;
type MODULE is
    record
        SIZE: INTEGER range 20 to 200;
        CRITICAL_DLY: TIME;
        NO_INPUTS: PIN_TYPE;
        NO_OUTPUTS: PIN_TYPE;
    end record;
```

Values can be assigned to a record type object using aggregates. For example,

```
variable NAND_COMP: MODULE;
-- NAND_COMP is an object of record type MODULE.
NAND_COMP := (50, 20 ns, 3, 2);
-- Implies 50 is assigned to SIZE, 20 ns is assigned
-- to CRITICAL_DLY, etc.
```

Values can be assigned to a record type object from another record type object of the same type using a single assignment statement. In the following example, each element of NAND_GENERIC is assigned the value of the corresponding element in NAND_COMP.

```
signal NAND_GENERIC: MODULE;
NAND_GENERIC <= NAND_COMP;
```

Each element of a record type object can also be assigned individually by using selected names. For example,

```
NAND_COMP.NO_INPUTS := 2;
```

Aggregate values can be assigned to record type objects using both positional and named associations. Since an aggregate does not specify its type, it can be either an array or a record aggregate, depending on its usage. For example,

```
CAB := (others=>'0');
```

If CAB is an array type object, the aggregate is treated as an array aggregate; on the other hand, if CAB is a record type object, the aggregate is a record aggregate where **others** refers to all the elements in the record.

3.3.4   Access Types

Values belonging to an access type are pointers to a dynamically allocated object of some other type. They are similar to pointers in Pascal and C languages. Examples of access type declarations are

```
-- MODULE is a record type declared in the previous sub-section.
type PTR is access MODULE;
type FIFO is array (0 to 63, 0 to 7) of BIT;
type FIFO_PTR is access FIFO;
```

PTR is an access type whose values are addresses that point to objects of type MODULE. Every access type may also have the value **null**, which means that it does not point to any object. Objects of an access type can only belong to the **variable** class. When an object of an access type is declared, the default value of this object is **null**. For example,

```
variable MOD1PTR, MOD2PTR: PTR; -- Default value is null.
```

Objects that access types point to, can be created using *allocators*. Allocators provide a mechanism to dynamically create objects of a specific type.

```
MOD1PTR := new MODULE;
```

The **new** in this assignment causes an object of type MODULE to be created and the pointer to this object is returned. The values of the elements of the MODULE record are the default values of each element; these are 20 (the left-most value of the implied subtype) for the SIZE element, TIME'LEFT for the CRITICAL_DLY element, and the value 0 (this is PIN_TYPE'LEFT) for the NO_INPUTS and NO_OUTPUTS elements. Initial values can also be assigned to a newly created object by explicitly specifying the values as shown in the following example.

> MOD2PTR := **new** MODULE'(25, 10 ns, 4, 9);

Objects of an access type can be referenced as

1. *scalar-obj-ptr*.**all**, if *scalar-obj-ptr* is a pointer to a scalar type object,
2. *array-obj-ptr* (*element-index*), if *array-obj-ptr* is a pointer to an array object,
3. *record-obj-ptr.element-name*, if *record-obj-ptr* is a pointer to a record object.

The elements of the object that MOD2PTR points to can be accessed as MOD2PTR.SIZE, MOD2PTR.CRITICAL_DLY, MOD2PTR.NO_INPUTS and MOD2PTR.NO_OUTPUTS, provided the pointer is not null.

For every access type, a procedure DEALLOCATE is implicitly declared. This procedure, when called, returns the storage occupied by the object to the host environment. For the PTR and FIFO_PTR access types declared earlier, the following DEALLOCATE procedures are implicitly declared:

> **procedure** DEALLOCATE (P: **inout** PTR);
> **procedure** DEALLOCATE (P: **inout** FIFO_PTR);

The execution of the following statement:

> DEALLOCATE(MOD2PTR);

causes the storage occupied by the object that MOD2PTR points to, to be deallocated and MOD2PTR is set to **null**.

Pointers can be assigned to other pointer variables of the same access type. Therefore,

> MOD1PTR := MOD2PTR;

is a legal assignment. Both MOD1PTR and MOD2PTR now point to the same object. Consider the following example.

```
type BITVEC_PTR is access BIT_VECTOR;
variable BITVEC1: BITVEC_PTR := new BIT_VECTOR'("1001");
```

BITVEC1 points to an object that is constrained to be of four bits. The bits can be accessed as BITVEC1(0) which is 1, BITVEC1(1) which is 0, and so on. Here is another example in which values are assigned to a dynamically allocated object using named association.

```
MOD2PTR := new MODULE'(CRITICAL_DLY=>10 ns, NO_INPUTS=>2,
                       NO_OUTPUTS=>3, SIZE=>100);
```

Access types are useful in modeling high-level behavior, especially that of regular structures like RAMs and FIFOs, where pointers can be used to access objects one at a time in a sequence.

3.3.5   Incomplete Types

It is possible to have an access type that points to an object that has elements which are also access types. This can lead to mutually dependent or recursive access types. Since a type must be declared before it is used, an incomplete type declaration can be used to solve this problem. An incomplete type declaration has the form

```
type type-name ;
```

Once an incomplete type has been declared, the *type-name* can now be used in any mutually dependent or recursive access type. However, a corresponding full type declaration must follow later. An example of a mutually dependent access type is

```
type COMP; -- Record contains component name and list of
            -- nets its connected to.
type NET;   -- Record contains net name and list of
            -- components it is connected to.
type COMP_PTR is access COMP;
type NET_PTR is access NET;
constant MODMAX: INTEGER := 100;
constant NETMAX: INTEGER := 2500;
type COMP_LIST is array (1 to MODMAX) of COMP_PTR;
type NET_LIST is array (1 to NETMAX) of NET_PTR;

type COMPLIST_PTR is access COMP_LIST;
type NETLIST_PTR is access NET_LIST;
-- Full type declarations for COMP and NET follow:
type COMP is
    record
        COMP_NAME: STRING(1 to 10);
```

```
                NETS: NETLIST_PTR;
            end record;
        type NET is
            record
                NET_NAME: STRING(1 to 10);
                COMPONENTS: COMPLIST_PTR;
            end record;
```

Here, COMP and NET have elements which access objects of type NET and COMP, respectively. An example of a recursive access type is

```
        type DFG;                -- A data flow graph node.
        type OP_TYPE is (ADD, SUB, MUL, DIV, SHIFT, ROTATE);
        type PTR is access DFG;
        type DFG is
            record
                OP_CODE: OP_TYPE;
                SUCC: PTR;      -- Successor node list.
                PRED: PTR;      -- Predecessor node list.
            end record;
```

PTR is an access type of DFG. It is also the type of an element in DFG. Here is another example.

```
        type MEM_RANGE is range 0 to 16383;
        type HOLE;              -- Represents available memory.
        type HOLE_PTR is access HOLE;
        type HOLE is
            record
                START_LOC, END_LOC: MEM_RANGE;
                PREV_HOLE, NEXT_HOLE: HOLE_PTR;
            end record;
```

3.3.6   File Types

Objects of file types represent files in the host environment. They provide a mechanism by which a VHDL design communicates with the host environment. The syntax of a file type declaration is

```
        type file-type-name is file of type-name;
```

The *type-name* is the type of values contained in the file. Here are two examples.

```
        type VECTORS is file of BIT_VECTOR;
        type NAMES is file of STRING;
```

A file of type VECTORS has a sequence of values of type BIT_VECTOR; a file of type NAMES has a sequence of strings as values in it.

A file is declared using a file declaration.The syntax of a file declaration is:

> **file** *file-name* : *file-type-name* **is** *mode string-expression* ;

The *string-expression* is interpreted by the host environment as the physical name of the file. The mode of a file, **in** or **out**, specifies whether it is an input or an output file, respectively. Input files can only be read while output files can only be written to.

Here are two examples of declaring files.

> **file** VEC_FILE: VECTORS **is in** "/usr/home/jb/uart/div.vec";
> **file** OUTPUT: NAMES **is out** "stdout";

VEC_FILE is declared to be a file that contains a sequence of bit vectors and it is an input file. It is associated with the file "/usr/home/jb/uart/div.vec" in the host environment. A file belongs to the **variable** class of objects. However, a file cannot be assigned values using a variable assignment statement. It can be read, written to, or tested for an end-of-file condition, only by using special procedures and functions that are implicitly declared for every file type; these are

> **procedure** READ (F: **in** *file-type-name*; VALUE: **out** *type-name*);
> -- Gets the next value in VALUE from file F.
>
> **procedure** WRITE (F: **out** *file-type-name*; VALUE: **in** *type-name*);
> -- Appends a given value in VALUE to file F.
>
> **function** ENDFILE (F: **in** *file-type-name*) **return** BOOLEAN;
> -- Returns false if a read on an input file F will be successful in getting
> -- another value, otherwise it returns true.

If *type-name* is an unconstrained array type, a different READ procedure is implicitly declared, which is of the form

> **procedure** READ (F: **in** *file-type-name*; VALUE: **out** *type-name*;
> LENGTH: **out** NATURAL);
> -- LENGTH returns the number of elements of the array that was read.

A file cannot be opened or closed explicitly and values within a file can only be accessed sequentially.

Here is a complete example of a test bench that reads vectors from a file,·
"fadd.vec", applies these vectors to the test component, a one-bit full adder,
and then writes back the results into another file, "fadd.out".

```
entity FA_TEST is end;

architecture IO_EXAMPLE of FA_TEST is
    component FULL_ADD
        port (CIN, A, B: in BIT; COUT, SUM: out BIT);
    end component;
    subtype STRING3 is BIT_VECTOR(0 to 2);
    subtype STRING2 is BIT_VECTOR(0 to 1);
    type IN_TYPE is file of STRING3;
    type OUT_TYPE is file of STRING2;
    file VEC_FILE: IN_TYPE is in "/usr/home/jb/vhdl_ex/fadd.vec";
    file RESULT_FILE: OUT_TYPE is
        out "/usr/home/jb/vhdl_ex/fadd.out";
    signal S: STRING3;
    signal Q: STRING2;
begin
    FA: FULL_ADD port map (S(0), S(1), S(2), Q(0), Q(1));

    process
        constant PROPAGATION_DELAY: TIME := 25 ns;
        variable IN_STR: STRING3;
        variable OUT_STR: STRING2;
    begin
        while (not ENDFILE (VEC_FILE)) loop
            READ (VEC_FILE, IN_STR);
            S <= IN_STR;
            wait for PROPAGATION_DELAY;
            OUT_STR := Q;
            WRITE (RESULT_FILE, OUT_STR);
        end loop;
        assert FALSE
            report "Completed.";
    end process;
end IO_EXAMPLE;
```

Two files, VEC_FILE and RESULT_FILE, are declared. VEC_FILE is an
input file and contains 3-bit strings, and RESULT_FILE is an output file into
which 2-bit strings are written. Input vectors are read one at a time until end
of file is reached. Each vector is applied and then the process waits for the full-
adder circuit to stabilize before sampling the adder output value which is
written to the output file. The assertion statement when executed simply
stops the simulation run since the assertion condition is always false. This

statement is not necessary if the VHDL simulator provides a facility to control the simulation run.

One file type, TEXT, is predefined in the language; this file type represents a file consisting of variable length ASCII strings. An access type, LINE, is also provided to point to such strings. Operations to read and write data from a single line are provided. Operations to read and write entire lines are also provided. The definitions for all these types and operations appear in the predefined package, TEXTIO.

3.4   Operators

The predefined operators in the language are classified into the following five categories:

1. Logical operators
2. Relational operators
3. Adding operators
4. Multiplying operators
5. Miscellaneous operators

The operators have increasing precedence going from category (1) to (5). Operators in the same category have the same precedence and evaluation is done left to right. Parentheses may be used to override the left to right evaluation.

3.4.1   Logical Operators

The six logical operators are

    and   or   nand   nor   xor   not

These operators are defined for the predefined types BIT and BOOLEAN. They are also defined for one-dimensional arrays of BIT and BOOLEAN. During evaluation, bit values '0' and '1' are treated as FALSE and TRUE values of the BOOLEAN type, respectively. The result of a logical operation has the same type as its operands. The **not** operator is a unary logical operator and has the same precedence as that of miscellaneous operators.

3.4.2   Relational Operators

These are

    =   /=   <   <=   >   >=

The result types for all relational operations is always BOOLEAN. The =
(equality) and the /= (inequality) operators are permitted on any type except
file types. The remaining four relational operators are permitted on any scalar
type (e.g., integer or enumerated types) or discrete array type (i.e., arrays in
which element values belong to a discrete type). When operands are discrete
array types, comparison is performed one element at a time from left to right.
For example,

BIT_VECTOR'('0', '1', '1') < BIT_VECTOR'('1', '0', '1')

is true, since the first element in the first array aggregate is less than the first
element in the second aggregate. Similarly, if

type MVL is ('U', '0', '1', 'Z');

then,

MVL'('U') < MVL'('Z')

is true since 'U' occurs to the left of 'Z'. Note that it is necessary to qualify the
aggregates and literals used in these examples since the literals are overloaded and their type cannot be determined from its use. Qualified expressions are
described in Chap. 10.

3.4.3   Adding Operators

These are

+   –   &

The operands for the + (addition) and – (subtraction) operators must be of the
same numeric type with the result being of the same numeric type. The addition and subtraction operators may also be used as unary operators, in which
case, the operand and the result type must be the same. The operands for the
& (concatenation) operator can be either a 1-dimensional array type or an element type. The result is always an array type. For example,

'0' & '1'

results in an array of characters "01".

'C' & 'A' & 'T'

results in the value "CAT".

"BA" & "LL"

creates an array of characters "BALL".

3.4.4   Multiplying Operators

These are

> *   /   **mod**   **rem**

The * (multiplication) and / (division) operators are predefined for both operands being of the same integer or floating point type. The result is also of the same type. The multiplication operator is also defined for the case when one of the operands is of a physical type and the second operand is of integer or real type. The result is of physical type.

For the division operator, division of an object of a physical type by either an integer or a real type object is allowed and the result type is of the physical type. Division of an object of a physical type by another object of the same physical type is also defined and it yields an integer value as a result.

The **rem** (remainder) and **mod** (modulus) operators operate on operands of integer types and the result is also of the same type. The result of a **rem** operation has the sign of its first operand and is defined as

> A rem B = A − (A / B) * B

The result of a **mod** operator has the sign of the second operand and is defined as

> A mod B = A − B * N   -- For some integer N.

3.4.5   Miscellaneous Operators

The miscellaneous operators are

> **abs**   **

The **abs** (absolute) operator is defined for any numeric type.

The ** (exponentiation) operator is defined for the left operand to be of integer or floating point type and the right operand (i.e., the exponent) to be of integer type only.

The **not** logical operator has the same precedence as the above two operators.

❏

CHAPTER 4 *Behavioral Modeling*

This chapter presents the behavioral style of modeling. In this modeling style, the behavior of the entity is expressed using sequentially executed, procedural type code, that is very similar in syntax and semantics to that of a high-level programming language like C or Pascal. A process statement is the primary mechanism used to model the procedural type behavior of an entity. This chapter describes the process statement and the various kinds of sequential statements that can be used within a process statement to model such behavior.

Irrespective of the modeling style used, every entity is represented using an entity declaration and at least one architecture body. The first two sections describe these in detail.

4.1 Entity Declaration

An entity declaration describes the external interface of the entity, that is, it gives the black-box view. It specifies the name of the entity, the names of inter-

face ports, their mode (i.e., direction), and the type of ports. The syntax for an
entity declaration is

```
entity entity-name is
    [ generic ( list-of-generics-and-their-types ) ; ]
    [ port ( list-of-interface-port-names-and-their-types ) ; ]
    [ entity-item-declarations ]
[ begin
    entity-statements ]
end [ entity-name ] ;
```

Generics are discussed in Chap. 7, and *entity-statements* are discussed in
Chap. 10. The *entity-name* is the name of the entity and the interface ports are
the signals through which the entity passes information to and from its external environment. Each interface port can have one of the following modes:

1. **in:** the value of an input port can only be read within the entity model.
2. **out:** the value of an output port can only be updated within
   the entity model; it cannot be read.
3. **inout:** the value of a bidirectional port can be read and updated within the entity model.
4. **buffer:** the value of a buffer port can be read and updated
   within the entity model. However, it differs from the **inout**
   mode in that it cannot have more than one source and that
   the only kind of signal that can be connected to it can be another buffer port or a signal with at most one source.

Declarations that are placed in the *entity-item-declarations* section are
common to all the design units that are associated with that entity declaration
(these may be architecture bodies and configuration declarations). Examples
of these are given in Chap. 10. An And-Or-Invert circuit is shown in Fig. 4.1
and its corresponding entity declaration is shown next.

```
entity AOI is
    port (A, B, C, D: in BIT; Z: out BIT);
end AOI;
```

The entity declaration specifies that the name of the entity is AOI and
that it has four input signals of type BIT and one output signal of type BIT.
Note that it does not specify the composition or functionality of the entity.

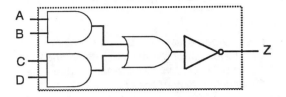

Figure 4.1 An And-Or-Invert circuit.

4.2   *Architecture Body*

An architecture body describes the internal view of an entity. It describes the functionality or the structure of the entity. The syntax of an architecture body is

> **architecture** *architecture-name* **of** *entity-name* **is**
>   [*architecture-item-declarations*]
> **begin**
>   *concurrent-statements ; these are* -->
>   *process-statement*
>   *block-statement*
>   *concurrent-procedure-call*
>   *concurrent-assertion-statement*
>   *concurrent-signal-assignment-statement*
>   *component-instantiation-statement*
>   *generate-statement*
> **end** [*architecture-name*] ;

The concurrent statements describe the internal composition of the entity. All concurrent statements execute in parallel, and therefore, their textual order of appearance within the architecture body has no impact on the implied behavior. The internal composition of an entity can be expressed in terms of structure, dataflow and sequential behavior. These are described using concurrent statements. For example, component instantiations are used to express structure, concurrent signal assignment statements are used to express dataflow and process statements are used to express sequential behavior. Each concurrent statement is a different element operating in parallel in a similar sense that individual gates of a design are operating in parallel.

The item declarations declare items that are available for use within the architecture body. The names of items declared in the entity declaration, including ports and generics, are available for use within the architecture body due to the association of the entity name with the architecture body by the statement

architecture *architecture-name* **of** *entity-name* **is** . . .

An entity can have many internal views, each of which is described using a separate architecture body. In general, an entity is represented using one entity declaration (that provides the external view) and one or more architecture bodies (that provide the internal view). Here are two examples of architecture bodies for the same AOI entity.

```
architecture AOI_CONCURRENT of AOI is
begin
    Z <= not ( (A and B) or (C and D) );
end AOI_CONCURRENT;

architecture AOI_SEQUENTIAL of AOI is
begin
    process (A, B, C, D)
        variable TEMP1, TEMP2: BIT;
    begin
        TEMP1 := A and B;                    -- statement 1
        TEMP2 := C and D;                    -- statement 2
        TEMP1 := TEMP1 or TEMP2;             -- statement 3
        Z <= not TEMP1;                      -- statement 4
    end process;
end AOI_SEQUENTIAL;
```

The first architecture body, AOI_CONCURRENT, describes the AOI entity using the dataflow style of modeling; the second architecture body, AOI_SEQUENTIAL, uses the behavioral style of modeling. In this chapter, we are concerned with describing an entity using the behavioral modeling style. A process statement, which is a concurrent statement, is the primary mechanism used to describe the functionality of an entity in this modeling style.

4.3   Process Statement

A process statement contains sequential statements that describe the functionality of a portion of an entity in sequential terms. The syntax of a process statement is

```
[ process-label : ] process [ ( sensitivity-list ) ]
    [ process-item-declarations ]
begin
```

```
            sequential-statements; these are -->
                variable-assignment-statement
                signal-assignment-statement
                wait-statement
                if-statement
                case-statement
                loop-statement
                null-statement
                exit-statement
                next-statement
                assertion-statement
                procedure-call-statement
                return-statement.
        end process [ process-label ] ;
```

A set of signals that the process is sensitive to is defined by the sensitivity list. In other words, each time an event occurs on any of the signals in the sensitivity list, the sequential statements within the process are executed in a sequential order, that is, in the order in which they appear (similar to statements in a high-level programming language like C or Pascal). The process then suspends after executing the last sequential statement and waits for another event to occur on a signal in the sensitivity list. Items declared in the item declarations part are available for use only within the process.

The architecture body, AOI_SEQUENTIAL, presented earlier, contains one process statement. This process statement has four signals in its sensitivity list and has one variable declaration. If an event occurs on any of the signals, A, B, C, or D, the process is executed. This is accomplished by executing statement 1 first, then statement 2, followed by statement 3, and then statement 4. After this, the process suspends (simulation does not stop, however) and waits for another event to occur on a signal in the sensitivity list.

4.4   Variable Assignment Statement

Variables can be declared and used inside a process statement. A variable is assigned a value using the variable assignment statement that typically has the form

        variable-object := expression ;

The expression is evaluated when the statement is executed and the computed value is assigned to the variable object instantaneously, that is, at the current simulation time.

Variables are created at the time of elaboration and retain their values throughout the entire simulation run (like static variables in C high-level programming language). This is because a process is never exited; it is either in an active state, that is, being executed, or in a suspended state, that is, waiting for a certain event to occur. A process is first entered at the start of simulation (actually, during the initialization phase of simulation) at which time it is executed until it suspends because of a **wait** statement (**wait** statements are described later in this chapter) or a sensitivity list.

Consider the following process statement.

```
process (A)
    variable EVENTS_ON_A: INTEGER := 0;
begin
    EVENTS_ON_A := EVENTS_ON_A + 1;
end process;
```

At start of simulation, the process is executed once. The variable EVENTS_ON_A gets initialized to 0 and then incremented by 1. After that, any time an event occurs on signal A, the process is activated and the single variable assignment statement is executed. This causes the variable EVENTS_ON_A to be incremented. At the end of simulation, variable EVENTS_ON_A contains the total number of events that occurred on signal A plus one.

Here is another example of a process statement.

```
signal A, Z: INTEGER;
. . .
PZ: process (A)                        -- PZ is a label for the process.
    variable V1, V2: INTEGER;
begin
    V1 := A - V2;                      -- statement 1
    Z <= - V1;                         -- statement 2
    V2 := Z + V1 * 2;                  -- statement 3
end process PZ;
```

If an event occurred on signal A at time T_1 and variable V2 was assigned a value, say 10, in statement 3, then when the next time an event occurs on signal A, say at time T_2, the value of V2 used in statement 1 would still be 10.

4.5   Signal Assignment Statement

Signals are assigned values using a signal assignment statement. The simplest form of a signal assignment statement is *signal-object* <= *expression* [**after** *delay-value*] ;

A signal assignment statement can appear within a process or outside of a process. If it occurs outside of a process, it is considered to be a concurrent signal assignment statement. This is discussed in the next chapter. When a signal assignment statement appears within a process, it is considered to be a sequential signal assignment statement and is executed in sequence with respect to the other sequential statements that appear within that process.

When a signal assignment statement is executed, the value of the expression is computed and this value is scheduled to be assigned to the signal after the specified delay. It is important to note that the expression is evaluated at the time the statement is executed (which is the current simulation time) and not after the specified delay. If no **after** clause is specified, the delay is assumed to be a default delta delay.

Some examples of signal assignment statements are

```
COUNTER <= COUNTER + "0010"; -- Assign after a delta delay.
PAR <= PAR xor DIN after 12 ns;
Z <= (A0 and A1) or (B0 and B1) or (C0 and C1) after 6 ns;
```

Delta Delay

A *delta delay* is a very small delay (infinitesimally small). It does not correspond to any real delay and actual simulation time does not advance. This delay models hardware where a minimal amount of time is needed for a change to occur, for example, in performing zero delay simulation. Delta delay allows for ordering of events that occur at the same simulation time during a simulation. Each unit of simulation time can be considered to be composed of an infinite number of delta delays. Therefore, an event always occurs at a real simulation time plus an integral multiple of delta delays. For example, events can occur at 15 ns, 15 ns + 1Δ, 15 ns + 2Δ, 15 ns + 3Δ, 22 ns, 22 ns + Δ, 27 ns, 27 ns + Δ, and so on.

Consider the AOI_SEQUENTIAL architecture body described in Sec. 4.2. Let us assume that an event occurs on input signal D (i.e., there is a change of value on signal D) at simulation time T. Statement 1 is executed first and TEMP1 is assigned a value immediately since it is a variable. Statement 2 is executed next and TEMP2 is assigned a value immediately. Statement 3 is executed next which uses the values of TEMP1 and TEMP2 computed in statements 1 and 2, respectively, to determine the new value for TEMP1. And finally, statement 4 is executed that causes signal Z to get the value of its right-hand-side expression after a delta delay, that is, signal Z gets its value only at time $T+\Delta$; this is shown in Fig. 4.2.

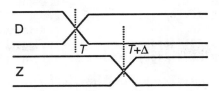

Figure 4.2 Delta delay.

Consider the process PZ described in the previous section. If an event occurs on signal A at time T, execution of statement 1 causes V1 to get a value, signal Z is then scheduled to get a value at time $T+\Delta$, and finally statement 3 is executed in which the old value of signal Z is used, that is, its value at time T, not the value that was scheduled to be assigned in statement 2. The reason for this is because simulation time is still at time T and has not advanced to time $T+\Delta$. Later when simulation time advances to $T+\Delta$, signal Z will get its new value. This example shows the important distinction between a variable assignment and a signal assignment statement. Variable assignments cause variables to get their values instantaneously while signal assignments cause signals to get their values at a later time (at least a delta delay later).

So far we have seen two examples of sequential statements, the variable assignment statement and the signal assignment statement. Other kinds of sequential statements are described next.

4.6   Wait Statement

As we saw earlier, a process may be suspended by means of a sensitivity list. That is, when a process has a sensitivity list, it always suspends after executing the last sequential statement in the process. The **wait** statement provides an alternate way to suspend the execution of a process. There are three basic forms of the **wait** statement.

> **wait on** *sensitivity-list* ;
> **wait until** *boolean-expression* ;
> **wait for** *time-expression* ;

They may also be combined in a single **wait** statement. For example,

> **wait on** *sensitivity-list* **until** *boolean-expression* **for** *time-expression* ;

Some examples of **wait** statements are

```
wait on A, B, C;                      -- statement 1
wait until (A = B);                   -- statement 2
wait for 10 ns;                       -- statement 3
wait on CLOCK for 20 ns;             -- statement 4
wait until (SUM > 100) for 50 ms;    -- statement 5
```

In statement 1, the execution of the **wait** statement causes the process to suspend and then it waits for an event to occur on signals A, B, or C. Once that happens, the process resumes execution from the next statement onwards. In statement 2, the process is suspended until the specified condition becomes true. When an event occurs on signal A or B, the condition is evaluated and if it is true, the process resumes execution from the next statement onwards, otherwise, it suspends again. When the **wait** statement in statement 3 is executed, say at time T, the process suspends for 10 ns and when simulation time advances to $T+10$ ns, the process resumes execution from the statement following the **wait** statement.

The execution of statement 4 causes the process to suspend and then it waits for an event to occur on the signal CLOCK for 20 ns. If no event occurs within 20 ns, the process resumes execution with the statement following the wait. In the last statement, the process suspends for a maximum of 50 ms until the value of signal SUM is greater than 100. The boolean condition is evaluated every time there is an event on signal SUM. If the boolean condition is not satisfied for 50 ms, the process resumes from the statement following the **wait** statement.

It is possible for a process not to have an explicit sensitivity list. In such a case, the process may have one or more **wait** statements. It must have at least one **wait** statement, otherwise, the process will never get suspended and would remain in an infinite loop during the initialization phase of simulation. It is an error if both the sensitivity list and a **wait** statement are present within a process. The presence of a sensitivity list in a process implies the presence of an implicit **"wait on** *sensitivity-list"* statement as the last statement in the process. An equivalent process statement for the process statement in the AOI_SEQUENTIAL architecture body is

```
process                              -- No sensitivity list.
    variable TEMP1, TEMP2: BIT;
begin
    TEMP1 := A and B;
    TEMP2 := C and D;
    TEMP1 := TEMP1 or TEMP2;
    Z <= not TEMP1;
    wait on A, B, C, D;              -- Replaces the sensitivity list.
end process;
```

Therefore, a process with a sensitivity list always suspends at the end of the process and when reactivated due to an event, resumes execution from the first statement in the process.

4.7   If Statement

An **if** statement selects a sequence of statements for execution based on the value of a condition. The condition can be any expression that evaluates to a boolean value. The general form of an **if** statement is

```
if boolean-expression then
    sequential-statements
[ elsif boolean-expression then       -- elsif clause; if stmt can have 0 or
    sequential-statements ]           -- more elsif clauses.
[ else                                -- else clause.
    sequential-statements ]
end if;
```

The **if** statement is executed by checking each condition sequentially until the first true condition is found; then, the set of sequential statements associated with this condition is executed. The **if** statement can have zero or more **elsif** clauses and an optional **else** clause. An **if** statement is also a sequential statement, and therefore, the previous syntax allows for arbitrary nesting of **if** statements. Here are some examples.

```
if SUM <= 100 then   -- This is a less-than-or-equal-to operator.
    SUM := SUM + 10;
end if;

if NICKEL_IN then
    DEPOSITED <= TOTAL_10;       -- This "<=" is a signal assignment
                                 -- operator.
elsif DIME_IN then
    DEPOSITED <= TOTAL_15;
elsif QUARTER_IN then
    DEPOSITED <= TOTAL_30;
else
    DEPOSITED <= TOTAL_ERROR;
end if;

if CTRL1 = '1' then
    if CTRL2 = '0' then
        MUX_OUT <= "0010";
    else
```

```
                        MUX_OUT <= "0001";
                end if;
        else
            if CTRL2 = '0' then
                MUX_OUT <= "1000";
            else
                MUX_OUT <= "0100";
            end if;
        end if;
```

A complete example of a 2-input **nor** gate entity using an **if** statement is shown next.

```
        entity NOR2 is
            port (A, B: in BIT; Z: out BIT);
        end NOR2;

        architecture NOR2 of NOR2 is     -- Architecture body can have
                                         -- same name as entity.
        begin
            P1: process (A, B)
                constant RISE_TIME: TIME := 10 ns;
                constant FALL_TIME: TIME := 8 ns;
                variable TEMP: BIT;
            begin
                TEMP := A nor B;
                if (TEMP = '1') then
                    Z <= TEMP after RISE_TIME;
                else
                    Z <= TEMP after FALL_TIME;
                end if;
            end process P1;
        end NOR2;
```

4.8   Case Statement

The format of a **case** statement is

```
        case expression is
            when choices => sequential-statements    -- branch #1
            when choices => sequential-statements    -- branch #2
            -- Can have any number of branches.
            [ when others => sequential-statements ] -- last branch
        end case;
```

The **case** statement selects one of the branches for execution based on the value of the expression. The expression value must be of a discrete type or of a one-dimensional array type. Choices may be expressed as single values, as a range of values, by using | (vertical bar: represents an "or"), or by using the **others** clause. All possible values of the expression must be covered in the **case** statement. The **others** clause can be used as a choice to cover the "catch-all" values and, if present, must be the last branch in the **case** statement. An example of a **case** statement is

```
type WEEK_DAY is (MON, TUE, WED, THU, FRI, SAT, SUN);
type DOLLARS is range 0 to 10;
variable DAY: WEEK_DAY;
variable POCKET_MONEY: DOLLARS;

case DAY is
    when TUE => POCKET_MONEY := 6;              -- branch 1
    when MON I WED => POCKET_MONEY := 2;        -- branch 2
    when FRI to SUN => POCKET_MONEY := 7;       -- branch 3
    when others => POCKET_MONEY := 0;           -- branch 4
end case;
```

Branch 2 is chosen if DAY has the value of either MON or WED. Branch 3 covers the values FRI, SAT, and SUN, while branch 4 covers the remaining value, THU. The **case** statement is also a sequential statement and it is, therefore, possible to have nested **case** statements. A model for a 4 * 1 multiplexer using a **case** statement is shown next.

```
entity MUX is
    port (A, B, C, D: in BIT; CTRL: in BIT_VECTOR(0 to 1);
            Z: out BIT);
end MUX;

architecture MUX_BEHAVIOR of MUX is
    constant MUX_DELAY: TIME := 10 ns;
begin
    PMUX: process (A, B, C, D, CTRL)
        variable TEMP: BIT;
    begin
        case CTRL is
            when "00" => TEMP := A;
            when "01" => TEMP := B;
            when "10" => TEMP := C;
            when "11" => TEMP := D;
        end case;
        Z <= TEMP after MUX_DELAY;
```

```
        end process PMUX;
      end MUX_BEHAVIOR;
```

4.9   Null Statement

The statement

```
    null ;
```

is a sequential statement that does not cause any action to take place and execution continues with the next statement. One example of this statement's use is in an if statement or in a case statement where for certain conditions, it may be useful or necessary to explicitly specify that no action needs to be performed.

4.10   Loop Statement

A loop statement is used to iterate through a set of sequential statements. The syntax of a loop statement is

```
      [ loop-label : ] iteration-scheme loop
          sequential-statements
      end loop [ loop-label ] ;
```

There are three types of iteration schemes. The first is the for iteration scheme that has the form

```
      for identifier in range
```

An example of this iteration scheme is

```
      FACTORIAL := 1;
      for NUMBER in 2 to N loop
          FACTORIAL := FACTORIAL * NUMBER;
      end loop;
```

The body of the for loop is executed (N–1) times, with the loop identifier, NUMBER, being incremented by 1 at the end of each iteration. The object NUMBER is implicitly declared within the for loop to belong to the integer type whose values are in the range 2 to N. No explicit declaration for the loop identifier is, therefore, necessary. The loop identifier, also, cannot be assigned any value inside the for loop. If another variable with the same name exists outside the **for** loop, these two variables are treated separately and the variable used inside the **for** loop refers to the loop identifier.

The range in a **for** loop can also be a range of an enumeration type such as

```
type HEXA is ('0', '1', '2', '3', '4', '5', '6', '7', '8', '9', 'A', 'B', 'C', 'D', 'E', 'F');
. . .
for NUM in HEXA'('9') downto HEXA'('0') loop
    -- NUM will take values in type HEXA from '9' through '0'.
    . . .
end loop;

for CHAR in HEXA loop
    -- CHAR will take all values in type HEXA from '0' through 'F'.
    . . .
end loop;
```

Notice that it is necessary to qualify the values being used for NUM [e.g., HEXA'('9')] since the literals '0' through '9' are overloaded, once being defined in type HEXA and the second time being defined in the predefined type CHARACTER. Qualified expressions are described in Chap. 10.

The second form of the iteration scheme is the **while** scheme that has the form

```
while boolean-expression
```

An example of the **while** iteration scheme is

```
J := 0; SUM := 10;
WH_LOOP: while J < 20 loop        -- This loop has a label, WH_LOOP.
    SUM := SUM * 2;
    J := J + 3;
end loop;
```

The statements within the body of the loop are executed sequentially and repeatedly as long as the loop condition, $J < 20$, is true. At this point, execution continues with the statement following the **loop** statement.

The third and final form of the iteration scheme is one where no iteration scheme is specified. In this form of **loop** statement, all statements in the loop body are repeatedly executed until some other action causes it to exit the loop. These actions can be caused by an **exit** statement, a **next** statement, or a **return** statement. Here is an example.

```
SUM := 1; J := 0;
L2: loop        -- This loop also has a label.
```

```
            J := J + 21;
            SUM := SUM * 10;
            exit when SUM > 100;
        end loop L2; -- This loop label, if present, must be the same
                     -- as the initial loop label.
```

In this example, the **exit** statement causes the execution to jump out of loop L2 when SUM becomes greater than 100. If the **exit** statement were not present, the loop would execute indefinitely.

4.11 *Exit Statement*

The **exit** statement is a sequential statement that can be used only inside a loop. It causes execution to jump out of the innermost loop or the loop whose label is specified. The syntax for an **exit** statement is

> **exit** [*loop-label*] [**when** *condition*] ;

If no loop label is specified, the innermost loop is exited. If the **when** clause is used, the specified loop is exited only if the given condition is true, otherwise, execution continues with the next statement. An alternate form for loop L2 described in the previous section is

```
        SUM := 1; J := 0;
        L3: loop
            J : = J + 21;
            SUM := SUM * 10;
            if (SUM > 100) then
                exit L3;            -- "exit;" also would have been sufficient.
            end if;
        end loop L3;
```

4.12 *Next Statement*

The **next** statement is also a sequential statement that can be used only inside a loop. The syntax is the same as that for the **exit** statement except that the keyword **next** replaces the keyword **exit**. Its syntax is

> **next** [*loop-label*] [**when** *condition*] ;

The **next** statement results in skipping the remaining statements in the current iteration of the specified loop and execution resumes with the first statement in the next iteration of this loop. If no loop label is specified, the innermost loop is assumed. In contrast to the **exit** statement that causes the loop to be terminated (i.e., exits the specified loop), the **next** statement causes the current loop iteration of the specified loop to be prematurely terminated and execution resumes with the next iteration. Here is an example.

```
for J in 10 downto 5 loop
    if (SUM < TOTAL_SUM) then
        SUM := SUM + 2;
    elsif (SUM = TOTAL_SUM) then
        next;
    else
        null;
    end if;
    K := K + 1;
end loop;
```

When the **next** statement is executed, execution jumps to the end of the loop (the last statement, K := K + 1, is not executed), decrements the value of the loop identifier, J, and resumes loop execution with this new value of J.

The **next** statement can also cause an inner loop to be exited. Here is such an example.

```
L4: for K in 10 downto 1 loop
    -- statements section 1
    L5: loop
        -- statements section 2
        next L4 when WR_DONE = '1';
        -- statements section 3
    end loop L5;
    -- statements section 4
end loop L4;
```

When WR_DONE = '1' becomes true, statements sections 3 and 4 are skipped and execution jumps to the beginning of the next iteration of loop L4. Notice that the loop L5 was terminated because of the result of **next** statement.

4.13 Assertion Statement

Assertion statements are useful in modeling constraints of an entity. For example, you may want to check if a signal value lies within a specified range, or check the setup and hold times for signals arriving at the inputs of an entity. If the check fails, an error is reported. The syntax of an assertion statement is

```
assert boolean-expression
  [ report string-expression ]
  [ severity expression ] ;
```

If the value of the boolean expression is false, the report message is printed along with the severity level. The expression in the severity clause must generate a value of type SEVERITY_LEVEL (a predefined enumerated type in the language with values NOTE, WARNING, ERROR, and FAILURE). The severity level is typically used by a simulator to initiate appropriate actions depending on its value. For example, if the severity level is ERROR, the simulator may abort the simulation process and provide relevant diagnostic information. At the very least, the severity level is displayed.

Here is a model of a D-type rising-edge-triggered flip-flop that uses assertion statements to check for setup and hold times.

```
entity DFF is
    port (D, CK: in BIT; Q, NOTQ: out BIT);
end DFF;

architecture CHECK_TIMES of DFF is
    constant HOLD_TIME: TIME := 5 ns;
    constant SETUP_TIME: TIME := 3 ns;
begin
    process (D, CK)
        variable LastEventOnD, LastEventOnCk: TIME;
    begin
        -- Check for hold time:
        if D'EVENT then
            assert (NOW = 0 ns) or
                    ((NOW - LastEventOnCk) >= HOLD_TIME)
                report "Hold time too short!"
                severity FAILURE;
            LastEventOnD := NOW;
        end if;

        -- Check for setup time:
        if (CK = '1') and CK'EVENT then
            assert (NOW = 0 ns) or
                    ((NOW - LastEventOnD) >= SETUP_TIME)
                report "Setup time too short!"
                severity FAILURE;
            LastEventOnCk := NOW;
        end if;

        -- Behavior of FF:
        if (CK = '1') and CK'EVENT then
```

```
                Q <= D;
                NOTQ <= not D;
            end if;
        end process;
    end CHECK_TIMES;
```

EVENT is a predefined attribute of a signal and is true if an event (a change of value) occurred on that signal at the time the value of the attribute is determined. Attributes are described in greater detail in Chap. 10. NOW is a predefined function that returns the current simulation time. In the previous example, the process is sensitive to signals D and CK. When an event occurs on either of these signals, the first if statement is executed. This checks to see if an event occurred on D. If so, the assertion is checked to make sure that the difference between the current simulation time and the last time an event occurred on signal CK is greater than a constant HOLD_TIME delay. If not, a report message is printed and the severity level is returned to the simulator. Similarly, the next if statement checks for the setup time. The last if statement describes the latch behavior of the D-type flip-flop. The setup and hold times have been modeled as constants in this example. These could also be modeled as generic parameters of the flip-flop. Generics are discussed in Chap. 7.

Here is another example that uses an assertion statement to check for spikes at the input of an inverter.

```
    package PACK1 is
        constant MIN_PULSE: TIME := 5 ns;
        constant PROPAGATE_DLY: TIME := 10 ns;
    end PACK1;

    use WORK.PACK1.all;
    entity INV is
        port (A: in BIT; NOT_A: out BIT);
    end INV;

    architecture CHECK_INV of INV is
    begin
        process (A)
            variable LastEventOnA: TIME := 0 ns;
        begin
            assert  (NOW = 0 ns) or
                    ((NOW - LastEventOnA) >= MIN_PULSE)
                report "Spike detected on input of inverter"
                severity WARNING;
            LastEventOnA := NOW;
            NOT_A <= not A after PROPAGATE_DLY;
        end process;
    end CHECK_INV;
```

Some other examples of assertion statements are

```
assert (DATA <= 255)
    report "Data out of range.";

assert (CLK = '0') or (CLK = '1');    -- CLK is of type ('X', '0', '1', 'Z').
```

In the last assertion statement example, the default report message "Assertion violation" is printed. The default severity level is ERROR if the severity clause is not specified as in the previous two examples.

4.14 More on Signal Assignment Statement

Earlier in this chapter, we saw a simple example of a signal assignment statement used inside a process that illustrated the delta delay model. In this section, we explain the signal assignment statement in greater detail to cover its more complex features. Aside from the delta delay model, there are two other types of delay models that can be used with signal assignments, inertial and transport.

4.14.1 Inertial Delay Model

Inertial delay models the delays often found in switching circuits. It represents the time for which an input value must be stable before the value is allowed to propagate to the output. In addition, the value appears at the output after the specified delay. If the input is not stable for the specified time, no output change occurs. When used with signal assignments, the input value is represented by the value of the expression on the right-hand-side and the output is represented by the target signal.

Figure 4.3 shows a simple example of a noninverting buffer with an inertial delay of 10 ns.

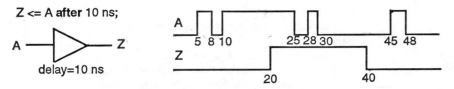

Figure 4.3 Inertial delay example.

Events on signal A that occur at 5 ns and 8 ns are not stable for the inertial delay duration and hence do not propagate to the output. Event on A at 10 ns remains stable for more than the inertial delay, and therefore, the value is propagated to the target signal Z after the inertial delay; Z gets the value '1' at 20 ns. Events on signal A at 25 ns and 28 ns do not affect the output since they are not stable for the inertial delay duration. Transition '1' to '0' at time 30 ns on signal A remains stable for at least the inertial delay duration, and therefore, a '0' is propagated to signal Z with a delay of 10 ns; Z gets the new value at 40 ns. Other events on A do not affect the target signal Z.

Since inertial delay is most commonly found in digital circuits, it is the default delay model. This delay model is often used to filter out unwanted spikes and transients on signals.

4.14.2 Transport Delay Model

Transport delay models the delays in hardware that do not exhibit any inertial delay. This delay represents pure propagation delay, that is, any changes on an input is transported to the output, no matter how small, after the specified delay. To use a transport delay model, the keyword **transport** must be used in a signal assignment statement. Figure 4.4 shows an example of a noninverting buffer using a transport delay of 10 ns.

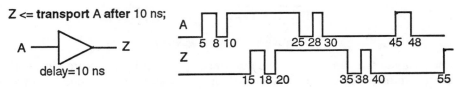

Figure 4.4 Transport delay example.

Ideal delay modeling can be obtained by using this delay model. In this case, spikes would be propagated through instead of being ignored as in the inertial delay case. Routing delays can be modeled using transport delay. An example of a routing delay model is

```
entity WIRE14 is
    port (A: in BIT; Z: out BIT);
end WIRE14;

architecture WIRE14_TRANSPORT of WIRE14 is
begin
    process (A)
    begin
        Z <= transport A after 0.1 ms;
    end process;
end WIRE14_TRANSPORT;
```

4.14.3 Creating Signal Waveforms

In all examples of signal assignment statements that we have seen so far, we have always assigned a single value to a signal; this need not be so. It is possible to assign multiple values to a signal, each with a different delay value. For example,

PHASE1 <= '0', '1' after 8 ns, '0' after 13 ns, '1' after 50 ns;

When this signal assignment statement is executed, say at time T, it causes four values to be scheduled for signal PHASE1, the value '0' is scheduled to be assigned at time $T+\Delta$, '1' at $T+8$ ns, '0' at $T+13$ ns, and '1' at $T+50$ ns. Thus, a waveform appears on the signal PHASE1 as shown in Fig. 4.5.

A more general syntax of a signal assignment statement is

signal-object <=   waveform-element , waveform-element ,
                             waveform-element , waveform-element ;
-- Can have any number of waveform elements.

Figure 4.5 A signal waveform.

Each waveform element has a value part, specified by an expression (called the waveform expression in this text), and a delay part, specified by an **after** clause that specifies the delay. The delays in the waveform elements must appear in increasing order. A waveform element is of the form

expression after time-expression

Any arbitrary waveform can, therefore, be easily created using a signal assignment statement.

4.14.4 Signal Drivers

What if there is more than one assignment to the same signal within a process? To understand how the waveform elements contribute to the effective value of a signal, it is important to understand the concept of a driver. Every signal assignment in a process creates a *driver* for that signal. The driver of a signal holds its current value and all its future values as a sequence of one or more transactions, where each transaction identifies the value to appear on the signal along with the time at which the value is to appear.

Consider the following signal assignment statement with three wave-form elements and the driver that is created for that signal.

```
process
begin
    . . .
    RESET <= 3 after 5 ns, 21 after 10 ns, 14 after 17 ns;
end process;
```

RESET ◄——— | curr@now | 3@T+5 ns | 21@T+10 ns | 14@T+17 ns |

All transactions on the driver are ordered in increasing order of time. A driver always contains at least one transaction, which could be the initial value of the signal. The value of a signal is the value of its driver (the case where a signal has more than one driver is considered in the next chapter). In the previous example, when the signal assignment statement is executed, say at time T, three new transactions are added to the driver for the RESET signal. The first transaction is the current value of the signal.

When simulation time advances to T+5 ns, the first transaction is deleted from the driver and RESET gets the value of 3. When time advances to T+10 ns, the second transaction is deleted and RESET gets the value of 21. When time advances to T+17 ns, the third transaction is deleted and RESET gets the value of 14.

What if there is another signal assignment to RESET in the same process? Since a signal inside a process can have only one driver, the transactions of the second signal assignment modify the transactions already present on the driver depending on whether inertial or transport delay model is used. We consider the transport delay case first.

Effect of Transport Delay on Signal Drivers

Here is an example of a process having three signal assignments to the same signal RX_DATA.

```
signal RX_DATA: NATURAL;
. . .
process
begin
    . . .
    RX_DATA <= transport 11 after 10 ns;
    RX_DATA <= transport 20 after 22 ns;
    RX_DATA <= transport 35 after 18 ns;
end process;
```

Assume that the statements are executed at time T. The transactions on the driver for RX_DATA are created as follows. When the first signal assignment is executed, the transaction, 11@T+10 ns, is added to the driver. After the second signal assignment is executed, the transaction, 20@T+ 22 ns, is appended to the driver since the delay of this transaction (= 22 ns) is larger than the delay of the pending transactions on the driver. The driver for RX_DATA looks like this

RX_DATA ◄───┤ curr@now │ 11@T+10 ns │ 20@T+22 ns │

When the third signal assignment statement is executed, the new transaction, 35@T+18 ns, causes the 20@T+22 ns transaction to be deleted and the new transaction is appended to the driver. The reason for this is because the delay for the new transaction (=18 ns) is less than the delay of the last transaction sitting on the driver (=22 ns). This effect is caused because transport delay is used. In general, a new transaction will delete all transactions sitting on a driver that are to occur at or later than the delay of the new transaction. Therefore, the driver for RX_DATA is changed to

RX_DATA ◄───┤ curr@now │ 11@T+10 ns │ 35@T+18 ns │

Here is another example.

```
process
    -- DATA_BUS is a signal of type BIT_VECTOR.
begin
    . . .
    DATA_BUS <= transport X"01" after 5 ns, X"FA" after 10 ns,
                X"E8" after 15 ns;
    DATA_BUS <= transport X"B5" after 12 ns;
end process;
```

When these statements are executed, the status of the driver for DATA_BUS after the first signal assignment is

DATA_BUS ◄──┤ curr@now │ X"01"@T+5 ns │ X"FA"@T+10 ns │ X"E8"@T+15 ns │

When the second signal assignment is executed, the new transaction, X"B5" @T+ 12 ns, causes the X"E8" @T+15 ns transaction to be deleted from the driver (because its delay value is larger than the delay of the new transaction). The remaining transactions on the driver are not deleted since their delays are less than the delay of the new transaction. Therefore, the final state of the driver after both the statements are executed is

DATA_BUS ←| curr@now | X"01"@T+5 ns | X"FA"@T+10 ns | X"B5"@T+12 ns |

The following summarizes the rules for adding a new transaction to a driver in the transport delay mode.

1. If the delay time of the new transaction is greater than those of all the transactions already present on the driver, then the new transaction is added at the end of the driver.

2. If the delay time of the new transaction is earlier than or equal to one or more transactions on the driver, then these transactions are deleted from the driver and the new transaction is added at the end of the driver.

Effect of Inertial Delay on Signal Drivers

When inertial delays are used, both the signal value being assigned and the delay value affect the deletion and addition of transactions. If the delay of the new transaction is earlier than an existing transaction, the latter is deleted and the new one is added at the end of the driver, regardless of the signal values of the two transactions. Note that this is the same as rule 2 for the transport delay case. On the other hand, if the delay of the new transaction is greater than an already existing one, the signal values of the two transactions are compared. If they are the same, the new transaction is simply added at the end of the driver, if not, the existing one is deleted before adding the new transaction. Deletion occurs for every existing transaction with a signal value that is different from the new transaction. The following examples will help clarify this.

Consider the following process statement.

```
process
begin
    TX_DATA <= 11 after 10 ns;
    TX_DATA <= 22 after 20 ns;
    TX_DATA <= 33 after 15 ns;
    wait;                          -- Suspends indefinitely.
end process;
```

The transaction, 11@10 ns, first gets added to the driver. The second transaction, 22@20 ns, causes the 11@10 ns transaction on the driver to be deleted because the signal value, that is, 22, of the new transaction is different from the value of the transaction on the driver, that is, 11. The state of the driver at this point is

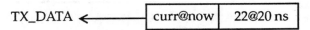

TX_DATA ← | curr@now | 22@20 ns |

The execution of the third signal assignment causes the transaction 22@20 ns to be deleted from the driver, since the delay of the new transaction (=15 ns) is less than the delay of the transaction on the driver (similar to the transport delay case). The final status of the driver is

TX_DATA ← | curr@now | 33@15 ns |

Let us consider another example.

```
process
begin
    ADDR_BUS <= 1 after 5 ns, 6 after 10 ns, 12 after 19 ns;
    ADDR_BUS <= 6 after 12 ns, 20 after 19 ns;
    wait;
end process;
```

The status of the driver for the ADDR_BUS signal after the first statement is executed is

ADDR_BUS ← | curr@now | 1@5 ns | 6@10 ns | 12@19 ns |

The execution of the second statement results in two new transactions. The first transaction, 6@12 ns, causes the 12@19 ns transaction to be deleted. Also, since the value of the new transaction (= 6) is the same as the value of the transaction 6@10 ns on the driver, the new transaction is added to the driver. The transaction 1@5 ns is deleted because its value is different. The transaction 20@19 ns is automatically added at the end of driver. The reason for this is that the language guarantees that if the first transaction of a signal assignment is added to the driver, all its subsequent transactions are imperatively added, that is, only the first waveform element in a signal assignment is interpreted as an inertial delay; the remaining waveform elements are interpreted as if they were transport delay elements.

The resulting driver is then

ADDR_BUS ←——	curr@now	6@10 ns	6@12 ns	20@19 ns

The summary of rules for adding a new transaction when inertial delay is used is

1. All transactions on a driver that are scheduled to occur at or after the delay of the new transaction are deleted (as in the transport case).

2. If the value of the new transaction is the same as the value of the transaction on the driver, the new transaction is added to the driver.

3. If the value of the new transaction is different from the values of one or more transactions on the driver, these transactions are deleted from the driver and the new transaction is added.

4. For a single signal assignment statement, if the first waveform element is added to the driver, all subsequent waveforms elements of that signal assignment are also added to the driver.

4.15   Other Sequential Statements

There are two other forms of sequential statements
1. Procedure call statement,
2. Return statement.

These are discussed in Chap. 8.

4.16   Multiple Processes

Since a process statement is a concurrent statement, it is possible to have more than one process within an architecture body. This makes it possible to capture the behavior of interacting processes, for example, that of interacting finite-state machines. Processes within an architecture body communicate with each other using signals that are visible to all the processes. Variables cannot be used to pass information between processes since their scope is limited to be within a process. Consider the following example of two interacting processes, RX, a receiver, and MP, a microprocessor. The RX process reads the serial input data and sends a READY signal informing that the data has been read in to the MP process . The MP process, after it assigns the data to the output, sends an acknowledge signal, ACK, back to the RX process to begin reading new input data. The block diagram for the two processes is shown in Fig. 4.6.

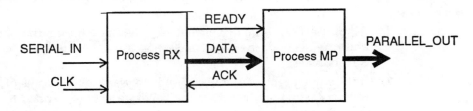

Figure 4.6 Two interacting processes.

The behavior for these two interacting processes is expressed in the following design description.

```
entity INTERACTING is
    port (SERIAL_IN, CLK: in BIT;
            PARALLEL_OUT: out BIT_VECTOR (0 to 7));
end INTERACTING;

architecture PROCESSES of INTERACTING is
    signal READY, ACK: BIT;
    signal DATA: BIT_VECTOR (0 to 7);
begin
    RX: process
    begin
        READ_WORD (SERIAL_IN, CLK, DATA);
        -- READ_WORD is a procedure described elsewhere that reads
        -- the serial data on every clock cycle and converts to a parallel
        -- data in signal DATA. It takes 10 ns to do this.
        READY <= '1';
        wait until ACK = '1';
        READY <= '0';
        wait for 50 ns;
    end process RX;
    MP: process
    begin
        wait for 25 ns;
        PARALLEL_OUT <= DATA;
        ACK <= '1', '0' after 25 ns;
        wait until READY = '1';
```

                    end process MP;
                    end PROCESSES;

   The interaction of these two processes via signals READY and ACK is
shown in the waveforms in Fig. 4.7.

   When multiple processes exist within an architecture body, it is possible
for more than one process to drive the same signal. In such a case, that signal
has multiple drivers (remember that a single process has only one driver for a
signal) and the effective value of the signal is obtained by using a resolution
function. This is discussed in the following chapter.

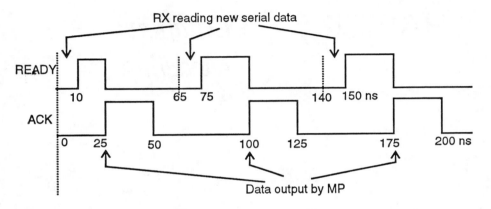

Figure 4.7 Handshaking protocol between the two processes.

CHAPTER 5   *Dataflow Modeling*

This chapter presents techniques for modeling the dataflow of an entity. A dataflow model specifies the functionality of the entity without explicitly specifying its structure. This functionality shows the flow of information through the entity, which is expressed primarily using concurrent signal assignment statements and block statements. This is in contrast to the behavioral style of modeling described in the previous chapter, in which the functionality of the entity is expressed using procedural type statements that are executed sequentially. This chapter also describes resolution functions and their usage.

5.1   *Concurrent Signal Assignment Statement*

One of the primary mechanisms for modeling the dataflow behavior of an entity is by using the concurrent signal assignment statement. An example of a dataflow model for a 2-input **or** gate, shown in Fig. 5.1, follows.

Figure 5.1 An **or** gate.

entity OR2 **is**
    port (signal A, B: in BIT; **signal** Z: **out** BIT);
    end OR2;

architecture OR2 **of** OR2 **is**
begin
    Z <= A **or** B **after** 9 ns;
    end OR2;

The architecture body contains a single concurrent signal assignment statement that represents the dataflow of the or gate. The semantic interpretation of this statement is that whenever there is an event (a change of value) on either signal A or B (A and B are signals in the expression for Z), the expression on the right is evaluated and its value is scheduled to appear on signal Z after a delay of 9 ns. The signals in the expression, A and B, form the "sensitivity list" for the signal assignment statement.

There are two other points to mention about this example. First, the input and output ports have their object class "signal" explicitly specified in the entity declaration. If it were not so, the ports would still have been signals, since this is the default and the only object class that is allowed for ports. The second point to note is that the architecture name and the entity name are the same. This is not a problem since architecture bodies are considered to be secondary units while entity declarations are primary units and the language allows secondary units to have the same names as the primary units.

An architecture body can contain any number of concurrent signal assignment statements. Since they are concurrent statements, the ordering of the statements is not important. Concurrent signal assignment statements are executed whenever events occur on signals that are used in their expressions. An example of a dataflow model for a 1-bit full-adder, whose external view is shown in Fig. 5.2, is presented next.

entity FULL_ADDER **is**
    port (A, B, CIN: **in** BIT; SUM, COUT: **out** BIT);
    end FULL_ADDER;

architecture FULL_ADDER **of** FULL_ADDER **is**
begin
    SUM <= (A **xor** B) **xor** CIN **after** 15 ns;

COUT <= (A and B) or (B and CIN) or (CIN and A) after 10 ns;
end FULL_ADDER;

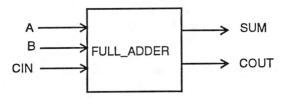

Figure 5.2 External view of a 1-bit full-adder.

Two signal assignment statements are used to represent the dataflow of the FULL_ADDER entity. Whenever an event occurs on signals A, B, or CIN, expressions of both the statements are evaluated and the value to SUM is scheduled to appear after 15 ns while the value to COUT is scheduled to appear after 10 ns. The **after** clause models the delay of the logic represented by the expression.

Contrast this with the statements that appear inside a process statement. Statements within a process are executed sequentially while statements in an architecture body are all concurrent statements and are order independent. A process statement is itself a concurrent statement. What this means is that if there were any concurrent signal assignment statements and process statements within an architecture body, the order of these statements also would not matter.

5.2   *Concurrent versus Sequential Signal Assignment*

In the previous chapter, we saw that signal assignment statements can also appear within the body of a process statement. Such statements are called *sequential* signal assignment statements, while signal assignment statements that appear outside of a process are called *concurrent* signal assignment statements. Concurrent signal assignment statements are event triggered, that is, they are executed whenever there is an event on a signal that appears in its expression, while sequential signal assignment statements are not event triggered and are executed in sequence in relation to the other sequential statements that appear within the process. To further understand the difference between these two kinds of signal assignment statements, consider the following two architecture bodies.

architecture SEQ_SIG_ASG of FRAGMENT1 is
  -- A, B and Z are signals.

```
begin
    process (B)
    begin -- Following are sequential signal assignment statements:
        A <= B;
        Z <= A;
    end process;
end;

architecture CON_SIG_ASG of FRAGMENT2 is
begin -- Following are concurrent signal assignment statements:
    A <= B;
    Z <= A;
end;
```

In architecture SEQ_SIG_ASG, the two signal assignments are sequential signal assignments. Therefore, whenever signal B has an event, say at time T, the first signal assignment statement is executed and then the second signal assignment statement is executed, both in zero time. However, signal A is scheduled to get its new value of B only at time $T+\Delta$ (the delta delay is implicit), and Z is scheduled to be assigned the old value of A (not the value of B) at time $T+\Delta$ also.

In architecture CON_SIG_ASG, the two statements are concurrent signal assignment statements. When an event occurs on signal B, say at time T, signal A gets the value of B after delta delay, that is, at time $T+\Delta$. When simulation time advances to $T+\Delta$, signal A will get its new value and this event on A (assuming there is a change of value on signal A) will trigger the second signal assignment statement that will cause the new value of A to be assigned to Z after another delta delay, that is, at time $T+2\Delta$. The delta delay model is explored in more detail in the next section.

Aside from the previous difference, the concurrent signal assignment statement is identical to the sequential signal assignment statement.

For every concurrent signal assignment statement, there is an equivalent process statement with the same semantic meaning. The concurrent signal assignment statement:

```
CLEAR <= RESET or PRESET after 15 ns;
-- RESET and PRESET are signals.
```

is equivalent to the following process statement:

```
process
begin
    CLEAR <= RESET or PRESET after 15 ns;
```

```
    wait on RESET, PRESET;
end process;
```

An identical signal assignment statement (this is now a sequential signal assignment) appears in the body of the process statement along with a **wait** statement whose sensitivity list comprises of signals used in the expression of the concurrent signal assignment statement.

5.3   Delta Delay Revisited

In a signal assignment statement, if no delay is specified or a delay of 0 ns is specified, a delta delay is assumed. Delta delay is an infinitesimally small amount of time. It is not a real time delta and does not cause real simulation time to change. The delta delay mechanism provides for ordering of events on signals that occur at the same simulation time. Consider the circuit shown in Fig. 5.3 and its corresponding model that follows.

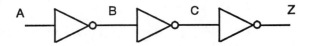

Figure 5.3 Three inverting buffers in series.

```
entity FAST_INVERTER is
    port (A: in BIT; Z: out BIT);
end;

architecture DELTA_DELAY of FAST_INVERTER is
    signal B, C: BIT;
begin -- Following statements are order independent:
    Z <= not C;              -- signal assignment #1
    C <= not B;              -- signal assignment #2
    B <= not A;              -- signal assignment #3
end;
```

The three signal assignments in the FAST_INVERTER entity use delta delays. When an event occurs on signal A, say at 20 ns, the third signal assignment is triggered which causes signal B to get the inverted value of A at 20 ns+1Δ. When time advances to 20 ns+1Δ, signal B changes. This triggers the second signal assignment, causing signal C to get the inverted value of B after another delta delay, that is, at 20 ns+2Δ. When simulation time advances to 20 ns+2Δ, the first signal assignment is triggered causing Z to get a new value at time 20 ns+3Δ. Even though the real simulation time stayed at 20 ns, Z was updated with the correct value through a sequence of delta-delayed events. This sequence of waveforms is shown in Fig. 5.4.

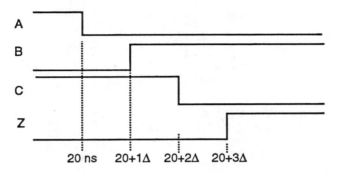

Figure 5.4 Delta delays in concurrent signal assignment statements.

A typical VHDL simulator maintains a list of events that is to occur in an event queue. The events in this queue are ordered not only on the real simulation time but also on the number of delta delays. Figure 5.5 shows a snapshot of an event queue in a VHDL simulator during simulation. Each event has associated with it a list of signal-value pairs that are to be scheduled. For example, the value '0' is to be assigned to signal Z when simulation time advances to 10 ns+2Δ.

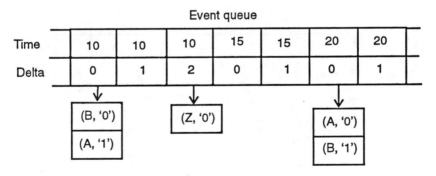

Figure 5.5 An event queue in a VHDL simulator.

Let us consider another example of delta delay. The dataflow model for the RS latch shown in Fig. 5.6 appears next.

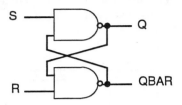

Figure 5.6 An RS latch.

```
entity RS_LATCH is
    port (R, S: in BIT := '1'; Q: buffer BIT := '1';
          QBAR: buffer BIT := '0');
end RS_LATCH;

architecture DELTA of RS_LATCH is
begin
    QBAR <= R nand Q;
    Q <= S nand QBAR;
end DELTA;
```

At start of simulation, both R and S have value '1' and Q and QBAR are at '1' and '0', respectively. Assume signal R changes from '1' to '0' at 5 ns. Figure 5.7 shows the sequence of events that occur as a result. After two delta delays, the circuit stabilizes with the final values of Q and QBAR being '0' and '1', respectively.

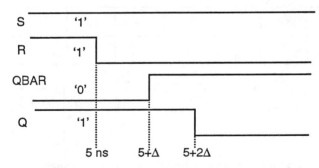

Figure 5.7 Sequence of events in the RS latch.

5.4   Multiple Drivers

Each concurrent signal assignment statement creates a driver for the signal being assigned. What happens when there is more than one assignment to the same signal? In this case, the signal has more than one driver and a mechanism is needed to compute the effective value of the signal. Consider the circuit shown in Fig. 5.8 and its corresponding dataflow model.

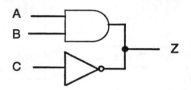

Figure 5.8 Two drivers driving signal Z.

entity TWO_DR_EXAMPLE **is**
    port (A, B, C: **in** BIT; Z: **out** BIT);
end TWO_DR_EXAMPLE;

architecture TWO_DR_EX_BEH **of** TWO_DR_EXAMPLE **is**
begin
    Z <= A **and** B **after** 10 ns;
    Z <= **not** C **after** 5 ns;
end; -- Effective value for signal Z has to be
      -- determined: not a legal VHDL model.

    In this example, there are two gates driving the output signal Z. How is the value of Z determined? It is determined by using a user-defined *resolution function* that considers the values of both the drivers for Z and determines the effective value. Consider the following architecture body.

architecture NO_ENTITY **of** DUMMY **is**
begin
    Z <= '1' **after** 2 ns, '0' **after** 5 ns, '1' **after** 10 ns;
    Z <= '0' **after** 4 ns, '1' **after** 5 ns, '0' **after** 20 ns;
    Z <= '1' **after** 10 ns, '0' **after** 20 ns;
end NO_ENTITY;

    In this case, there are three drivers for signal Z. Each driver has a sequence of transactions where each transaction defines the value to appear on the signal and the time at which it is to appear. The resolution function resolves the value for the signal Z from the current value of each of its drivers. This is shown pictorially in Fig. 5.9.

    The value of each driver is an input to the resolution function and based on the computation performed within the resolution function, the value returned by this function becomes the resolved value for the signal. The resolution function is user-written and it may perform any function. The function is not restricted to perform a wired-and or a wired-or operation; for example, it could be used to count the number of events on a signal.

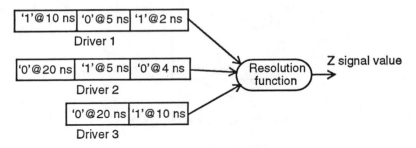

Figure 5.9 Resolving signal drivers.

A signal with more than one driver must have a resolution function associated with it, otherwise, it is an error. Such a signal is called a *resolved* signal. A resolution function is associated with a signal by specifying its name in the signal declaration. For example,

signal BUSY: WIRED_OR BIT;

is one way of associating the resolution function, WIRED_OR, with the signal BUSY. No arguments need be specified, since by default, the arguments for the function are the current values of all the drivers for that signal. The TWO_DR_EXAMPLE entity previously described is, therefore, incorrect; a resolution function must be specified for port Z such as

port (A,B, C: **in** BIT; Z: **out** WIRED_OR BIT);

Another way is by declaring a resolved subtype, that is, by including the name of the resolution function in the subtype declaration and then declaring the signal to be of that subtype. For example,

subtype RESOLVED_BIT **is** WIRED_OR BIT;
signal BUSY: RESOLVED_BIT;

The resolved signal Z in the TWO_DR_EXAMPLE entity can now be specified as

port (A, B, C: **in** BIT; Z: **out** RESOLVED_BIT);

The semantics of when a resolution function is invoked are as follows. Whenever an event occurs on a resolved signal, the resolution function associated with that signal is called with the values of all its drivers. The return value from the resolution function becomes the value for the resolved signal. In the example of architecture NO_ENTITY, the resolution function is invoked at time 2 ns with driver values '1', '0', and '0' (drivers 2 and 3 have '0' because that is assumed to be the initial value of Z). The function, WIRED_OR, is performed and the resulting resolved value of '1' is assigned to Z at 2 ns. Signal Z is scheduled to have another event at 4 ns, at which time the driver values, '1', '0', and '0', are passed to the resolution function which returns the value of '1' for signal Z. At time 5 ns, the driver values, '0', '1', and '0' are passed to the resolution function which returns the value '1'. At 10 ns, the driver values, '1', '1', and '1' are passed to the resolution function. Finally at time 20 ns, the driver values, '1', '0', and '0' are passed to the resolution function to determine the effective value for signal Z, which is '1'.

The resolution function has only one input parameter, which is a one dimensional unconstrained array. The input parameter type and the return type are the same type as the signal. The function typically computes a value from the various driver values, each element of the input array corresponding to one of the driver values. It should be noted that the identity of the driver is lost in the input array, that is, there is no way of knowing which driver is associated with which element of the input array. Here is an example of a WIRED_OR function that can be used as a resolution function.

```
function WIRED_OR (INPUTS: BIT_VECTOR) return BIT is
begin
    for J in INPUTS'RANGE loop
        if INPUTS(J) = '1' then
            return '1';
        end if;
    end loop;
    return '0';
end WIRED_OR;
```

There is nothing special about the syntax for a resolution function. It is identical to that of any other function (functions are described in Chap. 8). A function is recognized as a resolution function if it is associated with a signal in the signal declaration. In the previous example, we introduced a predefined attribute of an array object called RANGE. This attribute returns the range of the number of elements of the specified array object. For example, if there are four drivers when the WIRED_OR function is called, INPUTS'RANGE returns the range "0 to 3".

Drivers are also created for signals that are assigned within a process. The one difference is that irrespective of how many times a signal is assigned a value inside a process, there is only one driver for that signal in that process. Therefore, each process will create at most one driver for a signal. If a signal is assigned a value using multiple concurrent signal assignment statements (which can only appear outside a process), an equal number of drivers are created for that signal.

The following two sections present two other forms of the concurrent signal assignment statement: the conditional signal assignment statement and the selected signal assignment statement.

5.5   Conditional Signal Assignment Statement

The conditional signal assignment statement selects different values for the target signal based on the specified, possibly different, conditions (it is like an if statement). A typical syntax for this statement is

> target-signal <=   [*waveform-elements* **when** *condition* **else**]
> [*waveform-elements* **when** *condition* **else**]
> . . .
> *waveform-elements* ;

The semantics of this concurrent statement are as follows. Whenever an event occurs on a signal used either in any of the waveform expressions (recall that a waveform expression is the value expression in a waveform element) or in any of the conditions, the conditional signal assignment statement is executed by evaluating the conditions one at a time. For the first true condition found, the corresponding value (or values) of the waveform is scheduled to be assigned to the target signal. For example,

> Z <=   IN0 **after** 10 ns **when** S0 = '0' **and** S1 = '0' **else**
> IN1 **after** 10 ns **when** S0 = '1' **and** S1 = '0' **else**
> IN2 **after** 10 ns **when** S0 = '0' **and** S1 = '1' **else**
> IN3 **after** 10 ns;

In this example, the statement is executed any time an event occurs on signals IN0, IN1, IN2, IN3, S0, or S1. The first condition (S0='0' and S1='0') is checked; if false, the second condition (S0='1' and S1='0') is checked; if false, the third condition is checked; and so on. Assuming S0='0' and S1='1', then the value of IN2 is scheduled to be assigned to signal Z after 10 ns.

For a given conditional signal assignment statement, there is an equivalent process statement that has the same semantic meaning. Such a process statement has exactly one if statement and one **wait** statement within it. The signals in the sensitivity list for the **wait** statement is the union of signals in all the waveform expressions and the signals referenced in all the conditions. The equivalent process statement for these conditional signal assignment statement example is

```
process
begin
    if S0 = '0' and S1 = '0' then
        Z <= IN0 after 10 ns;
    elsif S0 = '1' and S1='0' then
        Z <= IN1 after 10 ns;
    elsif S0 = '0' and S1 = '1' then
        Z <= IN2 after 10 ns;
    else
        Z <= IN3 after 10 ns;
    end if;
    wait on IN0, IN1, IN2, IN3, S0, S1;
end process;
```

5.6 Selected Signal Assignment Statement

The selected signal assignment statement selects different values for a target signal based on the value of a select expression (it is like a **case** statement). A typical syntax for this statement is

```
with expression select          -- This is the select expression.
    target-signal <=    waveform-elements when choices ,
                        waveform-elements when choices ,
                        . . .
                        waveform-elements when choices ;
```

The semantics of a selected signal assignment statement are very similar to that of the conditional signal assignment statement. Whenever an event occurs on a signal in the select expression or on any signal used in any of the waveform expressions, the statement is executed. Based on the value of the select expression that matches the choice value specified, the value (or values) of the corresponding waveform is scheduled to be assigned to the target signal. Note that the choices are not evaluated in sequence. All possible values of the select expression must be covered by the choices that are specified not more than once. Values not covered explicitly may be covered by an "others" choice, which covers all such values. The choices may be a logical "or" of several values or may be specified as a range of values.

Here is an example of a selected signal assignment statement.

```
type OP is (ADD, SUB, MUL, DIV);
signal OP_CODE: OP;
. . .
with OP_CODE select
    Z <= A + B after ADD_PROP_DLY when ADD,
```

```
        A – B after SUB_PROP_DLY when SUB,
        A * B after MUL_PROP_DLY when MUL,
        A / B after DIV_PROP_DLY when DIV;
```

In this example, whenever an event occurs on signals, OP_CODE, A, or B, the statement is executed. Assuming the value of the select expression, OP_CODE, is SUB, the expression "A – B" is computed and its value is scheduled to be assigned to signal Z after SUB_PROP_DLY time.

For every selected signal assignment statement, there is also an equivalent process statement with the same semantics. In the equivalent process statement, there is one **case** statement that uses the select expression to branch. The list of signals in the sensitivity list of the **wait** statement comprises of all signals in the select expression and in the waveform expressions. The equivalent process statement for the previous example is

```
        process
        begin
            case OP_CODE is
                when ADD => Z <= A + B after ADD_PROP_DLY;
                when SUB => Z <= A – B after SUB_PROP_DLY;
                when MUL => Z <= A * B after MUL_PROP_DLY;
                when DIV => Z <= A / B after DIV_PROP_DLY;
            end case;
            wait on OP_CODE, A, B;
        end process;
```

5.7   Block Statement

A block statement is a concurrent statement. It can be used for three major purposes:

1. to disable signal drivers by using guards,
2. to limit signal scope,
3. to represent a portion of a design.

A block statement itself has no execution semantics but provides additional semantics for statements that appear within it. The syntax of a block statement is

```
        block-label : block [ ( guard-expression ) ]
                [ block-header ]
                [ block-declarations ]
        begin
```

```
       concurrent-statements
end block [ block-label ] ;
```

The *block-header*, if present, describes the interface of the block statement to its environment and is discussed in greater detail in Chap. 10. Any declarations appearing within the block are visible only within the block, that is, between block . . . end block. Any number of concurrent statements can appear within a block, possibly none. Block statements can be nested since a block statement is itself a concurrent statement. The block label present at the beginning of the block statement is necessary, however, the label appearing at the end of the block statement is optional, and if present, must be the same as the one used at the beginning of the block.

If a *guard-expression* appears in a block statement, there is an implicit signal called *GUARD* of type BOOLEAN declared within the block. The value of the GUARD signal is always updated to reflect the value of the guard expression. The guard expression must be of type BOOLEAN. Signal assignment statements appearing within the block statement can use this GUARD signal to enable or disable their drivers. Here is an example of a gated inverter.

```
B1: block (STROBE = '1')
begin
      Z <= guarded not A;
end block B1;
```

The signal GUARD that is implicitly declared within block B1 has the value of the expression (STROBE = '1'). The keyword **guarded** can optionally be used with signal assignment statements within a block statement. This keyword implies that only when the value of the GUARD signal is true (i.e., guard expression evaluates to true), the value of the expression "not A" is assigned to the target signal, Z. If the GUARD is false, events on A do not affect the value of signal Z. That is, the driver to Z for this signal assignment statement is disabled and signal Z retains its previous value. The block statement is very useful in modeling hardware elements that trigger on certain events, for example, flip-flops and clocked logic.

The only concurrent statements whose semantics are affected by the enclosing block statement are the *guarded assignments*, that is, the signal assignment statements that use the **guarded** option. The modified semantic meaning is as follows. Whenever an event occurs (an event is a change of value) on any signal used in the expression of a guarded assignment or on any signal used in the guard expression, the guard expression is evaluated. If the value is true, the signal assignment statement is executed and the target signal is scheduled to get a new value. If the value of the guard expression is false, the value of the target signal is unchanged.

Every guarded assignment has an equivalent process statement with identical semantics. Here is an example.

```
BG: block (guard-expression)
    signal SIG: BIT;
begin
    SIG <= guarded waveform-elements;
end block BG;

-- The equivalent process statement for the guarded assignment is:
BG: block (guard-expression)
    signal SIG: BIT;
begin
    process
    begin
        if GUARD then
            SIG <= waveform-elements;
        end if;
        wait on signals-in-waveform-elements, GUARD;
    end process;
end block BG;
```

The signal GUARD, even though implicitly declared, can be used explicitly within the block statement. For example,

```
B2: block ((CLEAR = '0') and (PRESET ='1'))
begin
    Q <= '1' when ( not GUARD ) else '0';
end block B2;
```

In this example, the signal assignment in the block statement is not a guarded assignment, and therefore, the driver to signal Q is never disabled. However, the value of Q is determined by the value of the GUARD signal because of its explicit use in the signal assignment statement. The value of the GUARD signal corresponds to the value of the guard expression "(CLEAR = '0') and (PRESET = '1')". This signal assignment statement is, therefore, executed any time an event occurs on either of the signals, CLEAR or PRESET.

It is also possible to explicitly declare a signal called GUARD, define an expression for it, and then use it within a guarded assignment. Here is an example.

```
B3: block
    signal GUARD: BOOLEAN;
begin
    GUARD <= CLEAR = '0' and PRESET = '1';
```

```
                    Q <= guarded DIN;
                end block B3;
```

The following example describes a 4 * 1 multiplexer using a block statement.

```
            use WORK.RF_PACK.WIRED_OR;
            entity MUX is
                port (DIN: in BIT_VECTOR(0 to 3); S: in BIT_VECTOR(0 to 1);
                    Z: out WIRED_OR BIT);
            end MUX;

            architecture BLOCK_EX of MUX is
                constant MUX_DELAY: TIME := 5 ns;
            begin
                B1: block (S = "00")
                begin
                    Z <= guarded DIN(0) after MUX_DELAY;
                end block B1;
                B2: block (S = "01")
                begin
                    Z <= guarded DIN(1) after MUX_DELAY;
                end block B2;
                    :
                    :
            end BLOCK_EX;
```

Notice that a resolution function is needed for signal Z since it has more than one driver. This function, WIRED_OR, is assumed to exist in a package RF_PACK that resides in library WORK.

Here is another example that models a rising-edge triggered D-type flip-flop.

```
            entity D_FLIP_FLOP is
                port (D, CLK: in BIT; Q, QBAR: out BIT);
            end D_FLIP_FLOP;

            architecture DFF of D_FLIP_FLOP is
            begin
                L1: block (CLK = '1' and (not CLK'STABLE))
                    signal TEMP: BIT;
                begin
                    TEMP <= guarded D;
                    Q <= TEMP;
                    QBAR <= not TEMP;
                end block L1;
            end DFF;
```

The guard expression uses a predefined attribute called STABLE. CLK'STABLE is a new signal of type BOOLEAN that is true as long as signal CLK has not had any event in the current delta time. This guard expression, therefore, implies a rising clock edge. The scope of the signal TEMP declared in block L1, has its scope restricted to be within the block. Of the three signal assignments, only the first one is a guarded assignment and, hence, controlled by the guard expression. The other two signal assignments are not controlled by the guard expression and are triggered purely on events occurring on signals in their expressions. When a rising clock edge appears on the signal CLK, say at time T, the value of D is assigned to signal TEMP after delta delay, that is, at time $T+\Delta$. If the value of TEMP is different from its previous value, the assignments to Q and QBAR will be triggered causing these signals to get new values after another delta delay, that is, at time $T+2\Delta$.

Other uses of the block statement are described in Chap. 10.

5.8   Concurrent Assertion Statement

Sequential assertion statements were discussed in the previous chapter. A concurrent assertion statement has exactly the same syntax as a sequential assertion statement. An assertion statement is a concurrent statement by virtue of its place of appearance within the model. If it appears inside of a process, it is a sequential assertion statement and is executed sequentially with respect to the other statements in the process; if it appears outside of a process, it is a concurrent assertion statement. The semantics of a concurrent assertion statement are as follows. Whenever an event occurs on a signal in the boolean expression of the assertion statement, the statement is executed.

Here is an example of a concurrent assertion statement used in a SR flip-flop model that makes a check to ensure that the input signals R and S are never simultaneously zero.

```
entity SR is
    port (S, R: in BIT; Q, NOTQ: out BIT);
end SR;

architecture SR_ASSERT of SR is
begin
    assert (not(S = '0' and R = '0'))
        report "Not valid inputs: R and S are both low"
        severity ERROR;
    -- Rest of model for SR flip-flop here.
end SR_ASSERT;
```

Anytime an event occurs on either of the signals, S or R, the assertion statement is executed and the boolean expression checked. If false, the report message is printed and the severity level is reported to the simulator for appropriate action.

❑

CHAPTER 6   *Structural Modeling*

This chapter describes the structural style of modeling. An entity is modeled as a set of components connected by signals, that is, as a netlist. The behavior of the entity is not explicitly apparent from its model. The component instantiation statement is the primary mechanism used for describing such a model of an entity.

6.1   An Example

Consider the circuit shown in Fig. 6.1 and its VHDL structural model.

```
entity GATING is
    port (A, CK, MR, DIN: in BIT; RDY, CTRLA: out BIT);
end GATING;

architecture STRUCTURE_VIEW of GATING is
    component AND2
        port (X, Y: in BIT; Z: out BIT);
    end component;
```

```
        component DFF
            port (D, CLOCK: in BIT; Q, QBAR: out BIT);
        end component;
        component NOR2
            port (A, B: in BIT; Z: out BIT);
        end component;
        signal S1, S2: BIT;
begin
        D1: DFF port map (A, CK, S1, S2);
        A1: AND2 port map (S2, DIN, CTRLA);
        N1: NOR2 port map (S1, MR, RDY);
end STRUCTURE_VIEW;
```

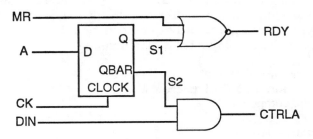

Figure 6.1 A circuit generating control signals.

Three components, AND2, DFF, and NOR2, are declared. These components are instantiated in the architecture body via three component instantiation statements, and the instantiated components are connected to each other via signals S1 and S2. The component instantiation statements are concurrent statements, and therefore, their order of appearance in the architecture body is not important. A component can, in general, be instantiated any number of times. However, each instantiation must have a unique component label; as an example, A1 is the component label for the AND2 component instantiation.

6.2   Component Declaration

A component instantiated in a structural description must first be declared using a component declaration. A component declaration declares the name and the interface of a component. The interface specifies the mode and the type of ports. The syntax of a simple form of component declaration is

```
component component-name
    port ( list-of-interface-ports ) ;
end component;
```

The *component-name* may or may not refer to the name of an already existing entity in a library. If it does not, it must be explicitly bound to an entity; otherwise, the model cannot be simulated. This is done using a configuration. Configurations are discussed in the next chapter.

The *list-of-interface-ports* specifies the name, mode, and type for each port of the component in a manner similar to that specified in an entity declaration. The names of the ports may also be different from the names of the ports in the entity to which it may be bound (different port names can be mapped in a configuration). In this chapter, we will assume that an entity of the same name as that of the component already exists and that the name, mode, and type of each port matches the corresponding ones in the component. Some examples of component declarations are

```
component NAND2
    port (A, B: in MVL; Z: out MVL);
end component;

component MP
    port (CK, RESET, RDN, WRN: in BIT;
          DATA_BUS: inout INTEGER range 0 to 255;
          ADDR_BUS: in BIT_VECTOR(15 downto 0));
end component;

component RX
    port (CK, RESET, ENABLE, DATAIN, RD: in BIT;
          DATA_OUT: out INTEGER range 0 to (2**8 - 1);
          PARITY_ERROR, FRAME_ERROR,
          OVERRUN_ERROR: out BOOLEAN);
end component;
```

Component declarations appear in the declarations part of an architecture body. Alternately, they may also appear in a package declaration. Items declared in this package can then be made visible within any architecture body by using the **library** and **use** context clauses. For example, consider the entity GATING described in the previous section. A package such as the one shown next may be created to hold the component declarations.

```
package COMP_LIST is
    component AND2
        port (X, Y: in BIT; Z: out BIT);
    end component;
    component DFF
```

```
            port (D, CLOCK: in BIT; Q, QBAR: out BIT);
        end component;
        component NOR2
            port (A, B: in BIT; Z: out BIT);
        end component;
    end COMP_LIST;
```

Assuming that this package has been compiled into design library DES_LIB, the architecture body can be rewritten as

```
    library DES_LIB;
    use DES_LIB.COMP_LIST.all;
    architecture STRUCTURE_VIEW of GATING is
        signal S1, S2: BIT;
        -- No need for specifying component declarations here, since they
        -- are made visible to architecture body using the context clauses.
    begin
        -- The component instantiations here.
    end STRUCTURE_VIEW;
```

The advantage of this approach is that the package can now be shared by other design units and the component declarations need not be specified inside every design unit.

6.3   Component Instantiation

A component instantiation statement defines a subcomponent of the entity in which it appears. It associates the signals in the entity with the ports of that subcomponent. A format of a component instantiation statement is

component-label : *component-name* **port map** (*association-list*) ;

The *component-label* can be any legal identifier and can be considered as the name of the instance. The *component-name* must be the name of a component declared earlier using a component declaration. The *association-list* associates signals in the entity, called *actuals*, with the ports of a component, called *locals*. An actual must be an object of class **signal**. Expressions or objects of class **variable** or **constant** are not allowed. An actual may also be the keyword **open** to indicate a port that is not connected.

There are two ways to perform the association of locals with actuals:

1. positional association,
2. named association.

In positional association, an *association-list* is of the form

$$actual_1, actual_2, actual_3, \ldots, actual_n$$

Each actual in the component instantiation is mapped by position with each port in the component declaration. That is, the first port in the component declaration corresponds to the first actual in the component instantiation, the second with the second, and so on. Consider an instance of a NAND2 component.

```
-- Component declaration:
component NAND2
    port (A, B: in BIT; Z: out BIT);
end component;
```

```
-- Component instantiation:
N1: NAND2 port map (S1, S2, S3);
```

N1 is the component label for the current instantiation of the NAND2 component. Signal S1 (which is an actual) is associated with port A (which is a local) of the NAND2 component, S2 is associated with port B of the NAND2 component, and S3 is associated with port Z. Signals S1 and S2 thus provide the two input values to the NAND2 component and signal S3 receives the output value from the component. The ordering of the actuals is, therefore, important.

If a port in a component instantiation is not connected to any signal, the keyword **open** can be used to signify that the port is not connected. For example,

```
N3: NAND2 port map (S1, open, S3);
```

The second input port of the NAND2 component is not connected to any signal. An input port may be left open only if its declaration specifies an initial value. For the previous component instantiation statement to be legal, a component declaration for NAND2 may appear like

```
component NAND2
    port (A, B: in BIT := '0'; Z: out BIT);
    -- Both A and B have an initial value of '0'; however, only
    -- the initial value of B is necessary in this case.
end component;
```

A port of any other mode may be left unconnected as long as it is not an unconstrained array.

In named association, an *association-list* is of the form

$$local_1 => actual_1, local_2 => actual_2, \ldots, local_n => actual_n$$

For example, consider the component NOR2 in the entity GATING described in the first section. The instantiation using named association may be written as

N1: NOR2 **port map** (B=>MR, Z=>RDY, A=>S1);

In this case, the signal MR (an actual), that is declared in the entity port list, is associated with the second port (port B, a local) of the NOR2 gate, signal RDY is associated with the third port (port Z) and signal S1 is associated with the first port (port A) of the NOR2 gate. In named association, the ordering of the associations is not important since the mapping between the actuals and locals are explicitly specified. An important point to note is that the scope of the locals is restricted to be within the port map part of the instantiation for that component; for example, the locals A, B, and Z of component NOR2 are relevant only within the port map of instantiation of component NOR2.

For either type of association, there are certain rules imposed by the language. First, the types of the local and the actual being associated must be the same. Second, the modes of the ports must conform to the rule that if the local is readable, so must the actual and if the local is writable, so must the actual. Since a signal locally declared is considered to be both readable and writable, such a signal may be associated with a local of any mode. If an actual is a port of mode **in**, it may not be associated with a local of mode **out** or **inout**; if the actual is a port of mode **out**, it may not be associated with a local of mode **in** or **inout**; if the actual is a port of mode **inout**, it may be associated with a local of mode **in, out,** or **inout.**

It is important to note that an actual of mode **out** or **inout** indicates the presence of a source for that signal, and therefore, must be resolved if that signal is multiply driven. A buffer port can never have more than one source; therefore, the only kind of actual that can be associated with a buffer port is another buffer port or a signal that has at most one source.

Another example of a component instantiation is

M1: MICRO **port map** (UDIN(3 **downto** 0), WRN, RDN, STATUS(0),
                    STATUS(1), UDOUT(0 **to** 7), TXDATA);

The first actual of the port map refers to a slice of the vectored UDIN signal, WRN and RDN are 1-bit signals, STATUS(0) and STATUS(1) refer to the 0th and 1st element of the STATUS array, UDOUT(0 **to** 7) refers to a slice of the UDOUT vector and TXDATA refers to an entire vector signal. This example shows that the signals used to interconnect components can also be

- slices,
- vectors, or,

- array elements.

6.4   Other Examples

Here is a complete structural model for a 9-bit parity generator circuit shown
in Fig. 6.2.

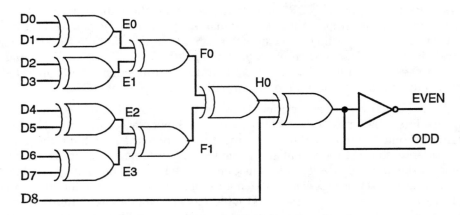

Figure 6.2 A 9-bit parity generator circuit.

```
entity PARITY_9_BIT is
    port (D: in BIT_VECTOR(8 downto 0); EVEN: out BIT;
          ODD: buffer BIT);
end PARITY_9_BIT;

architecture PARITY_STR of PARITY_9_BIT is
    component XOR2
        port (A, B: in BIT; Z: out BIT);
    end component;
    component INV2
        port (A: in BIT; Z: out BIT);
    end component;
    signal E0, E1, E2, E3, F0, F1, H0: BIT;
begin
    XE0: XOR2 port map (D(0), D(1), E0);
    XE1: XOR2 port map (D(2), D(3), E1);
    XE2: XOR2 port map (D(4), D(5), E2);
    XE3: XOR2 port map (D(6), D(7), E3);
    XF0: XOR2 port map (E0, E1, F0);
    XF1: XOR2 port map (E2, E3, F1);
    XH0: XOR2 port map (F0, F1, H0);
```

```
        XODD: XOR2 port map (H0, D(8), ODD);
        XEVEN: INV2 port map (ODD, EVEN);
    end PARITY_STR;
```

In this example, port ODD is of mode **buffer** since the value of this port is being read as well as written to inside the architecture. If this port were declared to be of mode **inout**, external signals defined outside the PARITY_9_BIT design would be able to drive this port which may not be desired.

An example of a decade counter using J-K flip-flops is shown in Fig. 6.3. Its structural model is described next.

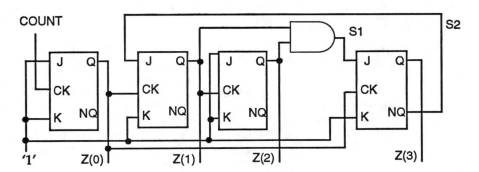

Figure 6.3 A decade counter.

```
    entity DECADE_CTR is
        port (COUNT: in BIT; Z: buffer BIT_VECTOR(0 to 3));
    end DECADE_CTR;

    architecture NET_LIST of DECADE_CTR is
        component JK_FF
            port (J, K, CK: in BIT; Q, NQ: buffer BIT);
        end component;
        component AND_GATE
            port (A, B: in BIT; C: out BIT);
        end component;
        signal S1, S2: BIT;
        signal S_HIGH: BIT := '1';
    begin
        A1: AND_GATE port map (Z(2), Z(1), S1);
        JK1: JK_FF port map (S_HIGH, S_HIGH, COUNT, Z(0), open);
        JK2: JK_FF port map (S2, S_HIGH, Z(0), Z(1), open);
        JK3: JK_FF port map (S_HIGH, S_HIGH, Z(1), Z(2), open);
        JK4: JK_FF port map (S1, S_HIGH, Z(0), Z(3), S2);
    end NET_LIST;
```

This example illustrates the point that only signals can be used as actuals inside a port map. If a constant, say '1', is to be set for one of the ports, as in instance JK1, it is necessary to define a signal, say S_HIGH, that contains this value and then use this signal as an actual for this port. It would be an error to use the constant value directly as an actual in a port map.

Structural models can be simulated only after the entities that the components represent are modeled and placed in a design library. The lowest level entities must be behavioral models. The simulation semantics of a component instantiation are best understood by an example. Consider the component instantiation A1 in the previous example. Assume that this instance is bound to an entity with the same name and identical port names. Its equivalent behavioral representation is

```
A1: block                        -- A block for each instantiation.
        port (A, B: in BIT; C: out BIT); -- Ports in component
                                 -- declaration.
        port map (C=>S1, A=>Z(2), B=>Z(1)); -- Association-list.
begin
     AND_GATE: block             -- The entity block.
               port (A, B: in BIT; C: out BIT); -- Ports of entity.
               port map (A=>A, B=>B, C=>C); -- Association of
                    -- component ports with entity ports.
                    -- Declarations that occur in entity declaration or
                    -- architecture body of AND_GATE entity.
     begin
          -- Behavior in architecture body for AND_GATE entity.
          -- For example,
          -- C <= A and B after 10 ns;
     end block AND_GATE;
end block A1;
```

As shown, a block statement can also have a port list and a port map list. The port list specifies the ports through which the block communicates with its external environment. The port map list specifies the mapping between the ports and the signals in the block's external enviroment that these ports connect to. More on this form of block statement is described in Chap. 10.

As a final example, consider the 3-bit up-down counter circuit shown in Fig. 6.4 and its structural model that appears next.

```
entity UP_DOWN is
    port (CLK, CNT_UP, CNT_DOWN: in BIT;
          A, B, C: buffer BIT);
end UP_DOWN;
```

```
architecture COUNTER of UP_DOWN is
    component JK_FF
        port (J, K, CK: in BIT; Q, QN: buffer BIT);
    end component;
    component AND2
        port (A, B: in BIT; C: out BIT);
    end component;
    component OR2
        port (A, B: in BIT; C: out BIT);
    end component;
    signal S1, S2, S3, S4, S5, S6, S7, S8: BIT;
    signal ONE: BIT := '1';
begin
    JK1: JK_FF port map (ONE, ONE, CLK, A, S1);
    A1: AND2 port map (CNT_UP, A, S2);
    A2: AND2 port map (S1, CNT_DOWN, S3);
    O1: OR2 port map (S2, S3, S4);
    JK2: JK_FF port map (ONE, ONE, S4, B, S5);
    A3: AND2 port map (B, CNT_UP, S7);
    A4: AND2 port map (S5, CNT_DOWN, S6);
    O2: OR2 port map (S7, S6, S8);
    JK3: JK_FF port map (ONE, ONE, S8, C, open);
end COUNTER;
```

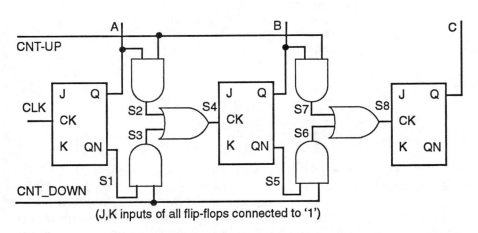

(J,K inputs of all flip-flops connected to '1')

Figure 6.4 A 3-bit up-down counter.

6.5   Resolving Signal Values

If outputs of two components drive a common signal, then the value of the signal must be resolved using a resolution function. This is similar to the case

of a signal being assigned using more than one concurrent signal assignment·
statement. For example, consider the circuit shown in Fig. 6.5 that shows two
and gates driving a common signal, RS1, which is inverted to produce the result in Z.

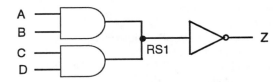

Figure 6.5 Two components driving a common signal.

```
entity DRIVING_SIGNAL is
    port (A, B, C, D: in BIT; Z: out BIT);
end DRIVING_SIGNAL;

-- PULL_UP is the name of a function defined in package RF_PACK that
-- has been compiled into the working library.
use WORK.RF_PACK.PULL_UP;
architecture RESOLVED of DRIVING_SIGNAL is
    signal RS1: PULL_UP BIT;
    component AND2
        port (IN1, IN2: in BIT; OUT1: out BIT);
    end component;
    component INV
        port (X: in BIT; Y: out BIT);
    end component;
begin
    A1: AND2 port map (A, B, RS1);
    A2: AND2 port map (C, D, RS1);
    I1: INV port map (RS1, Z);
end RESOLVED;
```

The key point here is that even though an assignment to signal RS1 is
not being made explicitly using signal assignment statements, the signal RS1
is being driven by two output ports, and therefore, must be resolved using a
resolution function. In the previous example, the PULL_UP resolution function is associated with signal RS1. This implies that the values of the outputs
of the **and** gates are passed through the resolution function before a value is
assigned to signal RS1. In general, each **out**, **inout**, and **buffer** port of a component creates a driver for the signal with which it is associated.

❑

CHAPTER 7   *Generics and Configurations*

This chapter introduces generics and provides examples to show how certain types of information can be passed into an entity using generics. Later sections in the chapter discuss the need for configurations and present the two alternate mechanisms provided by the language to configure, namely, the configuration specification and the configuration declaration.

7.1   *Generics*

It is often useful to pass certain types of information into a design description from its environment. Examples of such information are rise and fall delays, and size of interface ports. This is accomplished by using generics. Generics of an entity are declared along with its ports in the entity declaration. An example of a generic N-input **and** gate is shown next.

         entity AND_GATE **is**
            generic (N: NATURAL);

```
            port (A: in BIT_VECTOR(1 to N); Z: out BIT);
        end AND_GATE;

        architecture GENERIC_EX of AND_GATE is
        begin
            process (A)
                variable AND_OUT: BIT;
            begin
                AND_OUT := '1';
                for K in 1 to N loop
                    AND_OUT := AND_OUT and A(K);
                end loop;
                Z <= AND_OUT;
            end process;
        end GENERIC_EX;
```

In this example, the size of the input port has been modeled as a generic. By doing this, we have modeled an entire class of **and** gates with a variable number of inputs using a single behavioral description. The AND_GATE entity may now be used with a different number of input ports in different instantiations.

A generic declares a constant object of mode **in** (that is, the value can only be read), and can be used in the entity declaration and its corresponding architecture bodies. The value of this constant can be specified as a locally static expression in one of the following:

1. entity declaration
2. component declaration
3. component instantiation
4. configuration specification
5. configuration declaration

The value of a generic must be determinable at elaboration time, that is, a value for a generic must be explicitly specified at least once using any of the ones mentioned.

The value for a generic may be specified in the entity declaration for an entity as shown in this example. This is the default value for the generic. It can be overridden by others.

```
        entity NAND_GATE is
            generic (M: INTEGER := 2); -- M models the number of inputs.
            port (A: in BIT_VECTOR(M downto 1); Z: out BIT);
        end NAND_GATE;
```

Two other alternate ways of specifying the value of a generic are in a component declaration and in a component instantiation. The following examples demonstrates these.

```
entity ANOTHER_GEN_EX is
end;

architecture GEN_IN_COMP of ANOTHER_GEN_EX is
    -- Component declaration for NAND_GATE:
    component NAND_GATE
        generic (M: INTEGER);
        port (A: in BIT_VECTOR (M downto 1); Z: out BIT);
    end component;
    -- Component declaration for AND_GATE:
    component AND_GATE
        generic (N: NATURAL := 5);
        port (A: in BIT_VECTOR(1 to N); Z: out BIT);
    end component;
    signal S1, S2, S3, S4: BIT;
    signal SA: BIT_VECTOR (1 to 5);
    signal SB: BIT_VECTOR (2 downto 1);
    signal SC: BIT_VECTOR (1 to 10);
    signal SD: BIT_VECTOR (5 downto 0);
begin
    -- Component instantiations:
    N1: NAND_GATE generic map (6) port map (SD, S1);
    A1: AND_GATE generic map (N => 10) port map (SC, S3);
    A2: AND_GATE port map (SA, S4);
    -- N2: NAND_GATE port map (SB, S2);
end GEN_IN_COMP;
```

For the purposes of this discussion, we shall assume that the components NAND_GATE and AND_GATE are bound to the entities NAND_GATE and AND_GATE described earlier. The component declaration for AND_GATE specifies a value for the generic. When this component is instantiated and a new generic value is assigned using a generic map as in instance A1, the new value, that is, 10, overrides the value specified in the component declaration, that is, 5. When the AND_GATE component is instantiated and no generic map is specified as in instance A2, the value of the generic specified in the component declaration, that is, 5, is used. In the case of instance N1, again the value supplied by the generic map (i.e., 6) overrides the value assigned to the generic in the entity declaration for NAND_GATE (i.e., 2). The instance N2, shown as a comment, is illegal since neither the instantiation nor the declaration supply the value for the generic.

Values for generics may also be specified in a configuration specification or in a configuration declaration. We shall see this later in the section on configurations. The model of a **nor** gate with generic rise and fall delays is shown next.

```
entity NOR2 is
    generic (PT_HL, PT_LH: TIME);
    port (A, B: in BIT; Z: out BIT);
end NOR2;

architecture NOR2_DELAYS of NOR2 is
    signal TEMP: BIT;
begin
    TEMP <= not (A or B);
    Z <= TEMP after PT_HL when (TEMP = '0') else
        TEMP after PT_LH;
end NOR2_DELAYS;
```

Since no default values were provided for the generics in this case, the values must be provided later when this entity is instantiated or configured.

Consider an **or** gate constructed using two **nor** gates; each **nor** gate has the behavior described previously. The rise and fall delays are specified when the NOR2 component is instantiated. In the following example, different propagation delays are specified in each component instantiation statement.

```
entity OR2 is
    port (A, B: in BIT; C: out BIT);
end OR2;

architecture OR2_NOR2 of OR2 is
    component NOR2
        generic (PT_HL, PT_LH: TIME);
        port (A, B: in BIT; Z: out BIT);
    end component;
    signal S1: BIT;
begin
    N1: NOR2 generic map (5 ns, 3 ns) port map (A, B, S1);
    N2: NOR2 generic map (6 ns, 5 ns) port map (S1, S1, C);
end;
```

Other uses of generics include modeling ranges of subtypes, for example,

```
subtype ALUBUS is INTEGER range TOP downto 0;
-- TOP is a generic.
```

Generics can also be used to control the number of instantiations of a component in a generate statement (generate statements are discussed in Chap. 10).

7.2   Why Configurations?

A question that is often asked is why are configurations needed? There are two main reasons.

1. Sometimes it may be convenient to specify multiple views for a single entity and use any one of these for simulation. This can be easily done by specifying one architecture body for each view and using a configuration to bind the entity to the desired architecture body. For example, corresponding to an entity FULL_ADDER, there may be three architecture bodies, called FA_BEH, FA_STR, and FA_MIXED. Any one of these can be selected for simulation be specifying an appropriate configuration.

2. Similar to the previous case, it may be desirable to associate a component with any one of a set of entities. The component declaration may have its name and the names, types, and number of ports and generics different from those of its entities. For example, a declaration for a component used in a design may be

```
component OR2
    port (A, B: in BIT; Z: out BIT);
end component;
```

and the entities that the above component may possibly be bound to are

```
entity OR_GENERIC is
    port (N: out BIT; L, M: in BIT);
end OR_GENERIC;

entity OR_HS is
    port (X, Y: in BIT; Z: out BIT);
end OR_HS;
```

The component names and the entity names, as well as the port names and their order are different. In one case we may be interested in using the OR_HS entity for the OR2 component, and in another case, the OR_GENERIC entity. This can be achieved by appropriately specifying a configuration for the component. The advantage is that when components are used in a design, arbitrary names for components and their interface ports can be used and these can later be bound to specific entities prior to simulation.

A configuration is, therefore, used to bind

1. an architecture body to its entity declaration,
2. a component with an entity.

Note that a configuration does not have any simulation semantics associated with it; it only specifies how a top-level entity is organized in terms of lower level entities by specifying the bindings between the entities. The language provides two ways of performing this binding:

1. by using a configuration specification,
2. by using a configuration declaration.

7.3   Configuration Specification

A configuration specification is used to bind component instantiations to specific entities that are stored in design libraries. The specification appears in the declarations part of the architecture or block in which the components are instantiated. Binding of a component to an entity can be done on a per instance basis, or for all instantiations of a component, or for a selected set of instantiations of a component. Instantiations of different components can also be bound to the same entity.

Figure 7.1 shows a logic diagram for a 1-bit full-adder. Its structural model is described next.

```
library HS_LIB, CMOS_LIB;
entity FULL_ADDER is
    port (A, B, CIN: in BIT; SUM, COUT: out BIT);
end;

architecture FA_STR of FULL_ADDER is
    component XOR2
        port (A, B: in BIT; C: out BIT);
    end component;
    component AND2
        port (Z: out BIT; A0, A1: in BIT);
    end component;
    component OR2
        port (A, B: in BIT; C: out BIT);
    end component;
```

-- The following four statements are configuration specifications:
for X1, X2: XOR2
    use entity WORK.XOR2(XOR2BEH); -- Binding the entity with
        -- more than one instantiation of a component.
for A3: AND2
    use entity HS_LIB.AND2HS(AND2STR)
    port map (HS_B=>A1, HS_Z=>Z, HS_A=>A0); -- Binding the
        -- entity with a single instantiation of a component.
for all: OR2
    use entity CMOS_LIB.OR2CMOS(OR2STR); -- Binding the
        -- entity with all instantiations of OR2 component.
for others: AND2
    use entity WORK.A_GATE(A_GATE_BODY)
    port map (A0, A1, Z); -- Binding the entity with all unbound
        -- instantiations of AND2 component.
signal S1, S2, S3, S4, S5: BIT;
begin
    X1: XOR2 **port map** (A, B, S1);
    X2: XOR2 **port map** (S1, CIN, SUM);
    A1: AND2 **port map** (S2, A, B);
    A2: AND2 **port map** (S3, B, CIN);
    A3: AND2 **port map** (S4, A, CIN);
    O1: OR2 **port map** (S2, S3, S5);
    O2: OR2 **port map** (S4, S5, COUT);
end FA_STR;

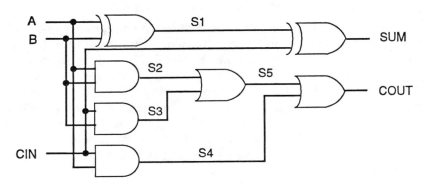

Figure 7.1 A 1-bit full-adder circuit.

The four **for** statements appearing in the declarative part of the architecture body are the configuration specifications. The first specification statement indicates that instances X1 and X2 of component XOR2 are bound to the entity represented by the entity-architecture pair, XOR2 and XOR2BEH, respectively, that resides in library WORK. The second specification binds the AND2 component with instantiation label A3 to the entity represented by the entity-architecture pair, AND2HS and AND2STR, respectively, that is present in design library HS_LIB. The mapping of the component (AND2) ports and the entity (AND2HS) ports is specified using named association; for example, port HS_A of the AND2HS entity is mapped to port A0 of the AND2 component. The third specification implies that for all instances of component OR2, use the entity represented by the specified entity-architecture pair that is present in the design library, CMOS_LIB. The last specification statement implies that all unbound instances of component AND2, that is, A1 and A2, are bound to the entity A_GATE using the architecture A_GATE_BODY, that resides in library WORK.

The previous example showed that different instances of the same component can be bound to different entities. Figure 7.2 depicts this binding.

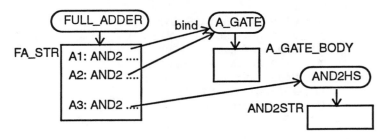

Figure 7.2 Different instances bound to different entities.

Similarly, it is also possible to bind different components to the same entity. An example is shown in Fig. 7.3. This figure shows that there is nothing special about the component name being AND2. By binding an instance of component AND2 to an entity called OR_GATE, this instance is being made to behave as specified in the architecture of entity OR_GATE. Using such a binding may cause confusion to the reader, even though it is syntactically correct, and it may be what was intended. Such bindings may sometimes be necessary, for example, while debugging a model, we may want to see the effect of specifying an **and** gate to behave like an **or** gate without changing the rest of the description.

This flexibility of being allowed to bind a component instance to any entity may result in a complex maze of bindings. An example is shown in Fig. 7.4.

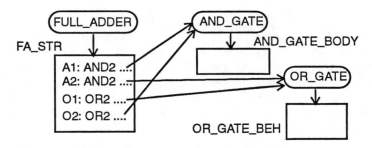

Figure 7.3 Different components bound to same entity.

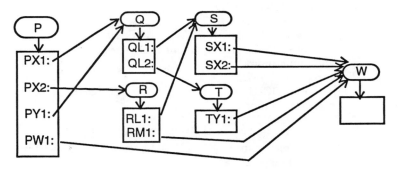

Figure 7.4 A complex maze of bindings.

Entity P has four component instances, PX1 and PX2 of component type PX, PY1 of component type PY, and PW1 of component type PW. Component instances PX1 and PY1 are bound to entity Q while PX2 is bound to R. Component instances QL1 and QL2 (of component type QL) in entity Q are bound to entities S and T, respectively. Component instances RL1 and RM1 in entity R are bound to entities S and W, respectively. All component instances in S and T, and component PW1 in entity P are bound to a single entity W. In other words, all the entities, P, Q, R, S, and T have been built hierarchically using a single primitive component, W.

The syntax of a configuration specification is

> **for** *list-of-comp-labels* : *component-name*
> **use** *binding-indication* ;

The *binding-indication* specifies the entity represented by the entity-architecture pair, and the generic and port bindings, and one of its forms is

```
entity entity-name [ ( architecture-name ) ]
   [ generic map ( generic-association ) ]
   [ port map ( port-association ) ]          -- Form 1
```

The list of component labels may be replaced with the keyword **all** to denote all instances of a component; it may also be the keyword **others** to specify all as yet unbound instances of a component. The generic map is used to specify the values for the generics or provide the mapping between the generic parameters of the component and the entity to which it is bound. The port map is used to specify the port bindings between the component and the bound entity. Additional examples of configuration specifications appear in the following architecture body.

```
architecture DUMMY of DUMMY is
   component NOR_GATE
      generic (RISE_TIME, FALL_TIME: TIME);
      port (S0, S1: in BIT; Q: out BIT);
   end component;
   component AND2_GATE
      port (DOUT: out BIT; DIN: in BIT_VECTOR);
   end component;
   for N1, N2: NOR_GATE
      use entity WORK.NOR2(NOR2_DELAYS)
      generic map (PT_HL => FALL_TIME, PT_LH => RISE_TIME)
      port map (S0, S1, Q);
   for all: AND2_GATE
      use entity WORK.AND2 (GENERIC_EX)
      generic map (10)
      port map (A => DIN, Z => DOUT);
   signal WR, RD, RW, S1, S2: BIT;
   signal SA: BIT_VECTOR (1 to 10);
begin
   N1: NOR_GATE generic map (2 ns, 3 ns) port map (WR, RD, RW);
   A1: AND2_GATE port map (S1, SA);
   N2: NOR_GATE generic map (4 ns, 6 ns)
                     port map (S1, SA(2), S3);
end DUMMY;
```

The entity declarations for the entities that are bound to components NOR_GATE and AND2_GATE are

```
entity NOR2 is
   generic (PT_HL, PT_LH: TIME);
   port (A, B: in BIT; Z: out BIT);
end NOR2;
```

```
entity AND2 is
    generic (N: NATURAL := 5);
    port (A: in BIT_VECTOR(1 to N); Z: out BIT);
end AND2;
```

In the binding for N1 and N2, the generic map specifies the mapping of generic names from the entity NOR2 to the component NOR_GATE using named association. The generic values supplied in the instantiations are, therefore, passed to the NOR2 entity through this mapping. The port binding is specified using positional association, that is, ports S0, S1, and Q of NOR_GATE component map to ports A, B, and Z, respectively, of the NOR2 entity. The configuration specification for the AND2_GATE specifies the value, 10, of the generic explicitly (using positional association) which overrides the default value, 5, specified in the entity declaration for the AND2 entity. The component declaration for AND2_GATE, in this case, should not specify any generics since the values are passed directly to the actual generics of the entity. The port mapping for the AND2_GATE is specified using named association.

How are the generic map and port map values in a component instantiation passed into its bound entity via the configuration specification? A look at the elaboration of a component instantiation helps us to understand this. Let us take the N1 instantiation in the previous architecture body as an example. Elaboration transforms this component instantiation into the following block statement.

```
N1: block                      -- A block for the component instantiation.
    generic (RISE_TIME, FALL_TIME: TIME); -- Generics of
        -- the component.
    generic map (RISE_TIME => 2 ns, FALL_TIME => 3 ns); -- Generic
        -- map in instantiation.
    port (S0, S1: in BIT; Q: out BIT); -- Ports of component.
    port map (S0 => WR, S1 => RD, Q => RW); -- Port map in
        -- instantiation.
begin
    NOR2: block                    -- A block for the bound entity.
        generic (PT_HL, PT_LH: TIME); -- Its generics.
        generic map (PT_HL => FALL_TIME, PT_LH => RISE_TIME);
            -- Generic map in configuration specification.
        port (A, B: in BIT; Z: out BIT); -- Its ports.
        port map (A => S0, B => S1, Z => Q); -- Port map in
            -- specification.
        -- Other declarations in the architecture
        -- body NOR2_DELAYS appear here.
    begin
        -- Statements in architecture body NOR2_DELAYS
        -- appear here.
```

```
        end block NOR2;
    end block N1;
```

The block N1 is created from the component instantiation of NOR_GATE. The generic map and port map for this block are the generic map and port map specified in the component instantiation for N1, that is, they specify the mapping between the values and signals in the component instantiation statement with the generics and ports of component NOR_GATE. The inner block with label NOR2 represents the entity NOR2 that the component instantiation N1 is bound to in the configuration specification. The generic map and port map of this block specify the generic map and port map that appear in the configuration specification, that is, they specify the mapping between the component NOR_GATE and the entity NOR2.

7.4   Configuration Declaration

Configuration specifications have to appear in an architecture body. Therefore, to change a binding, it is necessary to change the architecture body and re-analyze it. This may sometimes be cumbersome and time consuming. To avoid this, a configuration declaration may be used to specify a binding.

A configuration declaration is a separate design unit, therefore, it allows for late binding of components, that is, the binding can be performed after the architecture body has been written. It is also possible to have more than one configuration declaration for an entity, each of which defines a different set of bindings for components in a single architecture body, or possibly specifies a unique entity-architecture pair.

The typical format of a configuration declaration is

```
    configuration configuration-name of entity-name is
        block-configuration
    end [ configuration-name ] ;
```

It declares a configuration with the name, *configuration-name*, for the entity, *entity-name*. A *block-configuration* defines the binding of components in a block, where a block may be an architecture body, a block statement, or a generate statement. Bindings of components defined in a block statement and in a generate statement are discussed in Chap. 10. A block configuration is a recursive structure of the form

```
    for block-name
        component-configurations
        block-configurations
    end for ;
```

The *block-name* is the name of an architecture body, a block statement label, or a generate statement label. The top-level block is always an architecture body. A *component-configuration* binds components that appear in a block to entities and is of the form

```
for list-of-comp-labels : comp-name [ use binding-indication ; ]
    [ block-configuration ]
end for;
```

The block configuration that appears within a component configuration defines the bindings of components at the next level of hierarchy in the entity-architecture pair specified by the binding indication.

There are two other forms of binding indication in addition to the one shown in the previous section. These are

```
configuration configuration-name              -- Form 2
open                                           -- Form 3
```

In form 2, the binding indication specifies that the component instances are to be bound to a configuration of a lower level entity as specified by the configuration name. This implies that a configuration declaration with such a name must exist. In form 3, the binding indication indicates that the binding is not yet specified and that it is to be deferred. Both these forms of binding indication may also be used in a configuration specification.

Here is an example of a configuration declaration that specifies the component configurations for all component instances in architecture FA_STR of entity FULL_ADDER described in the previous section.

```
library CMOS_LIB;
configuration FA_CON of FULL_ADDER is
    for FA_STR
        use WORK.all;
        for A1, A2, A3: AND2
            use entity CMOS_LIB.BIGAND2 (AND2STR);
        end for;
        for others: OR2   -- use defaults, i.e. use OR2 from
                          -- library WORK.
        end for;
        for all: XOR2
            use configuration WORK.XOR2CON;
        end for;
    end for;
end FA_CON;
```

The configuration with name, FA_CON, binds architecture FA_STR with the FULL_ADDER entity. For components within this architecture body, instances A1, A2, and A3, are bound to the entity, BIGAND2, that exists in the design library, CMOS_LIB. For all instances of component OR2, the default bindings are used; these are the entities in the working library with the same names as the component names. The last component configuration shows a different type of binding indication. In this case, all component instances are bound to a configuration instead of an entity-architecture pair. All instances of component XOR2 are bound to a configuration with name XOR2CON, that exists in the working library. This type of binding may also be specified in a configuration specification.

The power of the configuration declaration lies in the fact that the sub-components in an entire hierarchy of a design can be bound using a single configuration declaration. For example, consider a full-adder circuit composed of two half-adders and an **or** gate.   The half-adder circuit is in turn composed of **xor** and **and** gates. The hierarchy for this full-adder is shown in Fig. 7.5.

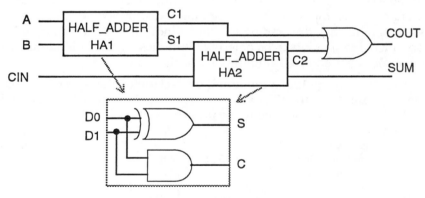

Figure 7.5 A hierarchical 1-bit full-adder.

The structural models for the full-adder and half-adder circuits are described next. A configuration declaration which specifies the bindings for components used in the entire hierarchy of the full-adder is also shown.

```
entity FULL_ADDER is
    port (A, B, CIN: in BIT; COUT, SUM: out BIT);
end FULL_ADDER;

architecture FA_WITH_HA of FULL_ADDER is
    component HALF_ADDER
        port (A, B: in BIT; SUM, CARRY: out BIT);
```

```
        end component;
        component OR2
            port (A, B: in BIT; Z: out BIT);
        end component;
        signal S1, C1, C2: BIT;
begin
        HA1: HALF_ADDER port map (A, B, S1, C1);
        HA2: HALF_ADDER port map (S1, CIN, SUM, C2);
        O1: OR2 port map (C1, C2, COUT);
end FA_WITH_HA;

entity HA is
        port (D0, D1: in BIT; S, C: out BIT);
end HA;

architecture HA_STR of HA is
        component XOR2
            port (X, Y: in BIT; Z: out BIT);
        end component;
        component AND2
            port (L. M: in BIT; N: out BIT);
        end component;
begin
        X1: XOR2 port map (D0, D1, S);
        A1: AND2 port map (D0, D1, C);
end HA_STR;

-- A configuration for the FULL_ADDER that is built using half-adders.
library ECL;
configuration FA_HA_CON of FULL_ADDER is
        for FA_WITH_HA              -- Top-level block configuration.
            for HA1, HA2: HALF_ADDER
                use entity WORK.HA(HA_STR)
                port map (D0=>A, D1=>B, S=>SUM, C=>CARRY);
                for HA_STR           -- Nested block configuration.
                    for all: XOR2
                        use entity WORK.XOR2(XOR2);
                    end for;
                    for A1: AND2
                        use configuration ECL.AND2CON;
                    end for;
                end for;
            end for;
            for O1: OR2
                use configuration WORK.OR2CON;
            end for;
```

```
      end for;
   end FA_HA_CON;
```

The top-level block configuration specifies the bindings of component instances present in the architecture body FA_WITH_HA. Instances HA1 and HA2 are bound to an entity specified by the entity-architecture pair, entity HA and architecture HA_STR. The nested block configuration specifies the binding of component instances present in the architecture body HA_STR. In this way, a configuration can be nested to any arbitrary depth and can be used to bind all components in a hierarchy.

The previous example shows that when components in a hierarchy are bound, a single configuration declaration may be used to replace a set of configuration specifications. If configuration specifications were used in the earlier example, they would have to be included separately in the architecture bodies, FA_WITH_HA and HA_STR, and then these bodies would have to be recompiled every time a binding is changed. Note that a component instance must not be bound both in a configuration specification and in a configuration declaration.

Configurations, therefore, provide the mechanism by which architecture bodies may contain technology-independent components. Technology-specific mappings can be specified separately using configuration declarations.

7.5   Default Rules

A large amount of overhead is introduced if the bindings for every component in a design must be individually specified. Fortunately, the language provides default binding rules. For each unbound component instance,

- an entity that is visible and has the same name as that of the component is used to bind to the instance; if no such entity exists, it is an error,
- the entity's most recently analyzed architecture is used,
- ports and generics are matched by names.

These default rules help to avoid writing specific bindings in cases where the component names are the same as the entity names. Another advantage of these default rules is that it allows for the usage of standard component names such as SN7400 and SN7402. In cases such as these, no bindings are necessary. However, a minimum configuration may be necessary. This could be of the form as shown.

```
library TTL_LIB;
configuration TLC_CON of TLC is
    for TLC_STRUCTURE
        use TTL_LIB.all;
    end for;
end TLC_CON;
```

TLC is an entity that has some component instantiations defined within its architecture body, TLC_STRUCTURE. The clause "**use** TTL_LIB.**all**" makes all
entities in library TTL_LIB visible. Therefore these will get bound to the component instances in the architecture body by virtue of the default rules.

❏

CHAPTER 8 *Subprograms and Overloading*

This chapter describes the two kinds of subprograms: procedures and functions. A function call can be used within an expression. A procedure call may be a sequential or a concurrent statement. It is possible for two or more subprograms to have the same name. This is called overloading. This chapter also presents this important concept and explains operator overloading as well.

8.1 Subprograms

A subprogram defines a sequential algorithm that performs a certain computation and executes in zero simulation time. There are two kinds of subprograms:

1. *Functions*: These are usually used for computing a single value.
2. *Procedures*: These are used to partition large behavioral descriptions. Procedures can return zero or more values.

A subprogram is defined using a *subprogram body*. The typical format for a subprogram body is

```
subprogram-specification is
    subprogram-item-declarations
begin
    subprogram-statements          -- Same as sequential-statements.
end [ subprogram-name ] ;
```

The *subprogram-specification* specifies the name of a subprogram and defines its interface, that is, it defines the formal parameter names, their class (i.e., **signal**, **variable**, or **constant**), their type, and their mode (whether they are **in**, **out**, or **inout**). Parameters of mode **in** are read-only parameters; these cannot be updated within a subprogram body. Parameters of mode **out** are write-only parameters; their values cannot be used but can only be updated within a subprogram body. Parameters of mode **inout** can be read as well as updated.

Actual values are passed to and from a subprogram via a subprogram call. Only a signal object may be used to pass a value to a parameter of the **signal** class. Only a variable object may be used to pass a value to a parameter of the **variable** class. A constant or an expression may be used to pass a value to a parameter of **constant** class. When parameters are of a **variable** or **constant** class, values are passed to the subprogram by value. Arrays may or may not be passed by reference. For signal objects, the reference to the signal, its driver, or both are passed into the subprogram. What this means is that any assignment to a signal in a procedure (signals cannot be assigned values in a function because the parameters are restricted to be of input mode) affects the actual signal driver immediately and is independent of whether the procedure terminates or not. For a signal of any mode, the signal-valued attributes, STABLE, QUIET, DELAYED, and TRANSACTION (attributes are discussed in Chap. 10), cannot be used in a subprogram body.

The type of an actual value in a subprogram call must match that of its corresponding formal parameter. If the formal parameter belongs to an unconstrained type, the size of this parameter is determined from the actual value that is passed in.

The *subprogram-item-declarations* part contains a set of declarations (e.g., type and object declarations) that are accessible for use locally within the subprogram. These declarations come into effect every time the subprogram is called. Variables are also created and initialized every time the subprogram is called. They remain in existence until the subprogram completes. This is in contrast with declarations in a process statement that get initialized only once, that is at start of simulation, and any declared variables persist throughout the entire simulation run.

The *subprogram-statements* part contains sequential statements that define the computation to be performed by the subprogram. A return statement, which is also a sequential statement, is a special statement that is allowed only within subprograms. The format of a return statement is

return [*expression*] ;

The return statement causes the subprogram to terminate and control is returned back to the calling object. All functions must have a return statement and the value of the expression in the return statement is returned to the calling program. For procedures, objects of mode **out** and **inout** return their values to the calling program.

The *subprogram-name* appearing at the end of a subprogram body, if present, must be the same as the function or procedure name specified in the subprogram specification part.

8.1.1   Functions

Functions are used to describe frequently used sequential algorithms that return a single value. This value is returned to the calling program using a return statement. Some of their common uses are as resolution functions, and as type conversion functions. The following is an example of a function body.

```
function LARGEST (TOTAL_NO: INTEGER; SET: PATTERN)
    return REAL is
    -- PATTERN is defined to be a type of 1-D array of
    -- floating-point values, elsewhere.
    variable RETURN_VALUE: REAL := 0.0;
begin
    for K in 1 to TOTAL_NO loop
        if SET(K) > RETURN_VALUE then
            RETURN_VALUE := SET(K);
        end if;
    end loop;
    return RETURN_VALUE;
end LARGEST;
```

Variable RETURN_VALUE comes into existence with an initial value of 0.0 every time the function is called. It ceases to exist after the function returns back to the calling program.

The general syntax of a subprogram specification for a function body is

function *function-name* (*parameter-list*) **return** *return-type*

The *parameter-list* describes the list of formal parameters for the function. The only mode allowed for the parameters is mode **in**. Also, only constants and signal objects can be passed in as parameters. The default object class is **constant**. For example, in function LARGEST, TOTAL_NO is a constant and its value cannot be modified within the function body. Another example of a function body is shown next. This function returns true if a rising edge has been detected on the input signal.

```
function VRISE (signal CLOCK_NAME: BIT) return BOOLEAN is
begin
      return (CLOCK_NAME = '1') and CLOCK_NAME'EVENT;
end VRISE;
```

A function call is an expression and can, therefore, be used in expressions. For example,

```
SUM := SUM + LARGEST(MAX_COINS, COLLECTION);
```

A function call has the form

function-name (list-of-actual-values)

The actual values may be associated by position (the first actual value corresponds to the first formal parameter, the second actual value corresponds to the second parameter, and so on) or they may be associated using named association (the association of actual values and formal parameters are explicitly specified). The function call in the last example used positional association. An equivalent function call using named association is

```
LARGEST (SET => COLLECTION, TOTAL_NO => MAX_COINS)
```

8.1.2   Procedures

Procedures allow decomposition of large behaviors into modular sections. In contrast to a function, a procedure can return zero or more values using parameters of mode **out** and **inout**. The syntax for the subprogram specification for a procedure body is

procedure *procedure-name (parameter-list)*

The *parameter-list* specifies the list of formal parameters for the procedure. Parameters may be constants, variables, or signals and their modes may be **in**, **out**, or **inout**. If the object class of a parameter is not explicitly specified, then the object class is by default a **constant** if the parameter is of mode **in**, else it is a variable if the parameter is of mode **out** or **inout**.

A simple example of a procedure body is shown next. It describes the behavior of an arithmetic logic unit.

```
type OP_CODE is (ADD, SUB, MUL, DIV, LT, LE, EQ);
. . .
procedure ARITH_UNIT (A, B: in INTEGER; OP: in OP_CODE;
                Z: out INTEGER; ZCOMP: out BOOLEAN) is
begin
    case OP is
        when ADD => Z := A + B;
        when SUB => Z := A – B;
        when MUL => Z := A * B;
        when DIV => Z := A / B;
        when LT => ZCOMP := A < B;
        when LE => ZCOMP := A <= B;
        when EQ => ZCOMP := A = B;
    end case;
end ARITH_UNIT;
```

The following is another example of a procedure body. This procedure rotates the specified signal vector ARRAY_NAME starting from bit START_BIT to bit STOP_BIT by the ROTATE_BY value. The object class for parameter ARRAY_NAME is explicitly specified. The variable FILL_VALUE is automatically initialized to '0' every time the procedure is called.

```
procedure ROTATE_LEFT
        (signal ARRAY_NAME: inout BIT_VECTOR;
        START_BIT, STOP_BIT: in INTEGER;
        ROTATE_BY: in INTEGER) is
        variable FILL_VALUE: BIT; --Initial value is BIT'LEFT which is '0'.
begin
    for MACVAR3 in 1 to ROTATE_BY loop
        FILL_VALUE := ARRAY_NAME(STOP_BIT);
        for MACVAR1 in STOP_BIT downto (START_BIT+1) loop
            ARRAY_NAME(MACVAR1) <=
                                ARRAY_NAME(MACVAR1-1);
        end loop;
        ARRAY_NAME(START_BIT) <= FILL_VALUE;
    end loop;
end ROTATE_LEFT;
```

Procedures are invoked by using procedure calls. A procedure call can either be a sequential statement or a concurrent statement; this is based on where the actual procedure call statement is present. If the call is inside a process statement or inside another subprogram, then it is a sequential procedure call statement, else it is a concurrent procedure call statement. The syntax of a procedure call statement is *procedure-name* (*list-of-actual-parameters*) ;

The actual parameters specify the expressions that are to be passed into the procedure and the names of objects that are to receive the computed values from the procedure. Actual parameters may be specified using positional association or named association. For example,

```
ARITH_UNIT (D1, D2, ADD, SUM, COMP);     -- Positional association.
ARITH_UNIT (Z=>SUM, B=>D2, A=>D1,
            OP=>ADD, ZCOMP=>COMP);       -- Named association.
```

A sequential procedure call statement is executed sequentially with respect to the sequential statements surrounding it inside a process or a subprogram. A concurrent procedure call statement is executed whenever an event occurs on one of the parameters which is a signal of mode **in** or **inout**. Semantically, a concurrent procedure call is equivalent to a process with a sequential procedure call and a **wait** statement that waits for an event on the signal parameters of mode **in** or **inout**. Here is an example of a concurrent procedure call and its equivalent process statement.

```
architecture DUMMY_ARCH of DUMMY is
    -- Following is a procedure body:
    procedure INT_2_VEC (signal D: out BIT_VECTOR;
        START_BIT, STOP_BIT: in INTEGER;
        signal VALUE: in INTEGER)
    begin
        -- Procedure behavior here.
    end INT_2_VEC;
begin
    -- This is an example of a concurrent procedure call:
    INT_2_VEC (D_ARRAY, START, STOP, SIGNAL_VALUE);
end DUMMY_ARCH;

-- is equivalent to:
architecture DUMMY_ARCH of DUMMY is
    procedure INT_2_VEC (signal D: out BIT_VECTOR;
        START_BIT, STOP_BIT: in INTEGER;
        signal VALUE: in INTEGER)
    begin
        -- Procedure behavior here.
    end INT_2_VEC;
begin
    process
    begin
        INT_2_VEC (D_ARRAY, START, STOP, SIGNAL_VALUE);
        -- This is now a sequential procedure call.
        wait on SIGNAL_VALUE;
```

```
        -- Since SIGNAL_VALUE is an input signal.
    end process;
  end DUMMY_ARCH;
```

A procedure can normally be used simultaneously as a concurrent and a sequential statement. However, if any of the procedure parameters are of the **variable** class, the procedure would be restricted to be used as a sequential procedural call, since variables can only be defined inside of a process. Concurrent procedure calls are useful in representing frequently used processes.

A procedure body can have a **wait** statement while a function cannot. Functions are used to compute values that are available instantaneously. Therefore, a function cannot be made to wait, for example, it cannot call a procedure with a **wait** statement in it. A process that calls a procedure with a **wait** statement cannot have a sensitivity list. This follows from the fact that a process cannot be sensitive to signals and also be made to wait simultaneously. Since a procedure can have a **wait** statement, any variables declared in the procedure retain their values through this wait period and cease to exist only when the procedure terminates.

8.1.3   Declarations

A subprogram body may appear in the declarative part of the block in which a call is made. This is not convenient if the subprogram is to be shared by many entities. In such cases, the subprogram body can be described at one place, possibly in a package body and then in the package declaration, the corresponding *subprogram declaration* is specified. If this package declaration is included in other design units using context clauses, the subprograms can then be used in these design units. A subprogram declaration describes the subprogram name and the list of parameters without describing the internal behavior of the subprogram, that is, it describes the interface for the subprogram. The syntax of a subprogram declaration is

subprogram-specification ;

Two examples of procedure and function declarations are shown next.

```
    procedure ARITH_UNIT (A, B: in INTEGER; OP: in OP_CODE;
                    Z: out INTEGER; ZCOMP: out BOOLEAN);
    function VRISE (signal CLOCK_NAME: BIT) return BOOLEAN;
```

Another reason subprogram declarations are necessary is to allow two subprograms to call each other recursively, for example,

```
procedure P () . . .
begin
    A := Q (B);    -- illegal function call.
end P;

function Q () . . .
begin
    P();
end Q;
```

The call to function Q in procedure P is illegal since Q has not yet been declared. This can be corrected by writing the function declaration for Q either before procedure P or inside the declarative part of procedure P.

8.2   Subprogram Overloading

Sometimes it is convenient to have two or more subprograms with the same name. In such a case, the subprogram name is said to be *overloaded*. For example, consider the following two declarations.

```
function COUNT (ORANGES: INTEGER) return INTEGER;
function COUNT (APPLES: BIT) return INTEGER;
```

Both functions are overloaded since they have the same name, COUNT, and have different parameter types. When a call to either function is made, it is easily possible to identify the exact function to which the call was made from the type of the actual parameters passed. For example, the function call

```
COUNT(20)
```

refers to the first function since 20 is of type INTEGER, while the function call

```
COUNT('1')
```

refers to the second function, since the type of actual parameter is BIT.

If two overloaded subprograms have the same parameter types and result types, then it is possible for one subprogram to hide the other subprogram. This can happen, for example, if a subprogram is declared within another subprogram's scope. Here is an example.

```
architecture HIDING of DUMMY_ENTITY is
    function ADD (A, B: BIT_VECTOR) return BIT_VECTOR is
    begin
        -- Body of function here.
    end ADD;
```

```
begin
    SUM_IN_ARCH <= ADD(IN1, IN2);
    process
        function ADD (C, D: BIT_VECTOR) return BIT_VECTOR is
        begin
            -- Body of function here.
        end ADD;
    begin
        SUM_IN_PROCESS <= ADD (IN1, IN2);
        SUM_IN_ARCH <= HIDING.ADD(IN1, IN2);
    end process;
end HIDING;
```

The function ADD declared in the architecture body is hidden within the process because of the second function ADD that is declared within the declarative part of the process. This function can still be accessed by qualifying the function name with the architecture name as shown in the second statement in the process.

It is also possible for two overloaded subprograms to be directly visible within a region, for example, caused by using **use** clauses. In such a case, a subprogram call may be ambiguous, and hence an error, if it is not possible to determine which of the overloaded subprograms is being called. Here is an example.

```
package P1 is
    function ADD (A, B: BIT_VECTOR) return BIT_VECTOR;
end P1;

package P2 is
    function ADD (X, Y: BIT_VECTOR) return BIT_VECTOR;
end P2;

use WORK.P1.all, WORK.P2.all;
architecture OVERLOADED of DUMMY_ENTITY is
begin
    SUM_CORRECT <= ADD (X => IN1, Y => IN2);
    SUM_ERROR <= ADD (IN1, IN2); -- An error.
end OVERLOADED;
```

The function call in the first signal assignment statement is not an error since it refers to the function declared in package P2, while the call in the second signal assignment statement is ambiguous and hence an error.

It is also possible for two subprograms to have the same parameter types and result types but have a different number of parameters. In this case, the number of actual values supplied in the subprogram call identifies the correct subprogram. Here is an example of such a set of functions that determine the smallest value from a set of 2, 4, or 8 integers.

> **function** SMALLEST (A1, A2: INTEGER) **return** INTEGER;
> **function** SMALLEST (A1, A2, A3, A4: INTEGER) **return** INTEGER;
> **function** SMALLEST (A1, A2, A3, A4, A5, A6, A7, A8: INTEGER)
>   **return** INTEGER;

A call such as

> . . . SMALLEST (4, 5) . . .

refers to the first function, while the function call

> . . . SMALLEST (20, 45, 52, 1, 89, 67, 91, 22) . . .

refers to the third function. This flexibility helps in writing code that is easy to decipher since the same subprogram name can be made to serve differently when used with a different set of inputs.

8.3   *Operator Overloading*

Operator overloading is one of the most useful features in the language. When a standard operator symbol is made to behave differently based on the type of its operands, the operator is said to be overloaded. The need for operator overloading arises from the fact that the predefined operators in the language are defined for operands of certain predefined types. For example, the **and** operation is defined for arguments of type BIT and BOOLEAN only. What if the arguments were of type MVL (where MVL is a user-defined enumeration type with values 'U', '0', '1' and 'Z')? In such a case, it is possible to redefine the **and** operation as a function that operates on arguments of type MVL. The **and** operator is then said to be overloaded. The operator in the expression

> S1 **and** S2

where S1 and S2 are of type MVL, would then refer to the **and** operation that was defined by the model writer as a function. The operator in the expression

> CLK1 **and** CLK2

where CLK1 and CLK2 are of type BIT, would refer to the predefined **and** operator.

Function bodies are written to define the behavior of overloaded operators. Such a function has, at most, two parameters; the first one refers to the left operand of the operator and the second parameter, if present, refers to the second operand. Here are some examples of function declarations for such function bodies.

```
type MVL is ('U', '0', '1', 'Z');
function "and" (L, R: MVL) return MVL;
function "or" (L, R: MVL) return MVL;
function "not" (R: MVL) return MVL;
```

Since the **and, or,** and **not** operators are predefined operator symbols, they have to be enclosed within double quotes when used as overloaded operator function names. Having declared the overloaded functions, the operators can now be called using two different types of notations:

1. standard operator notation,
2. standard function call notation.

Here are some examples of these two types of notations based on the overloaded operator function declarations that appeared earlier.

```
signal A, B, C: MVL;
signal X, Y, Z: BIT;

A <= 'Z' or '1';              -- #1: standard operator notation.
B <= "or" ('0', 'Z');        -- #2: function call notation.
X <= not Y;                  -- #3
Z <= X and Y;                -- #4
C <= (A or B) and (not C);   -- #5
Z <= (X and Y) or A;         -- #6
```

The **or** operator in the first statement refers to the overloaded operator because the type of the left operand is MVL. This is the standard operator notation since the overloaded operator symbol appears just like the standard operator symbol. An example of the function call notation is shown in the second statement in which the overloaded function, **or,** is explicitly called. The operators in the third and fourth statements refer to the predefined operators since their operands are of type BIT. The sixth statement would be an error assuming that there are no other overloaded **or** operators defined with the first parameter type of BIT and the second parameter type of MVL.

The last example brings up a very interesting point. In overloaded operator functions, it is not necessary for both operands to have the same type. In the previous case, if another **or** overloaded function with a declaration such as

function "or" (L: BIT; R: MVL) **return** BIT;

were defined, the sixth assignment statement would not be an error.

❑

CHAPTER 9   *Packages and Libraries*

This chapter explains packages and how compiled design units are stored in design libraries. It explains how the contents of design units stored in different libraries may be shared by several design units.

A package provides a convenient mechanism to store and share declarations that are common across many design units. A package is represented by

1. a package declaration, and optionally,
2. a package body.

9.1 Package Declaration

A package declaration contains a set of declarations that may possibly be shared by many design units. It defines the interface to the package, that is, it defines items that can be made visible to other design units, for example, a function declaration. A package body, in contrast, contains the hidden details of a package, for example, a function body.

The syntax of a package declaration is

package *package-name* **is**
    package-item-declarations --> These may be:
           -- subprogram declarations
           -- type declarations
           -- subtype declarations
           -- constant declarations
           -- signal declarations
           -- file declarations
           -- alias declarations
           -- component declarations
           -- attribute declarations
           -- attribute specifications
           -- disconnection specifications
           -- use clauses
end [*package-name*] ;

An example of a package declaration is given next.

package SYNTH_PACK **is**
    constant LOW2HIGH: TIME := 20 ns;
    type ALU_OP **is** (ADD, SUB, MUL, DIV, EQL);
    attribute PIPELINE: BOOLEAN;
    type MVL **is** ('U', '0', '1', 'Z');
    type MVL_VECTOR **is array** (NATURAL **range** <>) **of** MVL;
    subtype MY_ALU_OP **is** ALU_OP **range** ADD **to** DIV;
    component NAND2
        port (A, B: **in** MVL; C: **out** MVL);
    end component;
end SYNTH_PACK;

Items declared in a package declaration can be accessed by other design units by using the **library** and **use** context clauses. The set of common declarations may also include function and procedure declarations and deferred constant declarations. In this case, the behavior of the subprograms and the values of the deferred constants are specified in a separate design unit called the package body. Since the previous package example did not contain any subprogram declarations and deferred constant declarations, a package body was not necessary.

Consider the following package declaration.

use WORK.SYNTH_PACK.**all**;
package PROGRAM_PACK **is**
    constant PROP_DELAY: TIME;   -- A deferred constant.
    function "and" (L, R: MVL) **return** MVL;

```
      procedure LOAD (signal ARRAY_NAME: inout MVL_VECTOR;
                      START_BIT, STOP_BIT, INT_VALUE: in INTEGER);
   end PROGRAM_PACK;
```

In this case, a package body is required.

9.2   Package Body

A package body primarily contains the behavior of the subprograms and the values of the deferred constants declared in a package declaration. It may contain other declarations as well, as shown by the following syntax of a package body.

```
      package body package-name is
         package-body-item-declarations --> These are:
            -- subprogram bodies
            -- complete constant declarations
            -- subprogram declarations
            -- type and subtype declarations
            -- file and alias declarations
            -- use clauses
      end [ package-name ] ;
```

The package name must be the same as the name of its corresponding package declaration. A package body is not necessary if its associated package declaration does not have any subprogram or deferred constant declarations. The associated package body for the package declaration, PROGRAM_PACK, described in the previous section is

```
      package body PROGRAM_PACK is
         constant PROP_DELAY: TIME := 15 ns;
         function "and" (L, R: MVL) return MVL is
         begin
            return TABLE_AND(L, R);
            -- TABLE_AND is a 2-D constant defined elsewhere.
         end "and";
         procedure LOAD (signal ARRAY_NAME: inout MVL_VECTOR;
            START_BIT, STOP_BIT, INT_VALUE: in INTEGER) is
            -- Local declarations here.
         begin
            -- Procedure behavior here.
         end LOAD;
      end PROGRAM_PACK;
```

An item declared inside a package body has its scope restricted to be within the package body and it cannot be made visible in other design units. This is in contrast to items declared in a package declaration that can be accessed by other design units. Therefore, a package body is used to store private declarations that should not be visible, while a package declaration is used to store public declarations which other design units can access. This is very similar to declarations within an architecture body which are not visible outside of its scope while items declared in an entity declaration can be made visible to other design units. An important difference between a package declaration and an entity declaration is that an entity can have multiple architecture bodies with different names, while a package declaration can have exactly one package body, the names for both being the same.

A subprogram written in any other language can be made accessible to design units by specifying a subprogram declaration in a package declaration without a subprogram body in the corresponding package body. The association of this subprogram with its declaration in the package is not defined by the language and is, therefore, tool implementation-specific.

9.3   Design Libraries

A compiled VHDL description is stored in a design library. A design library is an area of storage in the file system of the host environment. The format of this storage is not defined by the language. Typically, a design library is implemented on a host system as a file directory and the compiled descriptions are stored as files in this directory. The management of the design libraries is also not defined by the language and is again tool implementation-specific.

An arbitrary number of design libraries may be specified. Each design library has a logical name with which it is referenced inside a VHDL description. The association of the logical names with their physical storage names is maintained by the host environment. There is one design library with the logical name, STD, predefined in the language; this library contains the compiled descriptions for the two predefined packages, STANDARD and TEXTIO. Exactly one design library must be designated as the working library with the logical name, WORK. When a VHDL description is compiled, the compiled description is always stored in the working library. Therefore, before compilation begins, the logical name WORK must point to one of the design libraries. Figure 9.1 shows a typical compilation scenario.

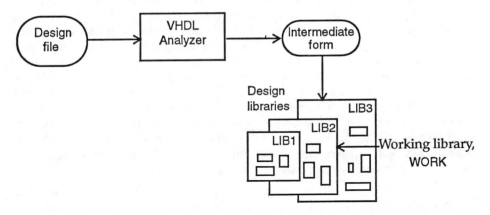

Figure 9.1 A typical compilation process.

The VHDL source is present in an ASCII file called the *design file*. This is processed by the VHDL analyzer, which after verifying the syntactic and semantic correctness of the source, compiles it into an intermediate form. The intermediate form is stored in the design library that has been designated as the working library.

9.4   Design File

The design file is an ASCII file containing the VHDL source. It can contain one or more design units, where a design unit is one of the following:

- entity declaration,
- architecture body,
- configuration declaration,
- package declaration,
- package body.

This means that each design unit can also be compiled separately.

A design library consists of a number of compiled design units. Design units are further classified as

1. *Primary* units: These units allow items to be exported out of the design unit. They are

   a. *entity declaration*: The items declared in an entity declaration are implicitly visible within the associated architecture bodies.

      b. *package declaration*: Items declared within a package dec-
laration can be exported to other design units using context clauses.

      c. *configuration declaration.*

  2. *Secondary* units: These units do not allow items declared
within them to be exported out of the design unit, that is,
these items cannot be referenced in other design units. These
are

      a. *architecture body*: A signal declared in an architecture
body, for example, cannot be referenced in other design
units.

      b. *package body.*

There can be exactly one primary unit with a given name in a single design library. Secondary units associated with different primary units can have
identical names in the same design library; also a secondary unit may have
the same name as its associated primary unit. For example, assume there exists an entity called AND_GATE in a design library. It may have an architecture body with the same name, and another entity, MY_GATE, in the same
design library may have an architecture body that also has the name,
AND_GATE.

Secondary units must coexist with their associated primary units in the
same design library, for example, an entity declaration and all of its architecture bodies must reside in the same library. Similarly, a package declaration
and its associated package body must reside in a single library.

Even though a configuration declaration is a primary unit, it must reside in the same library as the entity declaration to which it is associated.

9.5 Order of Analysis

Since it is possible to export items declared in primary units to other design
units, a constraint is imposed in the sequence in which design units must be
analyzed. A design unit that references an item declared in another primary
unit can be analyzed only after that primary unit has been analyzed. For example, if a configuration declaration references an entity, COUNTER, the entity declaration for COUNTER must be analyzed before the configuration
declaration.

A primary unit must be analyzed before any of its associated secondary
units. For example, an entity declaration must be analyzed before its architecture bodies are analyzed.

9.6   Implicit Visibility

An architecture body implicitly inherits all declarations in the entity since it is tied to that entity by virtue of the statement

architecture *architecture-name* **of** *entity-name* **is** . . .

Similarly, a package body implicitly inherits all items declared in the package declaration by virtue of its first statement

package body *package-name* **is** . . .

where the package name is the same as the one in the package declaration.

9.7   Explicit Visibility

Explicit visibility of items declared in other design units can be achieved using context clauses. There are two types of context clauses:

1.   **library** clause,
2.   **use** clause.

Context clauses are associated with design units and may be written just before the design unit to which visibility is to be made available. Figure 9.2 shows an example. Items specified in the context clause become visible only to the design unit that follows the context clause. This means that if a design file contains three design units, such as in the example shown in Fig. 9.3, then context clauses must be specified for each design unit. For example, the context clauses specified before design unit A makes them visible to design unit A only; context clauses specified before design unit B makes them visible to design unit B only.

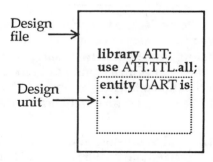

Figure 9.2 Context clause associated with following design unit.

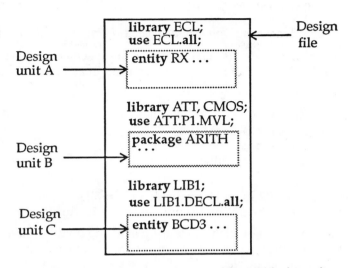

Figure 9.3 Separate context clauses with each design unit.

9.7.1 Library Clause

The **library** clause makes visible the logical names of design libraries that can be referenced within a design unit. The format of a **library** clause is

library *list-of-logical-library-names* ;

The following example of a library clause

library TTL, CMOS;

makes the logical names, TTL and CMOS, visible in the design unit that follows. Note that the **library** clause does not make design units or items present in the library visible, it makes only the library name visible (it is like a declaration for a library name). For example, it would be illegal to use the expression "TTL.SYNTH_PACK.MVL" within a design unit without first declaring the library name using the "**library** TTL;" clause.

The following library clause

library STD, WORK;

is implicitly declared for every design unit.

9.7.2 Use Clause

There are two main forms of the **use** clause.

                 use *library-name . primary-unit-name* ;   -- Form 1.

                 use *library-name . primary-unit-name . item* ;   -- Form 2.

   The first form of the use clause allows the specified primary unit name from the specified design library to be referenced in a design description. For example,

                 library CMOS;
                 use CMOS.NOR2;
                 configuration . . .
                         . . . **use entity** NOR2(. . .);
                 end;

Note that entity NOR2 must be available in compiled form in the design library, CMOS, before attempting to compile the design unit where it is used.

   The second form of the use clause makes the item declared in the primary unit visible and the item can, therefore, be referenced within the following design unit. For example,

                 library ATTLIB;
                 use ATTLIB.SYNTH_PACK.MVL;
                 -- MVL is a type declared in SYNTH_PACK package.
                 -- The package, SYNTH_PACK, is stored in the ATTLIB design library.
                 entity NAND2 **is**
                     port (A, B: **in** MVL; . . .) . . .

If all items within a primary unit are to be made visible, the keyword **all** can be used. For example,

                 use ATTLIB.SYNTH_PACK.**all;**

makes all items declared in package SYNTH_PACK in design library ATTLIB visible.

   Items external to a design unit can be accessed by other means as well. One way is to use a selected name. An example of using a selected name is

                 library ATTLIB;
                 use ATTLIB.SYNTH_PACK;
                 entity NOR2 **is**
                     port (A, B: **in** SYNTH_PACK.MVL; . . .) . . .

Since only the primary unit name was made visible by the use clause, the complete name of the item, that is, SYNTH_PACK.MVL must be specified. Another example is shown next. The type VALUE_9 is defined in package SIMPACK that has been compiled into the CMOS design library.

```
library CMOS;
package P1 is
    procedure LOAD (A, B: CMOS.SIMPACK.VALUE_9; . . . ) . . .
    . . .
end P1;
```

In this case, the primary unit name was specified only at the time of usage.

So far, we talked about exporting items across design libraries. What if it is necessary to export items from design units that are in the same library? In this case, there is no need to specify a **library** clause since every design unit has the following **library** clause implicitly declared.

```
library WORK;
```

The predefined design library STD contains the package STANDARD. The package STANDARD contains the declarations for the predefined types such as CHARACTER, BOOLEAN, BIT_VECTOR, and INTEGER. The following two clauses are also implicitly declared for every design unit:

```
library STD;
use STD.STANDARD.all;
```

Thus all items declared within the package STANDARD are available for use in every VHDL description.

❑

CHAPTER 10 *Advanced Features*

This chapter describes some of the more general features of the language that cannot be characterized as belonging to any specific modeling style. These include among others, attributes, type conversions, entity statements, aliases, generate statements, and guarded signals. The usage of block statements as a partitioning mechanism is also described.

10.1 Entity Statements

Certain statements that are common to all architecture bodies of an entity can be inserted into the entity declaration. Common declarations appear in the entity declarative part while other common statements appear in the entity statement part as shown.

```
entity entity-name is
    [ generic( . . . ); ]
    [ port ( . . . ); ]
    [ entity-item-declarations ]        -- Declarative part.
```

```
[ begin
        entity-statements ]                 -- Statements part.
  end [ entity-name ] ;
```

Entity-statements must be *passive* statements, that is, they must not assign values to any signals. The following statements are allowed as entity statements:

1. concurrent assertion statement,
2. concurrent procedure call (must be passive),
3. process statement (must be passive).

Entity statements can be used to monitor certain operating characteristics of an entity. For example, in an RS flip-flop, a check can be made to ensure that signals R and S are never high simultaneously. Here is a way of modeling this using an assertion statement.

```
entity RS_FLIPFLOP is
    port (R,S: in BIT; Q, QBAR: out BIT);
    constant FF_DELAY: TIME := 24 ns;
    type FF_STATE is (ONE, ZERO, UNKNOWN);
begin
    assert not (R = '1' and S = '1')
        report ("Not valid inputs!")
        severity ERROR;
end RS_FLIPFLOP;
```

The constant and type declarations in this example are examples of item declarations within an entity declaration. These item declarations are common to all the architecture bodies for that entity. Items declared by these declarations are also visible to all other design units associated with this entity declaration.

In the following example, the timing of a D flip-flop is checked using a concurrent procedure call that appears as an entity statement. This procedure will be called every time there is an event on input ports D and CLK, irrespective of the contents in the architecture bodies that are associated with this entity.

```
use WORK.MYPACK.CHECK_SETUP;
entity DFF is
    port (D, CLK: in BIT; Q, QBAR: out BIT);
    constant SETUP: TIME := 7 ns;
begin
    CHECK_SETUP (D, CLK, SETUP);
end DFF;
```

10.2   Generate Statements

Concurrent statements can be conditionally selected or replicated during the
elaboration phase using the generate statement. There are two forms of the
generate statement.

1. Using the for-generation scheme, concurrent statements can
   be replicated a predetermined number of times.
2. With the if-generation scheme, concurrent statements can be
   conditionally selected for execution.

The generate statement is interpreted during elaboration, and therefore,
has no simulation semantics associated with it. It resembles a macro expan-
sion. The generate statement provides for a compact description of regular
structures such as memories, registers, and counters.

The format of a generate statement using the for-generation scheme is

```
generate-label : for generate-identifier in discrete-range generate
       concurrent-statements
end generate [ generate-label ] ;
```

The values in the discrete range must be globally static, that is, they must be
computable at elaboration time. During elaboration, the set of concurrent
statements are replicated once for each value in the discrete range. These
statements can also use the generate identifier in their expressions and its value would be substituted during elaboration for each replication. There is an
implicit declaration for the generate identifier within the generate statement,
and therefore, no declaration for this identifier is required. The type of the
identifier is defined by the discrete range.

Consider the following representation of a 4-bit full-adder, shown in
Fig. 10.1, using the generate statement.

```
entity FULL_ADD4 is
    port (A, B: in BIT_VECTOR(3 downto 0); CIN: in BIT;
        SUM: out BIT_VECTOR(3 downto 0); COUT: out BIT);
end FULL_ADD4;

architecture FOR_GENERATE of FULL_ADD4 is
    component FULL_ADDER
        port (A, B, C: in BIT; COUT, SUM: out BIT);
    end component;
    signal CAR: BIT_VECTOR(4 downto 0);
begin
    CAR(0) <= CIN;
    GK: for K in 3 downto 0 generate
```

label   identifier   range

FA: FULL_ADDER **port map** (CAR(K), A(K), B(K),
CAR(K+1), SUM(K));
end generate GK;
COUT <= CAR(4);
end FOR_GENERATE;

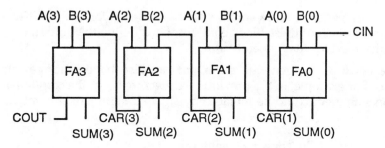

A(3) B(3)   A(2) B(2)   A(1) B(1)   A(0) B(0)   CIN

FA3   FA2   FA1   FA0

COUT   CAR(3)   CAR(2)   CAR(1)
SUM(3)   SUM(2)   SUM(1)   SUM(0)

Figure 10.1 A 4-bit full-adder.

After elaboration, the generate statement is expanded to

FA(3): FULL_ADDER **port map** (CAR(3), A(3), B(3), CAR(4), SUM(3));
FA(2): FULL_ADDER **port map** (CAR(2), A(2), B(2), CAR(3), SUM(2));
FA(1): FULL_ADDER **port map** (CAR(1), A(1), B(1), CAR(2), SUM(1));
FA(0): FULL_ADDER **port map** (CAR(0), A(0), B(0), CAR(1), SUM(0));

Components in a generate statement can be bound to entities using a generate block configuration. A block configuration is defined for each range of generate labels. Here is an example of such a binding using a configuration declaration.

configuration GENERATE_BIND **of** FULL_ADD4 **is**
  use WORK.all;   -- Example of a declaration in the
                       -- configuration declarative part.
  for FOR_GENERATE -- An architecture body block configuration.
    for GK(1)   -- A generate block configuration.
      for FA: FULL_ADDER
        use configuration WORK.FA_HA_CON;
      end for;
    end for;
    for GK(2 **to** 3)
      for FA: FULL_ADDER -- No explicit binding.
        -- Use defaults, i.e., use entity FULL_ADDER
        -- in working library.
      end for;
    end for;
    for GK(0)

```
            for FA: FULL_ADDER
                use entity WORK.FULL_ADDER(FA_DATAFLOW);
            end for;
        end for;
    end for;
end GENERATE_BIND;
```

There are three generate block configurations, one each for GK(1), GK(2 to 3), and for GK(0). Each of these block configurations define the bindings for the components valid for that generate index.

The body of the generate statement can also have other concurrent statements. For example, in the previous architecture body, the component instantiation statement could be replaced by signal assignment statements like this

```
G2: for M in 3 downto 0 generate
    SUM(M) <= (A(M) xor B(M)) xor CAR(M);
    CAR(M+1) <= (A(M) and B(M)) and CAR(M);
end generate G2;
```

The second form of the generate statement uses the if-generation scheme. The format for this type of generate statement is

```
generate-label : if expression generate
    concurrent-statements
end generate [ generate-label ] ;
```

The if-generate statement allows for conditional selection of concurrent statements based on the value of an expression. This expression must be a globally static expression, that is, the value must be computable at elaboration time.

Here is an example of a 4-bit counter, shown in Fig. 10.2, that is modeled using the if-generate statement.

```
entity COUNTER4 is
    port (COUNT, CLOCK: in BIT; Q:  buffer BIT_VECTOR(0 to 3));
end COUNTER4;

architecture IF_GENERATE of COUNTER4 is
    component D_FLIP_FLOP
        port (D, CLK: in BIT; Q: out BIT);
    end component;
begin
    GK: for K in 0 to 3 generate
        GK0: if K = 0 generate
            DFF: D_FLIP_FLOP port map (COUNT, CLOCK, Q(K));
```

```
        end generate GK0;
        GK1_3: if K > 0 generate
            DFF: D_FLIP_FLOP port map (Q(K-1), CLOCK, Q(K));
        end generate GK1_3;
      end generate GK;
    end IF_GENERATE;
```

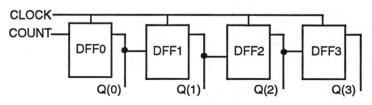

Figure 10.2 A 4-bit counter.

A simpler example is when a buffer is to be selected that has different delays based on the value of a constant. Here are the generate statements for such an example.

```
    GA: if USER_WANTS = LOW_DELAY generate
        Z <= A after 2 ns;
    end generate;
    GB: if USER_WANTS = MEDIUM_DELAY generate
        Z <= A after 10 ns;
    end generate;
    GC: if USER_WANTS = HIGH_DELAY generate
        Z <= A after 25 ns;
    end generate;
```

The if-generate statement is also useful in modeling repetitive structures, especially in modeling boundary conditions. An if-generate statement does not have an **else** or an **else-if** branch.

10.3 Aliases

An alias declares an alternate name for all or part of an existing object. It provides a convenient shorthand notation to write names for objects that have long names. It also provides a mechanism of referring to the same object in different ways depending on the context. For example,

signal S: BIT_VECTOR (31 **downto** 0);

can represent:

SIGN	EXPONENT	MANTISSA

31   30   23   0

or:

OPCODE	REG	BASE	OFFSET

31   26   23   18   0

The syntax for an alias declaration is

> **alias** *identifier* : *identifier-type* **is** *name* ;

For example,

> **variable** DATA_WORD: BIT_VECTOR(15 **downto** 0);
> **alias** DATA_BUS: BIT_VECTOR(7 **downto** 0) **is**
>   DATA_WORD(15 **downto** 8);
> **alias** STATUS: BIT_VECTOR(0 **to** 3) **is** DATA_WORD(3 **downto** 0);
> **alias** RESET: BIT **is** DATA_WORD(4);
> **alias** RX_READY: BIT **is** DATA_WORD(5);

Given these declarations, DATA_BUS can be used wherever DATA_WORD(15 **downto** 8) is used, RESET can be used wherever DATA_WORD(4) is used, and so on. It is important to note that assigning a value to an alias name is the same as assigning a value to the aliased name. The alias does not declare a new object but merely provides an alternate way of referring to the original object.

The alias of an array object may change the way in which the array is in-dexed, as shown in the alias declaration of STATUS. Only objects (signals, variables, and constants) can have aliases, not types. Alternate names can be provided for types by using subtype declarations.

10.4   Qualified Expressions

The type of an expression can be explicitly specified by qualifying the expression with its type. For example,

> INTEGER'(A * B + C)

qualifies the expression (A * B + C) to have an integer value. The qualification is useful for type checking and it does not imply any type conversion.

Apart from its type checking usefulness, type qualification can be used to qualify types for expressions whose types cannot be determined from their context. Consider the following two overloaded procedure declarations.

procedure CHAR2INT (A: **in** CHARACTER; Z: **out** INTEGER);
procedure CHAR2INT (A: **in** BIT; Z: **out** INTEGER);

A call to a procedure such as

CHAR2INT ('1', N);

is ambiguous since it is not clear which overloaded procedure is to be called. However, if the expression in the procedure call were modified to be

CHAR2INT (CHARACTER'('1'), N);

it is clear that this call refers to the first procedure.

10.5 Type Conversions

The language does allow for a very restricted set of type casting, that is, explicitly converting values between types. For example,

SUM := INTEGER (POLYWIDTH * 1.5);

will convert the real value obtained from POLYWIDTH * 1.5 to its equivalent integer value and assign it to SUM.

Type conversions are allowed between closely related types. These include among others, between integer and real, between array types that have the same dimensions and whose index types that are the same, and element types that are the same. Any other kind of type conversion, other than those predefined by the language, can be performed by using a user-defined function.

10.6 Guarded Signals

A *guarded* signal is a special type of a signal that is declared to be of a **register** or a **bus** kind in its declaration. A general form of a signal declaration is

signal *list-of-signals* : *resolution-function signal-type*
signal-kind [:= *expression*] ;

A guarded signal must be a resolved signal, that is, it must have a resolution function associated with it. Also, the signal can only be assigned values under the control of a guard expression, for example, using a guarded assignment (**guarded** option used in a concurrent signal assignment statement).

This implies that guarded signals can only be assigned values within block statements.

A guarded signal behaves differently from other signals in that when the guard expression is false, the driver to the guarded signal becomes disconnected after a specific time, called the *disconnect time*. On the other hand, in an unguarded signal, if the guard expression is false, any new events on the signals appearing in the expression do not influence the value of the target signal; the driver continues to drive the target signal with the old value. To understand this difference better, consider the following guarded block B1.

```
architecture GUARDED_EX of EXAMPLE is
    signal GUARD_SIG: WIRED_OR BIT register;
    signal UNGUARD_SIG: WIRED_AND BIT;
begin
    B1: block ( guard-expression )
    begin
        GUARD_SIG <= guarded expression1 ;
        UNGUARD_SIG <= guarded expression2 ;
    end block B1;
end GUARDED_EX;
```

Transforming the guarded signal assignment statement into its equivalent process statement, the block B1 now looks like this

```
B1: block ( guard-expression )
begin
    process
    begin
        if GUARD then
            GUARD_SIG <= expression1 ;
        else
            GUARD_SIG <= null; -- Disconnect driver
                               -- to GUARD_SIG.
        end if;
        wait on signals-in-expression1, GUARD;
    end process;
    process
    begin
        if GUARD then
            UNGUARD_SIG <= expression2 ;
        end if;
        wait on signals-in-expression2, GUARD;
    end process;
end block B1;
```

The process statement for the guarded signal, GUARD_SIG, has an explicit signal assignment statement that disconnects its driver, while there is no such statement for the unguarded signal, UNGUARD_SIG. As this example shows, a driver of a guarded signal can be explicitly disconnected by assigning a **null** value to the signal. Such a statement is called a *disconnection statement*.

Let us now explore the differences between a register and a bus signal. A bus signal represents a hardware bus in that when all drivers to the signal become disconnected (as might be the case on a real hardware bus), the value of the signal is determined by calling the resolution function with all the drivers off. A register signal, on the other hand, models a storage component (that is multiply driven) in which if all drivers to the signal become disconnected, the resolution function is not called and the value of the last active driver is retained. With a bus signal, the previous value is lost. Also, bus signals may either be ports of an entity or locally declared signals, whereas register signals can only be locally declared signals.

The disconnect time for a guarded signal can be specified using a *disconnection specification*. The syntax of a disconnection specification is

disconnect *guarded-signal-name* : *signal-type* **after** *time-expression* ;

This is an example of a disconnection specification.

disconnect GUARD_SIG: BIT **after** 8 ns;

This implies that the driver of signal GUARD_SIG will get disconnected 8 ns after the corresponding GUARD goes false.

The disconnection specification is useful in modeling decay times, for example, capacitance delay on buses. An alternate way of specifying disconnect time is by assigning a value **null** to the signal in a disconnection statement as shown.

S1 <= **null after** 10 ns;

This statement specifies that the driver of S1 will be disconnected after 10 ns. Thereafter, this driver does not contribute to the resolved value of the signal. However, such a statement can appear only as a sequential statement and the target signal must be a guarded signal.

Here is a more comprehensive example.

```
use WORK.RF_PACK.all;
-- Package RF_PACK contains functions WIRED_AND and WIRED_OR.
entity GUARDED_SIGNALS is
    port (CLOCK: in BIT; N: in INTEGER);
end;
```

```
       architecture EXAMPLE of GUARDED_SIGNALS is
            signal REG_SIG: WIRED_AND INTEGER register;
            signal BUS_SIG: WIRED_OR INTEGER bus;
            disconnect REG_SIG: INTEGER after 50 ns;
            disconnect BUS_SIG: INTEGER after 20 ns;
       begin
            BX: block (CLOCK='1' and (not CLOCK'STABLE))
            begin
                 REG_SIG <= guarded N after 15 ns;
                 BUS_SIG <= guarded N after 10 ns;
            end block BX;
       end EXAMPLE;
```

On a rising edge on the signal CLOCK, say at time T, the current value of N is scheduled to be assigned to signal REG_SIG after 15 ns, that is, at $T+15$ ns, and to signal BUS_SIG after 10 ns, that is, at $T+10$ ns. However, because of the disconnection specifications, the drivers to signals REG_SIG and BUS_SIG are scheduled to be disconnected after 15+50 ns, that is, at $T+65$ ns, and after 10+20 ns, that is, at $T+30$ ns, respectively. At time $T+30$ ns, the function WIRED_OR is called to determine the value for the signal BUS_SIG, even if all its drivers are off. At time $T+65$ ns, the driver to signal REG_SIG disconnects, the value on signal REG_SIG is retained and the resolution function, WIRED_AND, is not called (since there are zero drivers).

10.7 Attributes

An attribute is a value, function, type, range, signal, or a constant that can be associated with certain names within a VHDL description. These names could be among others, an entity name, an architecture name, a label, or a signal. For example, a record that contains the X and Y coordinates of a component placement could be associated with an entity name that describes the placement for that entity in a physical layout; a capacitance value can be associated with all signals of a specific type.

A large number of attributes are predefined in the language. These are described in Sec. 10.7.2. The language also provides the facility to associate user-defined attributes to names.

10.7.1 User-Defined Attributes

User-defined attributes are constants of any type. They are declared using attribute declarations. An *attribute declaration* declares an attribute name and its type and has the following form:

```
attribute attribute-name : value-type ;
```

For example,

```
type COMP_LOCATION is
    record
        X, Y: INTEGER;
    end record;
type INCHES is range 0 to 1000
    units
        micron;
    end units;
type FARADS is range 0 to 5000
    units
        pf;
    end units;
attribute PLACEMENT: COMP_LOCATION;
attribute LENGTH: INCHES;
attribute CAPACITANCE: FARADS;
```

These declared attributes have not yet been associated with any name. An *attribute specification* is used to associate an attribute with a name and to assign a value to the attribute. The syntax for an attribute specification is

```
attribute attribute-name of item-names : name-class is expression ;
```

The *item-names* is a list of one or more names of an entity, architecture, configuration, component, label, signal, variable, constant, type, subtype, package, procedure, or a function. The *name-class* indicates the class type, that is, whether it is an entity, architecture, label, or others. The attribute name must have been declared earlier using an attribute declaration. The attribute specification associates an attribute with a group of names that belong to a name class that has the value as specified by the expression (the value of expression must belong to the type of attribute). Some examples of attribute specifications are

```
attribute CAPACITANCE of CLK, RESET: signal is 20 pf;
attribute LENGTH of RX_READY: signal is 3 micron;
```

In the first example, the attribute CAPACITANCE is associated with two signals CLK and RESET, each of which has a value of 20 pf.

The item name in the attribute specification can also be replaced with the keyword **all** to indicate all names belonging to that name class. In the following example, the attribute CAPACITANCE is associated with all variables and the attribute value is set to 0 pf.

```
        attribute CAPACITANCE of all: variable is 0 pf;
```

After having created an attribute and then having associated it with a name, the value of the attribute can then be used in an expression by referring to

```
item-name ' attribute-name     -- The single quote is often read as "tick".
```

For example, RX_READY'LENGTH has the value of 3 micron. Here is a bigger example.

```
architecture NAND_PLACE of NAND_GATE is
    component NAND_COMP
        port (IN1, IN2: in BIT; OUT1: out BIT);
    end component;
    type COMP_LOCATION is
        record
            X, Y: INTEGER;
        end record;
    attribute PLACEMENT: COMP_LOCATION;
    attribute PLACEMENT of N1: label is (50, 45);
    signal PERIMETER: INTEGER;
    signal A, B, Z: BIT;
begin
    N1: NAND_COMP port map (A, B, Z);
    PERIMETER <= 2 * (N1'PLACEMENT.X +
                        N1'PLACEMENT.Y);
end NAND_PLACE;
```

User-defined attributes are useful for annotating VHDL models with tool-specific information.

10.7.2 Predefined Attributes

There are five classes of predefined attributes.

1. Value attributes: these return a constant value
2. Function attributes: calls a function that returns a value
3. Signal attributes: creates a new signal
4. Type attributes: returns a type name
5. Range attributes: returns a range

Value Attributes

If T is any scalar type or subtype,

- T'LEFT: returns the left bound, that is, the leftmost value, of T.
- T'RIGHT: returns the right bound, that is, the rightmost value, of T.
- T'HIGH: returns the upper bound, that is, the value at the highest position number, of T.
- T'LOW: returns the lower bound, that is, the value at the lowest position number, of T.

For example, if

```
type ALLOWED_VALUE is range 31 downto 0;
type WEEK_DAY is (SUN, MON, TUE, WED, THU, FRI, SAT);
subtype WORK_DAY is WEEK_DAY range FRI downto MON;
```

then the following equivalence relations are true:

```
ALLOWED_VALUE'LEFT = 31
ALLOWED_VALUE'HIGH = 31

ALLOWED_VALUE'RIGHT = 0
ALLOWED_VALUE'LOW = ALLOWED_VALUE'RIGHT
WEEK_DAY'LEFT = SUN;
WEEK_DAY'LOW = WEEK_DAY'LEFT
WEEK_DAY'RIGHT = SAT;
WEEK_DAY'HIGH = WEEK_DAY'RIGHT
WORK_DAY'RIGHT = MON;
WORK_DAY'LOW = WORK_DAY'RIGHT
WORK_DAY'LEFT = FRI;
WORK_DAY'HIGH = WORK_DAY'LEFT
```

If A is a constrained array object, then

- A'LENGTH(N) : returns the number of elements in the Nth dimension (N=1 if not specified).

For example, if

```
signal TX_BUS: MVL_VECTOR (7 downto 0);
```

then

```
TX_BUS'LENGTH = 8.
```

If BA is a block label or an architecture name, then

- BA'BEHAVIOR: is true if no structure is present, that is, there are no component instantiation statements.

- BA'STRUCTURE: is true if only structure is present, that is, it does not contain a nonpassive process statement or a concurrent statement whose equivalent process statement is nonpassive.

Function Attributes

These attributes represent functions that are called to obtain a value. They are often used to convert values from an enumeration or physical type to an integer type. If T is a discrete type, a physical type, or a subtype,

- T'POS(V): returns the position number of the value V in the ordered list of values of T.
- T'VAL(P): returns the value of the type that corresponds to position P.
- T'SUCC(V): returns the value of the parameter whose position is one larger than the position of value V in T.
- T'PRED(V): returns the value of the parameter whose position is one less than the position of value V in type T.
- T'LEFTOF(V): returns the value of the parameter that is to the left of value V in type T.
- T'RIGHTOF(V): returns the value of the parameter that is to the right of value V in type T.

For ascending ranges,

```
T'SUCC(X) = T'RIGHTOF(X)
T'PRED(X) = T'LEFTOF(X)
```

For descending ranges,

```
T'SUCC(X) = T'LEFTOF(X)
T'PRED(X) = T'RIGHTOF(X)
```

For example, if

```
type STATUS is (SILENT, SEND, RECEIVE);
subtype DELAY_TIME is TIME range 50 ns downto 10 ns;
```

then the following equivalence relations are true:

```
STATUS'POS(SEND) = 1
STATUS'VAL(2) = RECEIVE
DELAY_TIME'SUCC(21 ns) = 22 ns
DELAY_TIME'PRED(10 ns) is an error
DELAY_TIME'LEFTOF(29 ns) = 30 ns
```

```
DELAY_TIME'SUCC(29 ns) = DELAY_TIME'LEFTOF(29 ns)
DELAY_TIME'RIGHTOF(11 ns) = 10 ns
DELAY_TIME'PRED(11 ns) = DELAY_TIME'RIGHTOF(11 ns)
STATUS'SUCC(RECEIVE)  will cause a run-time error
STATUS'PRED(RECEIVE) = SEND
STATUS'LEFTOF(RECEIVE) = STATUS'PRED(RECEIVE)
STATUS'SUCC(SILENT) = SEND
STATUS'RIGHTOF(SILENT) = STATUS'SUCC(SILENT)
```

If A is a constrained array object, then

- A'LEFT(N): returns the left bound of the Nth dimension of the array.
- A'RIGHT(N): returns the right bound of the Nth dimension.
- A'LOW(N): returns the lower bound of the Nth dimension.
- A'HIGH(N): returns the upper bound of the Nth dimension.

For ascending ranges,

```
A'LEFT = A'LOW
A'RIGHT = A'HIGH
```

For descending ranges,

```
A'LEFT = A'HIGH
A'RIGHT = A'LOW
```

In all the previous cases, N=1 if not specified. Some more examples are shown next.

If

```
type COST_TYPE is array (7 downto 0, 0 to 3) of INTEGER;
variable COST_MATRIX: COST_TYPE;
```

then the following equivalence relations are true:

```
COST_MATRIX'LEFT(2) = 0
COST_MATRIX'LOW(1) = 0
COST_MATRIX'RIGHT(2) = 3
COST_MATRIX'HIGH(1) = 7
```

If S is a signal object, then

- S'EVENT: returns true if an event occurred on signal S in the current delta.
- S'ACTIVE: returns true if signal S is active in the current delta.

It is important to understand the difference between an event on a signal and a signal being active. A signal is said to be active when a new value is assigned to the signal, even if the new value is the same as the old value; while an event is said to have occurred only if the new value is different from the old value.

- S'LAST_EVENT: returns time elapsed since the last event on signal S.
- S'LAST_ACTIVE: returns time elapsed since the last time signal was active.
- S'LAST_VALUE: returns the value of S, before the last event.

The following examples show their usage in expressions:

```
signal CLOCK: BIT;
constant SETUP_TIME: TIME := 5 ns;
signal A: BIT;
signal COUNT: INTEGER;

(CLOCK = '1' and CLOCK'EVENT) -- Denotes a rising edge on
                               -- signal CLOCK.
(NOW – A'LAST_EVENT < SETUP_TIME) -- NOW is a predefined
     -- function that returns the current simulation time.
(COUNT = 20 and COUNT'LAST_VALUE = 10)
```

Signal Attributes

These attributes create new signals from the signals with which they are associated. These attributes, therefore, create implicit signals as compared to explicit signals that are created using signal declarations. If S is a signal object, then

- S'DELAYED (T): is a new signal that is the same type as signal S but delayed from S by time T. If T is not specified, a delay of 0 ns is assumed.
- S'STABLE (T): is a boolean signal that is true when signal S has not had any event for time T. If T is not specified, it implies current delta.
- S'QUIET (T): creates a boolean signal that is true when S has not been active for time T.
- S'TRANSACTION: creates a bit type signal that toggles its value every time signal S becomes active.

Assuming,

      signal CLOCK_SKEW, CTRL_A: BIT;

Figure 10.3 shows some examples of signal attributes.

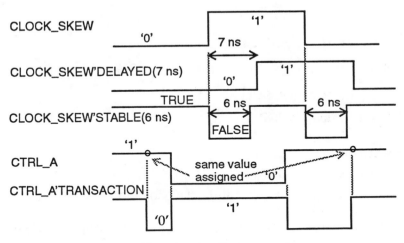

Figure 10.3 Signal attribute examples.

     It is important to understand the difference between function attributes for signals and signal attributes. Signal attributes create new signals, and therefore, cause events when used in concurrent statements; whereas function attributes for signals do not create new signals, and therefore, do not create new events. Signal attributes can, therefore, be used wherever a signal is expected, for example, in the sensitivity list of a process statement or as a signal parameter in a procedure. For example,

```
PSTABLE: process (A, B, CLK'STABLE)
begin
    . . .
end process;
```

It would be illegal to use CLK'EVENT since only signals are allowed in the sensitivity list of a process. Therefore, function attributes of signals should not be used in expressions where the intention is to create new events.

Type Attributes

If T is any type or subtype, T'BASE, which is the only type attribute, returns the base type of T. This attribute cannot be used in expressions as such since it returns a base type but it can be used in conjunction with other attributes. For example, if

```
type ALU_OPS is (ADDOP, SUBOP, MULOP, DIVOP, ANDOP,
                 NANDOP, OROP, NOROP);
subtype ARITH_OPS is ALU_OPS range ADDOP to DIVOP;
```

then

```
ARITH_OPS'BASE is ALU_OPS
```

which is the base type, and it can be used in an expression such as

```
ARITH_OPS'BASE'LEFT
```

which has the value ADDOP.

Range Attributes

If A is a constrained array object, then

- A'RANGE (N): returns the Nth index range of A (N=1, if not specified).
- A'REVERSE_RANGE(N): returns the Nth index range reversed.

For example, if

```
variable WBUS: MVL_VECTOR(7 downto 0);
```

then

```
WBUS'RANGE returns the range "7 downto 0" (quotations not included)
```

while

```
WBUS'REVERSE_RANGE returns the range "0 to 7".
```

The range attributes provide a mechanism for specifying the index constraint in **for** loops and for-generate statements in a parameterized way. For example, a use of this attribute in a **for** loop is shown next.

```
for INDEX in WBUS'REVERSE_RANGE loop
    . . .
end loop;
```

10.8 Aggregate Targets

It is possible for the target of a variable assignment statement or a signal assignment statement to be an aggregate target. An aggregate target represents a combination of one or more names that is of the array type or the record type.

Here is an example.

> **signal** A, B, C: BIT;
>
> (A, B, C) <= BIT_VECTOR'("100");

The left-hand side represents an aggregate target made up of three individual signals. The signal assignment statement indicates that signal A is assigned the value '1', and signals B and C are assigned the value '0'. Here is another example.

> **type** COUNT_REC **is**
>   **record**
>   INPUTS, OUTPUTS: POSITIVE;
>   **end record**;
> **variable** BOX1, BOX2: COUNT_REC;
> **variable** TOTAL_IN, TOTAL_OUT: POSITIVE;
> **function** "+" (A1, A2: COUNT_REC) **return** COUNT_REC;
>
> (TOTAL_IN, TOTAL_OUT) := BOX1 + BOX2;

In this case, variable TOTAL_IN gets the value of the INPUTS element of the overloaded function result, and TOTAL_OUT gets the value of the OUTPUTS element of the function result.

In general, an assignment to an aggregate target causes subelement values in the right-hand-side expression to be assigned to the corresponding subelements in the left-hand-side target.

10.9 More on Block Statements

One other use of a block statement is in representing a portion of a design. This means that an architecture body can be made up of a number of block statements, each representing a portion of a design, along with other concurrent statements. Block statements in turn can contain one or more concurrent statements, including other block statements. Block statements, thus, provide a mechanism for creating a hierarchy within an architecture body.

When a portion of a design is represented using a block statement, it is possible to use arbitrary names within the block and then to associate these names to those outside of that block by using the generic map and port map in the block header. The next example shows a description of a full-adder that has been partitioned into three blocks (where each could have been designed by a separate designer). Two of these blocks, HA1 and HA2, represent the two half-adders, and the block OR1 represents an **or** gate. Different styles of modeling are chosen in describing the half-adders and the **or** gate to show that block statements can contain any form of concurrent statements.

```
entity FULL_ADDER is
    generic (HA_DELAY: TIME := 5 ns);
    port (A, B, CIN: in BIT; SUM, COUT: out BIT);
end FULL_ADDER;

architecture BLOCK_VIEW of FULL_ADDER is
    signal S1, C1, C2: BIT;
begin
    HA1: block
        generic (CARRY_DELAY: TIME);
        generic map (CARRY_DELAY => HA_DELAY);
        port (IN1, IN2: in BIT; SUM, CARRY: out BIT);
        port map (IN1 => A, IN2 => B, SUM => S1, CARRY => C1);
    begin
        SUM <= (IN1 and (not IN2)) or (IN2 and (not IN1));
        CARRY <= IN1 and IN2 after CARRY_DELAY;
    end block HA1;

    HA2: block
        port (X, Y: in BIT; S, C: out BIT);
        port map (X => CIN, Y => S1, S => SUM, C => C2);
    begin
        process (X, Y)
        begin
            S <= X xor Y;
            C <= X and Y after HA_DELAY;
        end process;
    end block HA2;

    OR1: block
        port (A, B: in BIT; C: out BIT);
        port map (A => C1, C => COUT, B => C2);
        component OR_GATE
            port (X, Y: in BIT; Z: out BIT);
        end component;
    begin
        O1: OR_GATE port map (A, B, C);
    end block OR1;
end BLOCK_VIEW;
```

Block HA1 describes a half-adder using concurrent signal assignment statements. The generic and port map associate the local names (those within the block) to external names (names outside the block). Signal A, which is the input to the entity FULL_ADDER, is associated with signal IN1 used inside block HA1, signal S1 defined in the architecture body is associated with signal SUM declared within the HA1 block, and so on. Block HA2 describes a half-adder using a process statement, while block OR1 contains a component instantiation statement to represent an or gate. Port signals declared within each block are local to that block while signals declared in the architecture body and in the entity declaration are global to all the blocks. For example, signal SUM in HA1 refers to the signal SUM declared in that block and not to the output signal SUM. The HA_DELAY used in block HA2 is the generic declared in the entity declaration.

When components are instantiated inside a block statement, it is necessary to specify a block configuration for the block as well when writing the configuration declaration for such a design. Here is an example of a configuration declaration for the previous FULL_ADDER entity.

```
library CMOS_LIB;
configuration BLOCK_VIEW_CON of FULL_ADDER is
    for BLOCK_VIEW
        for HA1        -- A block configuration.
            -- Nothing to configure.
        end for;
        for HA2        -- A block configuration.
            -- Nothing to configure.
        end for;
        for OR1        -- A block configuration.
            for O1: OR_GATE
                use entity CMOS_LIB.OR2(OR2);
            end for;
        end for;
    end for;
end BLOCK_VIEW_CON;
```

Within the block configuration for the architecture body, there are three other block configurations, one for each of the block statements. Blocks HA1 and HA2 do not have any component instantiations and have, therefore, nothing to bind. It is not necessary to specify the block configurations for such blocks. The block OR1 has one component that is bound to an entity represented by the entity-architecture pair from library CMOS_LIB.

Since a block statement is just another concurrent statement, block statements can be nested. Here is an example.

```
B1: block
    signal A, B: BIT;
```

```
begin
  . . .
B2: block
      signal B, C: BIT;
    begin
      A <= B and C;          -- First signal assignment.
      C <= B1.B;             -- Second signal assignment.
    end block B2;
  end block B1;
```

The signal B used in the first signal assignment in block B2 refers to the signal B declared in that block. If the signal B declared in block B1 needs to be used within block B2, the signal must be explicitly qualified by the block label as shown in the second statement in block B2.

❑

CHAPTER 11 *Model Simulation*

This chapter describes the environment necessary for simulating hardware models written in VHDL. These models can be tested by writing test bench models which can themselves be described in VHDL. Some approaches to writing test bench models are also described in this chapter.

11.1 *Simulation*

Before beginning to model hardware, the first thing to decide is what type of simulation will be performed, that is, what values would be used during simulation. Would all objects (signals and variables) take values '0' or '1' only, or would they take values '0', '1', 'U', or 'Z', or use a 46-value logic? The number of values used during simulation will define the basic types that will be used to model hardware. This important decision has to be made prior to writing any model, since the predefined types that the language provides are not sufficient to model values such as 'U' (undefined) and 'Z' (high-impedance). The language, however, does provide the capability of creating user-defined types that can be used to model the values required for a particular simulation. In certain cases, it may be sufficient to model hardware using the predefined types of the language, for example, when modeling hardware at an abstract level where all data may be represented strictly as integers.

For the rest of this chapter and for the chapter following this, we shall assume that we are interested in performing a four-value simulation, 'U' to represent undefined, '0' to represent logic 0, '1' to represent logic 1, and 'Z' to represent high-impedance. The basic types are, therefore, defined as:

```
type MVL is ('U', '0', '1', 'Z');
type MVL_VECTOR is array (NATURAL range <>) of MVL;
```

The leftmost value of the MVL type is defined to be a 'U' so that all objects that are defined to be of this base type will have an initial value of 'U' at start of simulation. This accurately models real hardware.

These new basic types are still insufficient to model hardware. What is lacking is a set of operations that can operate on these types. Most of the operators in the language are defined for the predefined types only. Therefore, to allow operations on these new types, we need to provide overloaded operator functions for all the language operators that are needed to operate on these types. Often, it is useful to put all such information into a package. The following is an example of such a package, called ATT_PACKAGE.

```
package ATT_PACKAGE is
    type MVL is ('U', '0', '1', 'Z');
    type MVL_VECTOR is array (NATURAL range <>) of MVL;

    type MVL_1D_TABLE is array (MVL) of MVL;
    type MVL_2D_TABLE is array (MVL, MVL) of MVL;

    -- Truth tables for logical operators:
    constant TABLE_AND: MVL_2D_TABLE :=
        ((  'U',  '0',  'U',  'U'),
         (  '0',  '0',  '0',  '0'),
         (  'U',  '0',  '1',  'U'),
         (  'U',  '0',  'U',  'U'));
    constant TABLE_OR: MVL_2D_TABLE :=
        ((  'U',  'U',  '1',  'U'),
         (  'U',  '0',  '1',  'U'),
         (  '1',  '1',  '1',  '1'),
         (  'U',  'U',  '1',  'U'));
    -- and so on.
    -- Overloaded operator declarations on MVL type:
    function "and"    (L, R: MVL) return MVL;
    function "or"     (L, R: MVL) return MVL;
    -- and so on.
```

```
                    -- Overloaded operators for MVL_VECTOR type:
                    function "and"    (L, R: MVL_VECTOR) return MVL_VECTOR;
                    function "or"     (L, R: MVL_VECTOR) return MVL_VECTOR;
                    function "+"      (L, R: MVL_VECTOR) return MVL_VECTOR;
                    -- and so on.
                end ATT_PACKAGE;

                package body ATT_PACKAGE is
                    -- Function definitions for overloaded operators with MVL types:
                    function "and" (L, R: MVL) return MVL is
                    begin
                        return TABLE_AND(L, R);
                    end "and";
                    -- Functions for other overloaded operators can be similarly defined.
                    -- Function definitions for MVL_VECTOR types:
                    function "or" (L, R: MVL_VECTOR) return MVL_VECTOR is
                        variable RESULT: MVL_VECTOR(L'LENGTH-1 downto 0);
                    begin
                        assert L'LENGTH = R'LENGTH;
                        for K in RESULT'RANGE loop
                            RESULT(K) := TABLE_OR (L(K), R(K));
                        end loop;
                        return RESULT;
                    end "or";
                    -- Functions for other overloaded operators can be similarly defined.
                end ATT_PACKAGE;
```

The contents of package ATT_PACKAGE can now be made visible in other design units by using the **library** and **use** clauses. But first, the package must be compiled into a design library, say ATTLIB.

If a purely behavioral model is being simulated, the previous package might be sufficient. If structural models are to be simulated that reference primitive components defined in a certain library, it is useful to provide a package containing the component declarations for all components that reside in the library. There might be a separate package provided for each class of components, for example, a package that contains the component declarations for CMOS components, a package for all TTL 7400 series components, a package for ECL components, and so on. This would eliminate the need for writing component declarations in every structural description; all that would be necessary is to reference the component declarations package by using a **use** clause. Here is a template for such a package.

```
                library ATTLIB;
                use ATTLIB.ATT_PACKAGE.all;
                package CMOS_COMP is
                    component AOI21
```

```
                port (A1, A2, B: in MVL; Z: out MVL);
            end component;
            component FD1S3AX
                port (D, CKA, CKB: in MVL; Q, QN: out MVL);
            end component;
            component INRB
                port (A: in MVL; Z: out MVL);
            end component;
            -- Other components would be defined similarly.
        end CMOS_COMP;
```

This package also has to be compiled into a design library, say CMOSLIB.

There is yet another piece of information that is required before a structural model can be simulated. These are the behavioral models for any primitive components used in the structural model. If the primitive components as defined in the CMOS_COMP package are used, it is necessary to provide behavioral models for these primitive components. Three such examples are shown next.

```
        library ATTLIB;
        use ATTLIB.ATT_PACKAGE.all;
        entity AOI21 is
            port (A1, A2, B: in MVL; Z: out MVL);
        end AOI21;

        architecture BEH_MODEL of AOI21 is
        begin
            process (A1, A2, B)
                variable TEMP: MVL;
            begin
                TEMP := TABLE_AND(A1, A2);
                Z <= TABLE_NOR (TEMP, B);
            end process;
        end BEH_MODEL;

        library ATTLIB;
        use ATTLIB.ATT_PACKAGE.all;
        entity FD1S3AX is
            port (D, CKA, CKB: in MVL; Q, QN: out MVL);
        end FD1S3AX;

        architecture BEH_MODEL of FD1S3AX is
        begin
            process (D, CKA, CKB)
                variable TEMP: MVL;
            begin
```

```
                    if (CKA = '1' and CKA'EVENT) then
                            TEMP := TABLE_BUF (D);
                    end if;
                    Q <= TABLE_BUF (TEMP);
                    QN <= TABLE_NOT (TEMP);
               end process;
        end BEH_MODEL;

        library ATTLIB;
        use ATTLIB.ATT_PACKAGE.all;
        entity INRB is
               port (A: in MVL; Z: out MVL);
        end INRB;

        architecture BEH_MODEL of INRB is
        begin
               Z <= TABLE_NOT (A);
        end BEH_MODEL;
```

The behavioral descriptions for all the primitive library components also need to be compiled into a design library, say CMOSLIB. At this point, we are ready to begin modeling and simulating hardware.

11.2   Writing a Test Bench

A test bench is a model that is used to exercise and verify the correctness of a hardware model. The expressive power of the VHDL language provides us with the capability of writing test bench models also in the same language. A test bench has three main purposes:

1. to *generate* stimulus for simulation (waveforms),

2. to *apply* this stimulus to the entity under test and to monitor the output responses,

3. to *compare* output responses with expected known values.

Again, the language provides a large number of ways to write a test bench. In this section, we explore only some of these. A typical format of a test bench that drives an entity under test is

```
        entity TEST_BENCH is
        end;

        architecture TB_BEHAVIOR of TEST_BENCH is
               component ENTITY_UNDER_TEST
                    port ( list-of-ports-their-types-and-modes );
```

```
    end component;
    Local-signal-declarations ;
begin
    Generate-waveforms-using-behavioral-constructs ;
    Apply-to-entity-under-test ;
    EUT : ENTITY_UNDER_TEST port map ( port-associations ) ;
    Monitor-values-and-compare-with-expected-values ;
end TB_BEHAVIOR;
```

The application of stimulus to the entity under test is accomplished automatically by instantiating the entity in the test bench model and then specifying the appropriate interface signals. The next two subsections look at waveform generation and output response monitoring.

11.2.1 Waveform Generation

There are two main approaches in generating stimulus values:

1. create waveforms and apply stimulus at certain discrete time intervals,
2. generate stimulus based on the state of the entity, that is, based on the output response of the entity.

Two types of waveforms are typically needed. One is a repetitive pattern, for example in a clock, and the other is a sequential set of values.

Repetitive Patterns

A repetitive pattern with a constant on-off delay can be created using a concurrent signal assignment statement.

```
    A <= not A after 20 ns;          -- Signal A is assumed to be of type BIT.
```

The waveform created is shown in Fig. 11.1.

A clock with varying on-off period can be created using a process statement. The waveform created is shown in Fig. 11.1.

```
    -- Signal D_CLK is assumed to be a signal of type BIT.
    process
        constant OFF_PERIOD: TIME := 30 ns;
        constant ON_PERIOD : TIME := 20 ns;
    begin
        wait for OFF_PERIOD;
        D_CLK <= '1';
        wait for ON_PERIOD;
        D_CLK <= '0';
    end process;
```

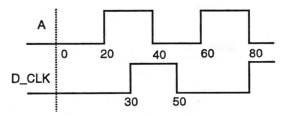

Figure 11.1 A repetitive pattern.

A problem with both of these approaches is that if the host environment provides no control over the amount of time simulation is to be performed, simulation would go on until time is equal to TIME'HIGH causing a lot of simulation time to be wasted. One way to avoid this is to put an assertion statement in the process that will cause the assertion to fail after a specific time. Here is such an example of an assertion statement.

```
assert (NOW <= 1000 ns)
    report "Simulation completed successfully"
    severity ERROR;
```

Assertion would fail when simulation time exceeds 1000 ns and simulation would stop (assuming that the simulator stops on getting a severity level of ERROR).

An alternate way to generate a clock with a varying on-off period is by using a conditional signal assignment statement. Here is an example.

```
D_CLK <=   '1' after OFF_PERIOD when D_CLK = '0' else
           '0' after ON_PERIOD;
-- D_CLK is a signal of type BIT.
-- OFF_PERIOD and ON_PERIOD are constants defined elsewhere.
```

A clock that is phase delayed from another clock can be generated by using the DELAYED predefined attribute. For example,

```
DLY_D_CLK <= D_CLK'DELAYED (10 ns);
```

The waveforms for D_CLK and DLY_D_CLK are shown in Fig. 11.2.

Two nonoverlapping clocks can be generated in a similar manner by making sure that the time specified for the DELAYED attribute is larger than the clock's on-period.

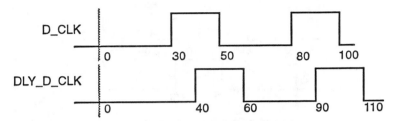

Figure 11.2 A phase-delayed clock.

A sequential set of values can also be generated for a signal by using multiple waveforms in a concurrent signal assignment statement. For example,

RESET <= '0', '1' **after** 100 ns, '0' **after** 180 ns, '1' **after** 210 ns;

The waveform generated on signal RESET is shown in Fig. 11.3.

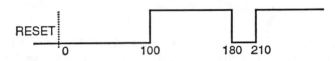

Figure 11.3 A nonrepetitive waveform.

This waveform can be made to repeat itself by placing the signal assignment statement inside a process statement along with a **wait** statement. The following example of a two-phase clock shows such a repeated waveform. Figure 11.4 shows the waveforms created.

```
signal CLK1, CLK2: MVL := '0';
. . .
TWO_PHASE: process
begin
        CLK1 <= 'U' after 5 ns, '1' after 10 ns, 'U' after 20 ns,
                '0' after 25 ns;
        CLK2 <= 'U' after 10 ns, '1' after 20 ns, 'U' after 25 ns,
                '0' after 30 ns;
    wait for 35 ns;
end process;
```

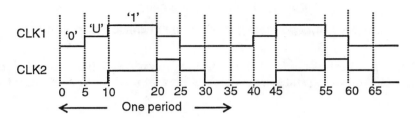

Figure 11.4 A complex repetitive waveform.

Using Vectors

Another way to apply stimulus to a set of signals is to store the set of vectors in a constant table or in an ASCII file. Here is an example that stores the input vectors in a table.

```
constant NO_OF_BITS: INTEGER := 4;
constant NO_OF_VECTORS: INTEGER := 5;
type TABLE_TYPE is array (1 to NO_OF_VECTORS) of
                        MVL_VECTOR(1 to NO_OF_BITS);
constant VECTOR_PERIOD: TIME := 100 ns;
constant INPUT_VECTORS: TABLE_TYPE :=
    ("1001", "1000", "0010", "0000", "0110");
signal INPUTS: MVL_VECTOR(1 to NO_OF_BITS);
signal A, B, C: MVL;
signal D: MVL_VECTOR(0 to 1);
```

Assume that the entity under test has four inputs, A, B, C, and D. If the vectors are to be applied at regular time intervals, a generate statement can be used as shown.

```
G1: for J in 1 to NO_OF_VECTORS generate
    INPUTS <= INPUT_VECTORS(J) after (VECTOR_PERIOD * J);
end generate G1;
A <= INPUTS(1);
B <= INPUTS(4);
C <= INPUTS(1);
D <= INPUTS(2 to 3);
```

If the vectors were to be applied at arbitrary intervals, a concurrent signal assignment statement with multiple waveforms can be used.

```
INPUTS <=  INPUT_VECTORS(1) after 10 ns,
           INPUT_VECTORS(2) after 25 ns,
           INPUT_VECTORS(3) after 30 ns,
```

```
                    INPUT_VECTORS(4) after 32 ns,
                    INPUT_VECTORS(5) after 40 ns;
```

Using this approach, it is possible to assign one vector column to more than one signal.

The input vectors could also be specified in an ASCII file as a sequence of values. The following statements define a file and read the vectors from the file.

```
process
    type VEC_TYPE is file of MVL_VECTOR;
    file VEC_FILE: VEC_TYPE is in "/usr/jb/EXAMPLE.vec";
    variable LENGTH: INTEGER;
    variable IN_VECTOR: MVL_VECTOR(1 to 4);
begin
    LENGTH := 4;          -- The number of bits to be read.
    while (not ENDFILE(VEC_FILE)) loop
        READ (VEC_FILE, IN_VECTOR, LENGTH);
        -- It is necessary to specify the LENGTH of the vector to be read
        -- since the file contains values of an unconstrained array type.
        :
        :
    end loop;
end process;
```

A complete test bench that uses the waveform application method is shown next. The entity being simulated is called DIV. The output value is written into a file for later comparison.

```
library ATTLIB;
use ATTLIB.ATT_PACKAGE.all;
entity DIV_TB is end;

architecture DIV_TB_BEH of DIV_TB is
    component DIV
        port (CK, RESET, TESTN: in MVL; ENA: out MVL);
    end component;
    signal CLOCK, RESET, TESTN, ENABLE: MVL;
    type VEC_TYPE is file of MVL_VECTOR;
    file OUTFILE: VEC_TYPE is out "/usr1/jb/div.vec.out";
    for D1: DIV use entity WORK.DIV;
begin
    CKP: process
    begin
        CLOCK <= '0';
        wait for 3 ns;
        CLOCK <= '1';
```

```
        wait for 5 ns;
        assert (NOW < 900 ns)
            report "Simulation completed successfully.";
    end process CKP;

    RESET <= '0', '1' after 110 ns;
    TESTN <= '0', '1' after 160 ns, '0' after 670 ns;
    -- Apply to entity under test:
    D1: DIV port map (CLOCK, RESET, TESTN, ENABLE);

    -- For every event on the ENABLE output signal, write to file.
    MONITOR: process (ENABLE)
    begin
        WRITE (OUTFILE, ENABLE);
    end process MONITOR;
end DIV_TB_BEH;
```

In the second approach for stimulus generation, the stimulus value generated is based on the state of the entity under test. This approach is useful in testing a finite state machine for which different input stimulus is applied based on the machine's state. Consider an entity in which the objective is to compute the factorial of an input number. The handshake mechanism between the entity under test and the test bench model is shown in Fig. 11.5.

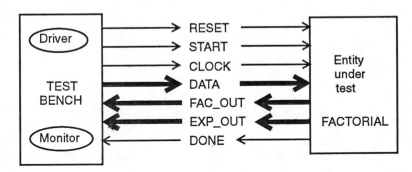

Figure 11.5 Handshake between test bench and entity under test.

The RESET input to the entity resets the factorial model to an initial state. The START signal is set after the DATA input is applied. When computation is complete, the output DONE signal is set to indicate that the computed result appears on the FAC_OUT and EXP_OUT outputs. The resulting factorial value is [FAC_OUT $* 2^{EXP\_OUT}$]. The test bench model provides input data on signal DATA starting from values 1 to 20 in increments of one. It applies the data, sets the START signal, waits for DONE signal, and then ap-

plies the next input data. Assertion statements are used to make sure that the
values appearing at the output are correct. The test bench description follows.

```
library ATTLIB; use ATTLIB.ATT_PACKAGE.all;
entity FAC_TB is
    constant IN_MAX: INTEGER := 5;
    constant OUT_MAX: INTEGER := 8;
end FAC_TB;

architecture FAC_TB_FUNC of FAC_TB is
    component FACTORIAL
        port (RESET, START, CLOCK: in MVL;
        DATA: in MVL_VECTOR(IN_MAX–1 downto 0);
        DONE: out MVL;
        FOUT, EOUT: out MVL_VECTOR(OUT_MAX–1 downto 0));
    end component;
    type FAC_STATE is (RESET_ST, START_ST,
                        APPL_DATA_ST, WAIT_RESULT_ST);
    signal CLK, RESET, START, DONE: MVL;
    signal DATA: MVL_VECTOR(7 downto 0) := (others => '0');
    signal FAC_OUT, EXP_OUT:
                        MVL_VECTOR(OUT_MAX–1 downto 0);
    signal NEXT_STATE: FAC_STATE; -- Starts with RESET_ST state.
    constant MAX_APPLY: POSITIVE := 20;
begin
    CLK_P: process
    begin
        CLK <= '0';
        wait for 4 ns;
        CLK <= '1';
        wait for 6 ns;
    end process CLK_P;

    process
        variable NUM_APPLIED: POSITIVE; -- Starting with 1.
    begin
        if ((CLK = '0') and CLK'EVENT) then -- Falling edge transition.
            case NEXT_STATE is
                when RESET_ST =>
                    RESET <= '1'; START <= '0';
                    NEXT_STATE <= APPL_DATA_ST;
                when APPL_DATA_ST =>
                    DATA <= INT2MVL(NUM_APPLIED, IN_MAX);
                    NEXT_STATE <= START_ST;
                when START_ST =>
                    START <= '1';
                    NEXT_STATE <= WAIT_RESULT_ST;
```

```
                          when WAIT_RESULT_ST =>
                              RESET <= '0'; START <= '0';
                              wait until (DONE = '1');
                              assert (NUM_APPLIED =
                              MVL2INT(FAC_OUT) *
                                           (2 ** MVL2INT(EXP_OUT)))
                                  report "Incorrect result from factorial model.";
                              NUM_APPLIED := NUM_APPLIED + 1;
                              if (NUM_APPLIED < MAX_APPLY) then
                                  NEXT_STATE <= APPL_DATA_ST;
                              else
                                  assert FALSE -- Stop simulation.
                                      report "Test completed successfully.";
                              end if;
                      end case;
                  end if;
              end process;

              -- Apply to entity under test:
              F1: FACTORIAL port map (RESET, START, CLK, DATA,
                      DONE, FAC_OUT, EXP_OUT);
          end FAC_TB_FUNC;
          -- Functions MVL2INT and INT2MVL are assumed to be
          -- defined in package ATT_PACKAGE.
```

11.2.2 Monitoring Behavior

In the test bench model for the FACTORIAL entity, we saw how the test bench can monitor the behavior of the entity and apply different patterns based on the output response. Another common way to monitor the output response of an entity is to apply a vector, sample the output after a specific time and then verify to make sure that the output response matches the expected values. Here is an example of such a test bench. The input and output vectors are stored in tables. Alternately, they could have been read from an ASCII file.

```
          library ATTLIB;
          use ATTLIB.ATT_PACKAGE.all;
          entity ANOTHER_DIV_TB is end;

          architecture APPLY_AND_SAMPLE of ANOTHER_DIV_TB is
              component DIV
                  port (CK, RESET, TESTN: in MVL; ENA: out MVL);
              end component;
              type MVL3 is array (1 to 3) of MVL;
              type MVL2_VECTOR is array (POSITIVE range <>,
                  POSITIVE range <>) of MVL;
```

```
                  constant INPUT_VECTORS: MVL2_VECTOR :=
                      ("100", "100", "100", "100", "110", "111", "011");
                  constant OUTPUT_VECTORS: MVL2_VECTOR :=
                      ("0", "0", "0", "0", "1");
                  constant STROBE_DELAY: TIME := 1 ns;
                  constant CYCLE_TIME: TIME := 80 ns;
                  signal CLOCK, RESET, TESTN, ENABLE: MVL;
              begin
                  APPLY: process
                  begin
                      for J in 1 to INPUT_VECTORS'LENGTH(1) loop
                          P_1(DRIVE_SIGNAL=>CLOCK,
                              SIGNAL_VALUE=>INPUT_VECTORS(J, 1),
                              DRIVE_DELAY=>20 ns, DRIVE_WIDTH=>30 ns);
                          -- Procedure P_1 generates a clock of specified
                          -- delay & width.
                          RESET <= INPUT_VECTORS(J, 2);
                          TESTN <= INPUT_VECTORS(J, 3);
                          wait for (CYCLE_TIME - STROBE_DELAY);
                          assert ENABLE = OUTPUT_VECTORS(J, 1);
                          wait for STROBE_DELAY;
                      end loop;
                  end process APPLY;
                  -- Entity under test:
                  D2: DIV port map (CLOCK, RESET, TESTN, ENABLE);
              end APPLY_AND_SAMPLE;
```

In this test bench example, the application of test vectors is expressed as a process. After a test vector is applied, the process suspends for time (CYCLE_TIME − STROBE_DELAY), samples the output and then checks to see if the expected output is equal to the specified output vector. The process then suspends for STROBE_DELAY time before reapplying the next vector.

❑

CHAPTER 12 *Hardware Modeling Examples*

This chapter describes a number of examples of hardware models using VHDL. As we have seen earlier, there is more than one way to model a particular entity using this language. In this chapter, we present one such approach for each entity being modeled. We shall be using the type MVL and the ATT_PACKAGE package, discussed in the previous chapter, for all the hardware models that are described in this chapter. The complete description of the ATT_PACKAGE package appears in Appendix C.

12.1 Modeling Entity Interface

The interface ports of an entity are specified using the entity declaration. The ports specify the names of signals that interact with the external environment of the entity. The semantics of each interface port is derived from the mode and type of the port. Here is an example of the external interface for an or-and-invert entity.

```
library ATTLIB; use ATTLIB.ATT_PACKAGE.all;
entity OAI32 is
    port (A1, A2, A3, B1, B2: in MVL; Z: out MVL);
end OAI32;
```

This entity declaration specifies that the entity OAI32, has five input ports and one output port, all of type MVL, that is, the ports can have values 'U', '0', '1' or 'Z'. An example of an entity interface for a 4-bit counter is shown next.

```
library ATTLIB; use ATTLIB.ATT_PACKAGE.all;
entity COUNTER4 is
    port (COUNT, CLOCK: in MVL;
          Q: out MVL_VECTOR(3 downto 0));
end COUNTER4;
```

This entity declaration declares two 1-bit inputs and a 4-bit output for entity COUNTER4. Its external view is shown in Fig. 12.1.

Figure 12.1 An external view of a 4-bit counter.

12.2 Modeling Simple Elements

A basic hardware element is a wire. A wire can be modeled in VHDL as a signal. Consider a 4-bit **and** gate whose behavior is described next.

```
library ATTLIB; use ATTLIB.ATT_PACKAGE.all;
entity AND4 is end;

architecture AND4_DF of AND4 is
    signal A, B, C: MVL_VECTOR(3 downto 0);
begin
    A <= B and C after 5 ns;
end AND4_DF;
```

The gate delay for the **and** gate is specified to be 5 ns. An interesting point to note is that the previous architecture body is a legal VHDL description in spite of the fact that there are no inputs and outputs of the entity. The hardware represented by this behavior is shown in Fig. 12.2.

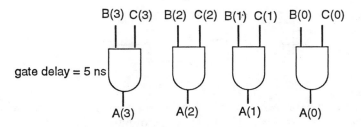

Figure 12.2 A 4-bit **and** gate.

This example and the one following show that boolean equations can be modeled as expressions in concurrent signal assignment statements. Wires can be modeled as signal objects. For example, in the following description, signal F represents a wire that connects the output of the **not** operator to the input of the **xor** operator. The circuit represented by the architecture is shown in Fig. 12.3.

```
architecture BOOLEAN_EX of B_EX is
    signal D, E, F, G: MVL;
begin
    D <= F xor G;
    F <= not E;
end BOOLEAN_EX;
```

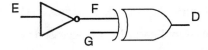

Figure 12.3 A combinational circuit.

Consider the following behavior and its corresponding hardware representation shown in Fig. 12.4.

```
architecture LOOP1 of ASYNCHRONOUS is
    signal A, B, C, D: MVL;
begin
    C <= A or D;
    A <= B nand C;
end LOOP1;
```

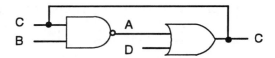

Figure 12.4 An asynchronous loop.

This circuit has an asynchronous loop and if the model were simulated with a certain set of signal values (B='1', C='1', D='0'), simulation time would never advance since the simulator would always be iterating between the two signal assignments. The iteration time would be two delta delays. Therefore, extra caution must be exercised when values are assigned to signals and when these same signals are used in expressions.

In certain cases, it is desirable to have such an asynchronous loop. An example of such an asynchronous loop is shown next; the statement represents a periodic waveform with a cycle of 20 ns. Its hardware representation is shown in Fig. 12.5.

A <= **not** A **after** 10 ns;

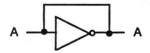

Figure 12.5 A clock generator.

Elements of a vector signal can also be accessed, either as a single element or as a slice. For example,

signal A: MVL;
signal C: MVL_VECTOR(0 **to** 4);
signal B, D: MVL_VECTOR(5 **downto** 0);
. . .
D(4 **downto** 0) <= B(5 **downto** 1) **or** C;
D(5) <= A **and** B(5);

The first signal assignment implies D(4) <= B(5) **or** C(0), D(3) <= B(4) **or** C(1), and so on.

Single bit signals and vector signals can be concatenated to form larger vector signals. For example,

signal C, CC: MVL_VECTOR(7 **downto** 0);
signal CX: MVL;

```
. . .
C <= CX & CC(6 downto 0);
```

It is also possible to refer to an element of a vector signal whose index value is computable only at simulation run time. For example,

```
A <= B(K);
```

implies a decoder whose output is signal A, and K specifies the selection address. B is a vector of values of the same type as signal A. The object B models the behavior of the decoder.

Shift operations are easily modeled using the concatenation operator. For example,

```
signal A, Z: MVL_VECTOR(0 to 7);
. . .
Z <= A(1 to 7) & A(0);              -- A left rotate operation.
Z <= A(7) & A(0 to 6);              -- A right rotate operation.
Z <= A(1 to 7) & '0';               -- A left shift operation.
Z <= A(K to 7) & A(0 to (K-1));     -- A k-left rotate operation.
```

Subfields of a vector signal, called slices, can also be accessed. For example, consider a 32-bit instruction register, INSTR_REG, in which the first 16 bits denote address, next 8 bits represent opcode, and the remaining 8 bits represent the index. Given the following declarations:

```
type MEMORY_TYPE is array (0 to 1023, 31 downto 0) of MVL;
signal INSTR_REG: MVL_VECTOR(31 downto 0);
signal ADDRESS: MVL_VECTOR(15 downto 0);
signal OP_CODE, INDEX: MVL_VECTOR(7 downto 0);
signal MEMORY: MEMORY_TYPE;
signal PROG_CTR: MVL_VECTOR(0 to 9);
```

then one way to read the subfield information from the INSTR_REG is to use three concurrent signal assignment statements. The slices of the instruction register are assigned to specific signals.

```
INSTR_REG <= MEMORY (MVL2INT(PROG_CTR));
-- MVL2INT is a function that translates MVL_VECTOR value to integer.
ADDRESS <= INSTR_REG(15 downto 0);
OP_CODE <= INSTR_REG(23 downto 16);
INDEX <= INSTR_REG(31 downto 24);
. . .
PROCEDURE_CALL(ADDRESS, OP_CODE, INDEX);
```

An alternate way is to declare the subfields of the instruction register as aliases instead of as separate signals.

```
alias ADDRESS: MVL_VECTOR(15 downto 0) is
    INSTR_REG(15 downto 0);
alias OP_CODE: MVL_VECTOR(7 downto 0) is
    INSTR_REG(23 downto 16);
alias INDEX: MVL_VECTOR(7 downto 0) is
    INSTR_REG(31 downto 24);
```

In this case, the explicit assignments to the three subfields are not necessary.

```
INSTR_REG <= MEMORY (MVL2INT(PROG_CTR));
...
PROCEDURE_CALL (ADDRESS, OP_CODE, INDEX);
```

12.3 Different Styles of Modeling

This section gives examples of the three different modeling styles provided by the language: dataflow, behavioral, and structural. Consider the circuit shown in Fig. 12.6 that saves the value of the input A into a register and then multiplies it with input C.

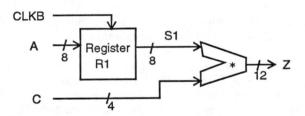

Figure 12.6 A buffered multiplier.

The entity declaration that declares the interface signals for the circuit is

```
library ATTLIB; use ATTLIB.ATT_PACKAGE.all;
entity SAVE_MULT is
    port (A: in MVL_VECTOR(0 to 7); C: in MVL_VECTOR(0 to 3);
        CLKB: in MVL; Z: out MVL_VECTOR(0 to 11));
end SAVE_MULT;
```

The first modeling style is the dataflow style in which concurrent signal assignment statements are used to model the circuit.

```
architecture DATA_FLOW of SAVE_MULT is
    signal S1: MVL_VECTOR(0 to 7);
begin
    Z <= S1 * C; -- The multiplication operator is overloaded to
```

```
                    -- operate on MVL_VECTORs of different sizes.
        R1: block (CLKB='1' and (not CLKB'STABLE))
        begin
            S1 <= guarded A;
        end block R1;
    end DATA_FLOW;
```

This representation does not directly imply any structure, but implicitly describes it. However, its functionality is very clear. The flip-flop has been modeled using a block statement.

The second way to describe the circuit is to model it as a sequential process.

```
        architecture SEQUENTIAL of SAVE_MULT is
            signal S1: MVL_VECTOR(0 to 7);
        begin
            process (A, C, CLKB)
            begin
                if (CLKB='1' and (not CLKB'STABLE)) then
                    S1 <= A;
                end if;
                Z <= S1 * C;
            end process;
        end SEQUENTIAL;
```

This model also describes the behavior but does not imply any structure, explicitly or implicitly. In this case, the flip-flop has been modeled using an **if** statement.

The third way to describe the SAVE_MULT circuit is to model it as a netlist assuming the existence of an 8-bit register and an 8-bit multiplier.

```
        architecture NET_LIST of SAVE_MULT is
            component REG8
                port (DIN: in MVL_VECTOR(0 to 7); CLK: in MVL;
                    DOUT: out MVL_VECTOR(0 to 7));
            end component;
            component MULT8
                port (A, B: in MVL_VECTOR(0 to 7);
                    Z: out MVL_VECTOR(0 to 15));
            end component;
            signal S1, S3: MVL_VECTOR(0 to 7);
            signal S2: MVL_VECTOR(0 to 15);
        begin
            R1: REG8 port map (A, CLKB, S1);
            M1: MULT8 port map (S1, S3, S2);
            Z <= S2 (4 to 15);
```

```
        S3 <= "0000" & C;      -- This assignment is necessary since
                -- an expression cannot be specified directly in a port map.
    end NET_LIST;
```

This description explicitly describes the structure but the behavior is un-known. This is because the REG8 and MULT8 component names are arbitrary and they could have any behavior associated with them. The signal assign-ment to Z is necessary since the multiplier was assumed to produce a 16-bit output.

Of these three different modeling styles, the behavioral style of model-ing is generally the fastest to simulate, if simulation time is critical.

12.4 Modeling Regular Structures

Let us assume that we want to construct a 10-deep 8-bit stack using 8-bit reg-isters. The stack has an input port and an output port and a control signal that specifies whether to pop or to push data. Overflow and underflow conditions are ignored. Ten 8-bit registers model the stack. The input to each register is connected from either the top register or from the bottom register depending on whether to push or pop. Since this basically involves a replication of the register 10 times, a generate statement can be used to model the stack. Here is the model.

```
        library ATTLIB; use ATTLIB.ATT_PACKAGE.all;
        entity STACK is
            port (DATAIN: in MVL_VECTOR(7 downto 0);
                    DATAOUT: out MVL_VECTOR(7 downto 0);
                    CLK, STCK_CTRL: in MVL);
        end STACK;

        architecture GENERATE_EX of STACK is
            type STACK_TYPE is array (1 to 10) of
                                        MVL_VECTOR(7 downto 0);
            signal REGIN: MVL_VECTOR(7 downto 0);
            signal DATA: STACK_TYPE;
            component REG8
                port (DIN: in MVL_VECTOR(0 to 7);
                    DOUT: out MVL_VECTOR(0 to 7); CLK: in MVL);
            end component;
        begin
            G1: for K in 1 to 10 generate   -- 10 is top of stack, 1 is bottom.
                G2: if (K = 10) generate
                    REGIN <=    DATAIN when STCK_CTRL = '1'
                                else DATA(K−1);
```

```
                        end generate G2;
                        G3: if K > 1 and K < 10 generate
                                REGIN <=    DATA(K+1) when STCK_CTRL = '1' -- PUSH
                                            else DATA(K–1);                       -- POP
                        end generate,G3;
                        G4: if K = 1 generate
                                REGIN <=    DATA(K+1) when STCK_CTRL = '1'
                                            else (others=>'U');
                        end generate G4;
                        FF8: REG8 port map (REGIN, DATA(K), CLK);
                        end generate G1;
                        DATAOUT <= DATA(10);          -- Output is connected to
                                                      -- top of stack.

              end GENERATE_EX;
```

The generate statement is expanded by unrolling the loop during elaboration time. When variable K has a value of 1, the input to the bottom-most register is 'U', if the stack is being popped; when K is 10, the input to the top-most register is the input to the stack, DATAIN. The output of the top-most register is the output of the stack.

12.5 Modeling Delays

Consider a 3-input **nor** gate. Its behavior can be modeled using a concurrent signal assignment statement such as

```
        -- A, B, C and Z are signals of type MVL.
        Z <= not (A or B or C) after 12 ns;
```

This statement models the **nor** gate with an inertial delay of 12 ns. This delay represents the time from when an event occurs on signal A, B, or C until the result value appears on signal Z. An event could be any value change, for example, 'U'->'Z', 'U'->'0', or '1'->'0'.

If the rise time, that is, the transition time for '0'->'1', and the fall time, that is, the transition time for '1'->'0', were to be explicitly modeled, a different mechanism is needed. Consider the following conditional signal assignment.

```
        signal Z, A: BIT;
        . . .
        Z <= not A after 12 ns when A = '1' else
             not A after 14 ns;                  -- when A = '0';
```

If an event occurs on signal A (it can only be a '0'->'1' or a '1'->'0' transition since the signal type is BIT), the inverted value of A will appear on signal Z after 12 ns if signal A had the transition '0'->'1' (12 ns is then the fall time), else Z will get its value after 14 ns if the transition on signal A is from '1'->'0' (14 ns is then the rise time). Such a model is sufficient for BIT types but is insufficient when a signal type has more than two values, for example, when using an MVL type. In such a case, the following example illustrates an approach to model rise and fall times, independently.

```
library ATTLIB; use ATTLIB.ATT_PACKAGE.all;
entity NOR3 is
    port (A, B, C: in MVL; Z: out MVL);
end NOR3;

architecture TIMES of NOR3 is
begin
    process (A, B, C)
        variable OLD_Z, NEW_Z: MVL;
        constant RISE_TIME: TIME := 8 ns;
        constant FALL_TIME: TIME := 10 ns;
    begin
        NEW_Z := not (A or B or C);
        if (OLD_Z = '0') and (NEW_Z = '1') then
            Z <= NEW_Z after RISE_TIME;
        elsif (OLD_Z = '1') and (NEW_Z = '0') then
            Z <= NEW_Z after FALL_TIME;
        else
            Z <= NEW_Z after MAX(RISE_TIME, FALL_TIME);
            -- Function MAX returns the maximum of the two time
            -- values. It is declared in the package ATT_PACKAGE.
        end if;
        OLD_Z := NEW_Z;
    end process;
end TIMES;
```

There is nothing special in the previous example. The old value of signal Z is saved. When a new value for Z is computed, a check is made to see what type of transition occurred. Based on whether a rising or a falling edge occurred, the computed value is assigned to the signal Z after the appropriate delay. The rise and fall times are specified using constant declarations in this example. They could also have been declared elsewhere, for example, in an entity declaration or in a package declaration or as generics for the NOR3 entity such as

```
entity NOR3 is
    generic (RISE_TIME: TIME := 8 ns; FALL_TIME: TIME := 10 ns);
    port (A, B, C: in MVL; Z: out MVL);
end NOR3;
```

12.6 Modeling Conditional Operations

Operations that occur under certain conditions can be modeled using either a
selected signal assignment statement, a conditional signal assignment statement, an **if** statement, or a **case** statement. Let us consider a 3-bit decoder circuit. Its behavior can be modeled using a conditional signal assignment as
shown below.

```
library ATTLIB; use ATTLIB.ATT_PACKAGE.all;
entity DECODER is
    port (CTRL: in MVL_VECTOR(0 to 2);
        Z: out MVL_VECTOR(0 to 7));
    constant DECODER_DELAY: TIME := 24 ns;
end DECODER;

architecture CONDITIONAL_EX of DECODER is
begin
    G1: for K in 0 to 7 generate
        Z(K) <= '0' after DECODER_DELAY
                    when MVL2INT(CTRL) = K else
                '1' after DECODER_DELAY;
        -- MVL2INT is a function declared in the package
        -- ATT_PACKAGE; it converts an MVL_VECTOR value into
        -- an integer value.
    end generate G1;
end CONDITIONAL_EX;
```

A multiplexer can be modeled using a process statement. The value of
the select lines are first determined and based on this value, a **case** statement
selects the appropriate input that is to be assigned to the output.

```
library ATTLIB; use ATTLIB.ATT_PACKAGE.all;
entity MULTIPLEXER is
    generic (MUX_DELAY: TIME := 15 ns);
    port (SEL: in MVL_VECTOR(0 to 1); A, B, C, D: in MVL;
        MUX_OUT: out MVL);
end MULTIPLEXER;

architecture PROCESS_MUX of MULTIPLEXER is
begin
    P1: process (SEL, A, B, C, D)
        variable TEMP: MVL;
    begin
        case SEL is
            when "00" => TEMP := A;
            when "01" => TEMP := B;
```

```
            when "10" => TEMP := C;
            when "11" => TEMP := D;
        end case;
        MUX_OUT <= TEMP after MUX_DELAY;
    end process P1;
end PROCESS_MUX;
```

12.7 Modeling Synchronous Logic

So far in this chapter, most of the examples that we have seen are that of combinational logic. As far as synchronous logic is concerned, there is no explicit object in the language that declares registers or memories. The semantics of the language, however, provides for signals to be interpreted as registers or memories depending on how the values to these signals are assigned. There are again a large number of ways in which synchronous logic can be modeled. Some of these are

- by controlling the signal assignment,
- by using a guarded assignment,
- by using a **register** kind signal.

Consider the following example that shows how controlling a signal assignment can model a synchronous, edge-triggered D-type flip-flop.

```
library ATTLIB; use ATTLIB.ATT_PACKAGE.all;
entity D_FLIP_FLOP is
    port (D, CLOCK: in MVL; Q: out MVL);
end D_FLIP_FLOP;

architecture SYNCHRONOUS of D_FLIP_FLOP is
begin
    process (CLOCK)
    begin
        if ((CLOCK = '1') and CLOCK'EVENT) then -- Rising edge.
        -- Alternately "if ((CLOCK = '1') and
        -- (not CLOCK'STABLE)) then".
            Q <= D after 5 ns;
        end if;
    end process;
end SYNCHRONOUS;
```

The semantics of the process statement indicates that when there is a rising edge on signal CLOCK, Q will get the value of D after 5 ns, else the value of signal Q does not change (a signal retains its value until it is assigned a new value). Even though Q and D are signals, the behavior in the process statement expresses the semantics of a D-type flip-flop. Given this entity, an 8-bit register can be modeled as follows:

```
library ATTLIB; use ATTLIB.ATT_PACKAGE.all;
entity REGISTER8 is
    generic (START: INTEGER := 0; STOP: INTEGER := 7);
    port (D: in MVL_VECTOR(START to STOP);
        Q: out MVL_VECTOR(START to STOP); CLOCK: in MVL);
end REGISTER8;

architecture COMPONENT_BEH of REGISTER8 is
    component D_FLIP_FLOP
        port (D, CLOCK: in MVL; Q: out MVL);
    end component;
begin
    G_LABEL: for K in START to STOP generate
        DFF: D_FLIP_FLOP port map (D(K), CLOCK, Q(K));
        -- This component instantiation statement could very well have
        -- been replaced by the process statement that appears
        -- in the architecture body of the D_FLIP_FLOP entity.
    end generate G_LABEL;
end COMPONENT_BEH;
```

Consider a gated cross-coupled latch circuit shown in Fig. 12.7 and its dataflow model.

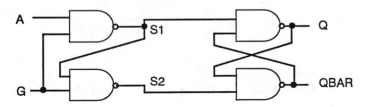

Figure 12.7 A gated latch.

```
library ATTLIB; use ATTLIB.ATT_PACKAGE.all;
entity GATED_FF is
    port (A, G: in MVL; Q, QBAR: buffer MVL);
end GATED_FF;

architecture IMPLICIT_LATCH of GATED_FF is
    signal S1, S2: MVL;
begin
    S1 <= A nand G;
    S2 <= S1 nand G;
    Q <= QBAR nand S1;
```

```
                QBAR <= Q nand S2;
            end IMPLICIT_LATCH;
```

In this example, the concurrent signal assignment statements do not have any conditions associated with them but the semantics of the behavior implies a latch. Note that the outputs of the gated flip-flop are of mode **buffer** since they are being assigned to and being read within the architecture body.

A memory can be modeled as a 2-dimensional array of flip-flops. Consider a generic RAM model in which each memory element is a GATED_FF component that was described earlier. ASIZE is the number of bits on the address port and DSIZE is the number of bits on the data port of the RAM.

```
library ATTLIB; use ATTLIB.ATT_PACKAGE.all;
entity RAM_GENERIC is
    generic (ASIZE, DSIZE: INTEGER);
    port (ADDRESS: in MVL_VECTOR(ASIZE-1 downto 0);
          DATA_IN: in MVL_VECTOR(DSIZE-1 downto 0);
          DATA_OUT: buffer MVL_VECTOR(DSIZE-1 downto 0));
end RAM_GENERIC;

architecture COMPONENT_BEH of RAM_GENERIC is
    component GATED_FF
        port (A, G: in MVL; Q, QBAR: buffer MVL := '0');
    end component;
    component DECODER
        generic (SELECT_SIZE: INTEGER);
        port (ADDR: out
                    MVL_VECTOR(2**SELECT_SIZE-1 downto 0);
              SEL_CTRL: in
                    MVL_VECTOR(SELECT_SIZE-1 downto 0));
    end component;
    signal ADDR_SELECT: MVL_VECTOR(2**ASIZE-1 downto 0);
begin
    D1: DECODER generic map (ASIZE)
                port map (ADDR_SELECT, ADDRESS);
    L1: for J in 0 to 2**ASIZE-1 generate
        L2: for K in 0 to DSIZE-1 generate
            GFF: GATED_FF port map (DATA_IN(K),
                ADDR_SELECT(J), DATA_OUT(K), open);
        end generate L2;
    end generate L1;
end COMPONENT_BEH;
```

The keyword **open** in the instantiation of the gated latch indicates that the QBAR port of the gated latch is not connected to any other signal.

Synchronous logic can also be modeled using guarded assignments. For example, a level-sensitive D flip-flop can be modeled as

```
library ATTLIB; use ATTLIB.ATT_PACKAGE.all;
entity LEVEL_SENS_DFF is
    port (STROBE, D: in MVL; Q, QBAR: out MVL);
end LEVEL_SENS_DFF;

architecture GUARDED_BEH of LEVEL_SENS_DFF is
    signal TEMP: MVL;
begin
    B1: block (STROBE = '1') -- STROBE is the name of the clock input.
    begin
        TEMP <= guarded D;
        Q <= TEMP;
        QBAR <= not TEMP;
    end block B1;
end GUARDED_BEH;
```

When STROBE is '1', any events on signal D are transferred to TEMP and eventually to Q, but when STROBE becomes '0', the value in TEMP (also in Q and QBAR) is retained and any change in input D no longer affects the value of signal TEMP.

It is important to understand the semantics of a signal assignment to determine the inference of synchronous logic. Consider the difference between the following two architecture bodies, BODY1 and BODY2.

```
architecture BODY1 of NO_NAME is
    signal A: MVL;
begin
    A <= not A;
end BODY1;

architecture BODY2 of NO_NAME is
    signal A, CLOCK: MVL;
begin
    process (A, CLOCK)
    begin
        if (CLOCK = '0' and CLOCK'EVENT) then
            A <= not A;
        end if;
    end process;
end BODY2;
```

Architecture BODY1 implies the circuit shown in Fig. 12.8 while architecture BODY2 implies the circuit shown in Fig. 12.9.

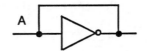

Figure 12.8 No latch implied.

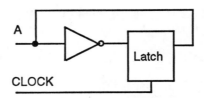

Figure 12.9 A latch implied.

If architecture BODY1 were simulated as is, simulation will go into an endless loop due to the zero delay asynchronous loop (simulation time does not advance) and each execution of the concurrent signal assignment statement will keep triggering itself after a delta delay. Whereas in architecture BODY2, the value of A is latched only on the falling edge of the CLOCK signal and thereafter, any changes on A (input of latch) do not affect the output of latch.

A signal declared to be of the **register** kind also models a latch. If all drivers to such a signal are disconnected, the signal retains its old value, thereby implying the semantics of a latch. Consider the circuit shown in Fig. 12.10 in which a capacitive latch is loaded with different values based on the two mutually exclusive clock signals. The disconnect time models the decay time for the capacitive latch.

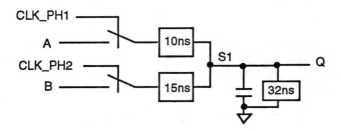

Figure 12.10 A capacitive latch.

library ATTLIB; **use** ATTLIB.ATT_PACKAGE.**all**;
entity REGISTER_SIGNAL **is**
    port (A, B, CLK_PH1, CLK_PH2: **in** MVL; Q: **out** MVL);
end REGISTER_SIGNAL;

```
architecture EXAMPLE of REGISTER_SIGNAL is
    signal S1: WIRED_OR MVL register;
    disconnect S1: MVL after 32 ns;
begin
    B1: block (CLK_PH1 = '1')
    begin
        S1 <= guarded A after 10 ns;
    end block B1;
    B2: block (CLK_PH2 = '1')
    begin
        S1 <= guarded B after 15 ns;
    end block B2;
    Q <= S1;
end EXAMPLE;
```

12.8   State Machine Modeling

State machines can usually be modeled using a **case** statement in a process. The state information is stored in a signal. The multiple branches of the **case** statement contain the behavior for each state. Here is an example of a simple multiplication algorithm represented as a state machine. When RESET signal is high, the accumulator ACC and the counter COUNT are initialized. When RESET goes low, multiplication starts. If the bit of the multiplier MPLR in position COUNT is '1', the multiplicand MCND is added to the accumulator. Next, the multiplicand is left-shifted by one bit and the counter is incremented. If COUNT is 16, multiplication is complete and the DONE signal is set high. If not, the COUNT bit of the multiplier MPLR is checked and the process repeated. The state diagram is shown in Fig. 12.11 and the corresponding state machine model is shown next.

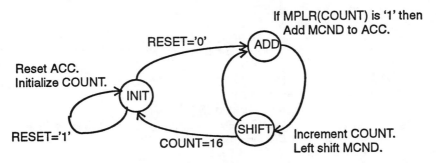

Figure 12.11 State diagram for multiplier.

```vhdl
library ATTLIB; use ATTLIB.ATT_PACKAGE.all;
entity MULTIPLY is
    port (MPLR, MCND: in MVL_VECTOR(15 downto 0);
        -- MPLR is multiplier, MCND is multiplicand.
        CLOCK, RESET: in MVL;
        DONE: out MVL; ACC: buffer MVL_VECTOR(31 downto 0));
end MULTIPLY;

architecture STATE_MACHINE of MULTIPLY is
    type STATE_TYPE is (INIT, ADD, SHIFT);
    signal MPY_STATE: STATE_TYPE; -- Initial state is INIT.
begin
    process
        variable COUNT: NATURAL;
        variable MCND_TEMP: MVL_VECTOR(31 downto 0);
    begin
        wait until (CLOCK = '0' and CLOCK'EVENT);
        -- Alternately, "wait until (CLOCK = '0' and
        -- not CLOCK'STABLE);";
        -- Both are equivalent in this context.
        case MPY_STATE is
            when INIT =>
                if RESET = '1' then
                    MPY_STATE <= INIT;
                    -- The above statement is not really necessary
                    -- since MPY_STATE will retain its old value.
                else
                    ACC <= (others => '0');
                    COUNT := 0;
                    MPY_STATE <= ADD;
                    DONE <= '0';
                    MCND_TEMP(15 downto 0) := MCND;
                    MCND_TEMP(31 downto 16) := (others => '0');
                end if;
            when ADD =>
                if (MPLR(COUNT) = '1') then
                    ACC <= ACC + MCND_TEMP;
                end if;
                MPY_STATE <= SHIFT;
            when SHIFT =>
                -- Left-shift MCND:
                MCND_TEMP := MCND_TEMP(30 downto 0) & '0';
                COUNT := COUNT + 1;
                if (COUNT = 16) then
                    MPY_STATE <= INIT;
                    DONE <= '1';
                else
```

```
                        MPY_STATE <= ADD;
                 end if;
           end case;
         end process;
      end STATE_MACHINE;
```

The signal MPY_STATE holds the state of the model. Initially the model is in state INIT and stays in this state as long as signal RESET is '1'. When RESET gets the value '0', the accumulator ACC is cleared, the counter COUNT is reset and the multiplicand MCND is loaded into a temporary variable MCND_TEMP, and model advances to state ADD. When model is in ADD state, the multiplicand in MCND_TEMP is added to ACC only if the bit at the COUNT position of the multiplier is a '1', and then the model advances to state SHIFT. In this state, the multiplier is left shifted once, counter is incremented and if the counter value is 16, signal DONE is set to '1' and model returns to state INIT. At this time, ACC contains the result of the multiplication. If the counter value was less than 16, the model repeats itself going through states ADD and SHIFT until the counter value becomes 16.

State transitions occur at every falling clock edge; this is specified by the **wait** statement. The mode of signal ACC is set to **buffer** since the value is read and updated within the model.

12.9   Interacting State Machines

Interacting state machines can be described as separate processes communicating via common signals. Consider the state transition diagram shown in Fig. 12.12 for two interacting processes, TX, a transmitter, and MP, a microprocessor. If process TX is not busy, process MP sets the data to be transmitted on a data bus and sends a signal, LOAD_TX, to process TX to load the data and to begin transmitting. A signal, TX_BUSY, is set by process TX during transmission to indicate that it is busy and that it cannot receive any further data from process MP.

A skeleton model for these two interacting processes is shown next. Only the control signals and state transitions are shown. Data manipulation code is not described.

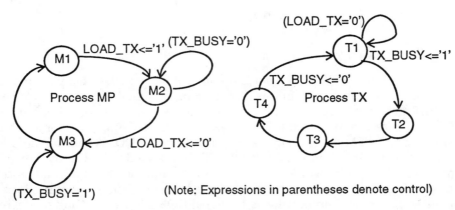

(Note: Expressions in parentheses denote control)

Figure 12.12 State diagram of two interacting processes.

```
architecture INTERACTING of FSM1 is
    type MP_STATE_TYPE is (M1, M2, M3);
    type TX_STATE_TYPE is (T1, T2, T3, T4);
    signal MP_STATE: MP_STATE_TYPE;
    signal TX_STATE: TX_STATE_TYPE;
    signal LOAD_TX, TX_BUSY: BIT;
    -- CLOCK is an input signal.
begin
    MP: process
    begin
        wait until (CLOCK = '0' and CLOCK'EVENT);
        case MP_STATE is
            when M1 =>              -- Load data on data bus.
                LOAD_TX <= '1';
                MP_STATE <= M2;
            when M2 =>              -- Wait for acknowledge.
                if TX_BUSY = '1' then
                    MP_STATE <= M3;
                    LOAD_TX <= '0';
                end if;
            when M3 =>              -- Wait for TX to finish.
                if TX_BUSY = '0' then
                    MP_STATE <= M1;
                end if;
        end case;
    end process MP;
    TX: process (CLOCK)
    begin
        if (CLOCK = '0' and CLOCK'EVENT) then
            case TX_STATE is
```

```
            when T1 =>        -- Wait for data to load.
              if LOAD_TX = '1' then
                 TX_STATE <= T2;
                 TX_BUSY <= '1'; -- Read data from data bus.
              end if;
            when T2 =>        -- Transmitting data.
              TX_STATE <= T3;
            when T3 =>
              TX_STATE <= T4;
            when T4 =>        -- Transmission completed.
              TX_BUSY <= '0';
              TX_STATE <= T1;
         end case;
       end if;
     end process TX;
   end INTERACTING;
```

Two different ways of modeling a falling clock edge are shown in the two processes, MP and TX. Both are equivalent in this case since all statements in the processes are synchronized to the clock edge. However, if there were some asynchronous statements, it would be necessary to use the if statement style. The wait statement style could also be used, but then two separate processes would have to be used, one for the synchronous part and one for the asynchronous part. The sequence of actions for the previous entity is shown in Fig. 12.13.

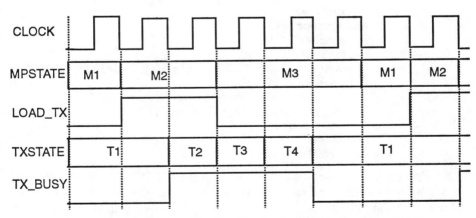

Figure 12.13 Sequence of actions for the two interacting processes.

Consider another example of two interacting processes, DIV, a clock divider, and RX, a receiver. In this case, process DIV generates a new clock, and process RX goes through its sequence of states synchronized to this new clock. The state diagram is shown in Fig. 12.14.

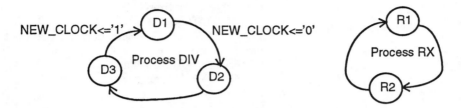

Figure 12.14 DIV generates clock for RX.

```
architecture ANOTHER_EXAMPLE of FSM2 is
    type DIV_STATE_TYPE is (D1, D2, D3);
    type RX_STATE_TYPE is (R1, R2);
    signal DIV_STATE: DIV_STATE_TYPE;
    signal RX_STATE: RX_STATE_TYPE;
    signal NEW_CLOCK: BIT;
    -- Signal CLOCK is an input port.
begin
    DIV: process
    begin
        wait until (CLOCK = '1' and CLOCK'EVENT);
        case DIV_STATE is
            when D1 => DIV_STATE <= D2; NEW_CLOCK <= '0';
            when D2 => DIV_STATE <= D3;
            when D3 => NEW_CLOCK <= '1'; DIV_STATE <= D1;
        end case;
    end process DIV;
    RX: process
    begin
        wait until (NEW_CLOCK = '0' and NEW_CLOCK'EVENT);
        case RX_STATE is
            when R1 => RX_STATE <= R2;
            when R2 => RX_STATE <= R1;
        end case;
    end process RX;
end ANOTHER_EXAMPLE;
```

Process DIV generates a new clock, NEW_CLOCK, as it goes through its sequence of states. The state transitions in this process occur on the rising edge of the signal CLOCK. Process RX is executed every time a falling edge on the NEW_CLOCK signal occurs. The sequence of waveforms for these interacting state machines is shown in Fig. 12.15.

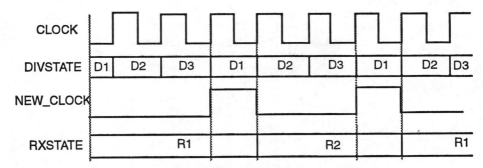

Figure 12.15 Interaction between processes, RX and DIV.

12.10 Modeling Moore FSM

The output of a Moore finite state machine (FSM) depends only on the state and not on its inputs. This type of behavior can be modeled using a single process with a **case** statement that switches on the state value. An example of a state transition diagram for a Moore finite state machine is shown in Fig. 12.16 and its corresponding behavior model appears next.

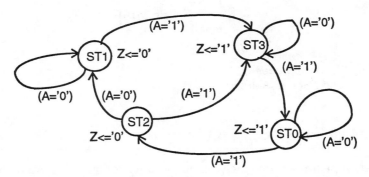

Figure 12.16 State diagram of a Moore machine.

```
library ATTLIB; use ATTLIB.ATT_PACKAGE.all;
entity MOORE_FSM is
    port (A, CLOCK: in BIT; Z: out MVL);
end MOORE_FSM;

architecture FSM_EXAMPLE of MOORE_FSM is
    type STATE_TYPE is (ST0, ST1, ST2, ST3);
    signal MOORE_STATE: STATE_TYPE;
```

```
begin
    process (CLOCK)
    begin
        if (CLOCK = '0' and CLOCK'EVENT) then
            case MOORE_STATE is
                when ST0 =>
                    Z <= '1';
                    if (A = '1') then
                        MOORE_STATE <= ST2;
                    end if;
                when ST1 =>
                    Z <= '0';
                    if (A = '1') then
                        MOORE_STATE <= ST3;
                    end if;
                when ST2 =>
                    Z <= '0';
                    if (A = '0') then
                        MOORE_STATE <= ST1;
                    else
                        MOORE_STATE <= ST3;
                    end if;
                when ST3 =>
                    Z <= '1';
                    if (A = '1') then
                        MOORE_STATE <= ST0;
                    end if;
            end case;
        end if;
    end process;
end FSM_EXAMPLE;
```

12.11 Modeling Mealy FSM

In a Mealy type finite state machine, the outputs not only depend on the state of the machine but also on its inputs. This type of finite state machine can also be modeled in a similar style as the Moore example case, that is, using a single process. To show the variety of the language, a different style is used to model a Mealy machine. In this case, we use two processes, one process that models the synchronous aspect of the finite state machine and the second process models the combinational part of the finite state machine. Here is an example of a state transition table, shown in Fig. 12.17, and its corresponding behavior model.

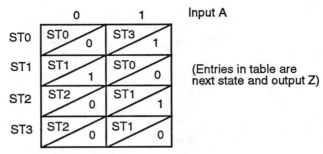

Present state

Figure 12.17 State transition table for a Mealy machine.

```
library ATTLIB; use ATTLIB.ATT_PACKAGE.all;
entity MEALY_FSM is
    port (A, CLOCK: in BIT; Z: out MVL);
end MEALY_FSM;


architecture YET_ANOTHER_EXAMPLE of MEALY_FSM is
    type MEALY_TYPE is (ST0, ST1, ST2, ST3);
    signal P_STATE, N_STATE: MEALY_TYPE;
begin
    SEQ_PART: process (CLOCK)
    begin
        -- Synchronous section:
        if (CLOCK = '0' and CLOCK'EVENT) then
            P_STATE <= N_STATE;
        end if;
    end process SEQ_PART;
    COMB_PART: process (P_STATE, A)
    begin
        case P_STATE is
            when ST0 =>
                if (A = '1') then
                    Z <= '1'; N_STATE <= ST3;
                else
                    Z <= '0';
                end if;
            when ST1 =>
                if (A = '1') then
                    Z <= '0'; N_STATE <= ST0;
                else
                    Z <= '1';
                end if;
```

```
                    when ST2 =>
                        if (A = '0') then
                            Z <= '0';
                        else
                            Z <= '1'; N_STATE <= ST1;
                        end if;
                    when ST3 =>
                        Z <= '0';
                        if (A = '0') then
                            N_STATE <= ST2;
                        else
                            N_STATE <= ST1;
                        end if;
            end case;
        end process COMB_PART;
    end YET_ANOTHER_EXAMPLE;
```

In this type of finite state machine, it is important to put the input signals in the sensitivity list for the combinational part process, since the outputs may directly depend on the inputs independent of the clock. Such a condition does not occur in a Moore finite state machine since outputs depend only on states and state changes occur synchronously.

12.12 A Simplified Blackjack Program

This section presents a state machine description of a simplified blackjack program. The blackjack program is played with a deck of cards. Cards 2 to 10 have values equal to their face value, and an ace has a value of either 1 or 11. The object of the game is to accept a number of random cards such that the total score (sum of values of all cards) is as close to 21 without exceeding 21.

When a new card is inserted, signal CARD_RDY is true and signal CARD_VALUE has the value of the card. The signal REQUEST_CARD indicates when the program is ready to accept a new card. If a sequence of cards is accepted such that total exceeds 21, signal LOST is set to true indicating that it has lost, else the signal WON is set to true indicating that the game has been won. The state sequencing is controlled by the signal CLOCK. This external interface of the blackjack program, shown in Fig. 12.18, is expressed using the following entity declaration.

```
        entity BLACKJACK is
            port (CARD_RDY: in BOOLEAN; CARD_VALUE: in INTEGER;
                REQUEST_CARD, WON, LOST: out BOOLEAN;
                CLOCK: in BIT);
        end BLACKJACK;
```

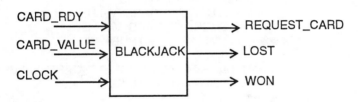

Figure 12.18 External view of blackjack program.

The behavior of the program is described in the following architecture body. The program accepts cards until its score is at least 17. The first ace is counted as a 11 unless the score exceeds 21 in which case 10 is subtracted so that the value for an ace of 1 is used. Three registers are used to store the state of the program: TOTAL to hold the sum, CURRENT_CARD_VALUE to hold the value of the card read (which could be 1 through 10), and ACE_AS_11 to remember whether an ace was counted as a 11 instead of a 1. The state of the blackjack program is stored in signal BJ_STATE.

```
architecture STATE_MACHINE of BLACKJACK is
    type STATE_TYPE is (INITIAL_ST, GETCARD_ST, REMCARD_ST,
            ADD_ST, CHECK_ST, WIN_ST, BACKUP_ST, LOSE_ST);
    signal BJ_STATE: STATE_TYPE;
begin
    process
        variable CURRENT_CARD_VALUE, TOTAL: INTEGER;
        variable ACE_AS_11: BOOLEAN;
    begin
        wait until (CLOCK = '0' and CLOCK'EVENT);
        case BJ_STATE is
            when INITIAL_ST =>
                TOTAL := 0; ACE_AS_11 := FALSE; WON <= FALSE;
                LOST <= FALSE; BJ_STATE <= GETCARD_ST;
            when GETCARD_ST =>
                REQUEST_CARD <= TRUE;
                if CARD_RDY then
                    CURRENT_CARD_VALUE := CARD_VALUE;
                    BJ_STATE <= REMCARD_ST;
                end if;            -- Else stay in GETCARD_ST state.
            when REMCARD_ST => -- Wait for card to be removed.
                if CARD_RDY then
                    REQUEST_CARD <= FALSE;
                else
                    BJ_STATE <= ADD_ST;
                end if;
            when ADD_ST =>
```

```
              if (not ACE_AS_11) and
                  (CURRENT_CARD_VALUE = 1) then
                  CURRENT_CARD_VALUE := 11;
                  ACE_AS_11 := TRUE;
              end if;
              TOTAL := TOTAL + CURRENT_CARD_VALUE;
              BJ_STATE <= CHECK_ST;
          when CHECK_ST =>
              if (TOTAL < 17) then
                  BJ_STATE <= GETCARD_ST;
              elsif (TOTAL < 22) then
                  BJ_STATE <= WIN_ST;
              else
                  BJ_STATE <= BACKUP_ST;
              end if;
          when BACKUP_ST =>
              if ACE_AS_11 then
                  TOTAL := TOTAL - 10; ACE_AS_11 := FALSE;
                  BJ_STATE <= CHECK_ST;
              else
                  BJ_STATE <= LOSE_ST;
              end if;
          when LOSE_ST =>
              LOST <= TRUE; REQUEST_CARD <= TRUE;
              if CARD_RDY then
                  BJ_STATE <= INITIAL_ST;
              end if;              -- Else stay in this state.
          when WIN_ST =>
              WON <= TRUE; REQUEST_CARD <= TRUE;
              if CARD_RDY then
                  BJ_STATE <= INITIAL_ST;
              end if;              -- Else stay in this state.
        end case;
      end process;
    end STATE_MACHINE;
```

12.13 Hierarchy in Design

A hierarchy in a design is managed by using component instantiation and component declaration statements. Given a large design, one could decompose a design into a number of smaller subdesigns. The components (same as a subdesign) at each level would instantiate components at lower levels in the hierarchy. The description of components at any level could be in any design style, that is, dataflow, behavioral, structural, or mixed. For example, all components could be described as sequential processes initially, and as each component at each level is synthesized, it may be described using the structural style. Consider the hierarchical design shown in Fig. 12.19.

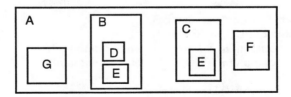

Figure 12.19 A hierarchical design.

Design A is composed of four components, B, C, F, and G. Subdesign B is composed of components D, E, and some glue behavioral logic. Subdesign C is composed of component E and some other behavioral logic. Component E is used by components B and C. Initially, there would be a separate entity declaration plus architecture body for each component A, B, C, D, E, F, and G. As each component is synthesized to its primitive gate level, different architecture bodies for each component are developed. A skeleton model for this large design example is shown next.

```
--Library and use clauses, if any.
entity A is  port ( . . . ) end A;

architecture A_INTERNALS of A is
     component B port ( . . . ) end component;
     component C port ( . . . ) end component;
     component F port ( . . . ) end component;
     component G port ( . . . ) end component;
begin
     B_COMP1: B port map ( . . . );
     C_COMP1: C port map ( . . . );
     F_COMP1: F port map ( . . . );
     G_COMP1: G port map ( . . . );
     -- There might be other glue logic here, for example, high
     -- power drivers for the I/O for A, etc.
end A _INTERNALS;

entity F is port ( . . . ) end F;
architecture F_INTERNALS of F is
begin
     -- Behavior of F.
end F_INTERNALS;

entity G is port ( . . . ) end;
architecture G_INTERNALS of G is
```

```
begin
    -- Behavior of G.
end G_INTERNALS;

entity B is port ( . . . ) end B;
architecture B_INTERNALS of B is
    component D port ( . . . ) end component;
    component E port ( . . . ) end component;
begin
    D_COMP1: D port map ( . . . );
    E_COMP1: E port map ( . . . );
    -- Remaining behavior of B.
end B_INTERNALS;

entity C is port ( . . . ) end C;
architecture C_INTERNALS of C is
    component E port ( . . . ) end component;
begin
    E_COMP2: E port map ( . . . );
    -- Other behavior of C.
end C_INTERNALS;

entity D is port ( . . . ) end D;
architecture D_INTERNALS of D is
begin
    -- Behavior of D.
end D_INTERNALS;

entity E is port ( . . . ) end E;
architecture E_INTERNALS of E is
begin
    -- Behavior of E.
end E_INTERNALS;
```

Each entity (entity declaration plus an architecture body) could be placed in a separate text file and compiled into a working library. Having described the entire system behavior for design A, it could then be simulated and verified. There is no need to specify a configuration if all the entities are compiled into the working library, since the default bindings will be used (see Sec. 7.5).

Next the synthesis of each component could either proceed top-down, that is, translate behavior of design A to structure, then for B, C, D, E, F, G, or it can proceed bottom-up, that is, synthesize subdesign E and D before B or C. Say component E is synthesized into a structure either using available synthesis tools or by a manual design process, this structure could be saved in a new architecture body that is still associated with the same entity declaration E. For example,

```
architecture E_2 of E is
begin
    -- Structure of E.
end E_2;
```

To simulate this new architecture, a configuration declaration would have to be written that would bind entity E to architecture E_2. For example,

```
configuration E_CON of E is
    for E_2
    end for;
end E_CON;
```

Configuration E_CON would now be verified on a stand-alone basis. This would verify the entity E using architecture E_2. To simulate the entire design A again, references to component E in design B and C must bind its instantiations to the new architecture for E. This could be done using a configuration specification that is added to the architecture body for both B and C, such as

```
for comp-label : E use configuration WORK.E_CON;
```

If the architecture bodies for B and C cannot be changed, a configuration declaration can be written for design A as shown next.

```
configuration A_CON of A is
    for B
        for E_COMP1: E
            use configuration WORK.E_CON;
        end for;
    end for;
    for C
        for E_COMP2: E
            use configuration WORK.E_CON;
        end for;
    end for;
    -- For unbound components, use default rules (see Sec. 7.5).
end A_CON;
```

The basic idea is that every time a component is synthesized into its structure, a new architecture body is created that is associated with the same entity declaration. A configuration declaration or a configuration specification can be written to bind the new architecture with the component one level above in the hierarchy.

It is not necessary to keep the subdesigns of an entire design in a single design library. However, all architecture bodies of a component must reside in the same library. This is because they must reside with their corresponding entity declaration. If components reside in different libraries, configuration specifications would have to be written (the default rules work for only components in one library, that is, working library) and these will be made visible to their next higher level component by using context clauses. For example, if component E were to reside in library JOHNS_LIB, then the configuration specification appearing in the architecture for subdesign C might be

```
library JOHNS_LIB;
architecture C_2 of C is
    for E_COMP2: E use configuration JOHNS_LIB.E_CON;
begin
    . . .
end C_2;
```

❑

APPENDIX A   *Predefined Environment*

This appendix describes the predefined environment of the language. The set of reserved words for the language is listed in the first section. The next two sections give the source code listing for the predefined packages STANDARD and TEXTIO. The predefined attributes have already been described in Chap. 10. All information in this appendix has been reprinted from the IEEE Std 1076-1987 IEEE Standard VHDL Language Reference Manual.[1]

A.1   Reserved Words

The following identifiers are reserved words in the language (also called keywords), and therefore, cannot be used as identifiers in a VHDL description.

---

1. Reprinted here from the IEEE Std VHDL LRM 1076-1987 by permission from IEEE.

abs	access	after	alias
all	and	architecture	array
assert	attribute		
begin	block	body	buffer
bus			
case	component	configuration	constant
disconnect	downto		
else	elsif	end	entity
exit			
file	for	function	
generate	generic	guarded	
if	in	inout	is
label	library	linkage	loop
map	mod		
nand	new	next	nor
not	null		
of	on	open	or
others	out		
package	port	procedure	process
range	record	register	rem
report	return		
select	severity	signal	subtype
then	to	transport	type
units	until	use	
variable			

wait   **when**   **while**   **with**

xor

A.2   Package STANDARD

The package STANDARD is a predefined package that contains the definitions for the predefined types and functions of the language. A source code
listing of this package follows.

```
package STANDARD is
  -- Predefined enumeration types:
  type BOOLEAN is (FALSE, TRUE);
  type BIT is ('0', '1');
  type CHARACTER is (

    NUL,  SOH,  STX,  ETX,  EOT,  ENQ,  ACK,
    BEL,  BS,   HT,   LF,   VT,   FF,   CR,
    SO,   SI,   DLE,  DC1,  DC2,  DC3,  DC4,
    NAK,  SYN,  ETB,  CAN,  EM,   SUB,  ESC,
    FSP,  GSP,  RSP,  USP,

    ' ',  '!',  '"',  '#',  '$',  '%',  '&',
    ''',  '(',  ')',  '*',  '+',  ',',  '-',
    '.',  '/',  '0',  '1',  '2',  '3',  '4',
    '5',  '6',  '7',  '8',  '9',  ':',  ';',
    '<',  '=',  '>',  '?',

    '@',  'A',  'B',  'C',  'D',  'E',  'F',
    'G',  'H',  'I',  'J',  'K',  'L',  'M',
    'N',  'O',  'P',  'Q',  'R',  'S',  'T',
    'U',  'V',  'W',  'X',  'Y',  'Z',  '[',
    '\',  ']',  '^',  '_',

    '`',  'a',  'b',  'c',  'd',  'e',  'f',
    'g',  'h',  'i',  'j',  'k',  'l',  'm',
    'n',  'o',  'p',  'q',  'r',  's',  't',
    'u',  'v',  'w',  'x',  'y',  'z',  '{',
    '|',  '}',  '~',  DEL
  );

  type SEVERITY_LEVEL is (NOTE, WARNING,
                          ERROR, FAILURE);
```

```
-- Predefined numeric types:
type INTEGER is range implementation_defined;
type REAL is range implementation_defined;

-- Predefined type TIME:
type TIME is range implementation_defined
    units
        fs;                              -- femtosecond
        ps    = 1000 fs;                 -- picosecond
        ns    = 1000 ps;                 -- nanosecond
        us    = 1000 ns;                 -- microsecond
        ms    = 1000 us;                 -- microsecond
        sec   = 1000 ms;                 -- seconds
        min   = 60 secs;                 -- minutes
        hr    = 60 min;                  -- hours
    end units;

-- Function that returns the current simulation time:
function NOW return TIME;

-- Predefined numeric subtypes:
subtype NATURAL is INTEGER range 0 to INTEGER'HIGH;
subtype POSITIVE is INTEGER range 1 to INTEGER'HIGH;

-- Predefined array types:
type STRING is array (POSITIVE range <>) of CHARACTER;
type BIT_VECTOR is array (NATURAL range <>) of BIT;
end STANDARD;
```

A.3   Package TEXTIO

Package TEXTIO contains declarations of types and subprograms that support formatted ASCII I/O operations. A source code listing of the package follows.

```
package TEXTIO is
    -- Type definitions for text I/O:
    type LINE is access STRING;   -- A line is a pointer to a
                                  -- STRING value.
    type TEXT is file of STRING;  -- A file of variable-length
                                  -- ASCII records.
    type SIDE is (RIGHT, LEFT);   -- For justifying output data
                                  -- within fields.
    subtype WIDTH is NATURAL;     -- For specifying widths of
                                  -- output fields.
```

-- Standard text files:
file INPUT: TEXT **is in** "STD_INPUT";
file OUTPUT: TEXT **is out** "STD_OUTPUT";

-- Input routines for standard types:
procedure READLINE (F: **in** TEXT; L: **out** LINE);

procedure READ (L: **inout** LINE; VALUE: **out** BIT;
                GOOD: **out** BOOLEAN);
procedure READ (L: **inout** LINE; VALUE: **out** BIT);

procedure READ (L: **inout** LINE; VALUE: **out** BIT_VECTOR;
                GOOD: **out** BOOLEAN);
procedure READ (L: **inout** LINE; VALUE: **out** BIT_VECTOR);

procedure READ (L: **inout** LINE; VALUE: **out** BOOLEAN;
                GOOD: **out** BOOLEAN);
procedure READ (L: **inout** LINE; VALUE: **out** BOOLEAN);

procedure READ (L: **inout** LINE; VALUE: **out** CHARACTER;
                GOOD: **out** BOOLEAN);
procedure READ (L: **inout** LINE; VALUE: **out** CHARACTER);

procedure READ (L: **inout** LINE; VALUE: **out** INTEGER;
                GOOD: **out** BOOLEAN);
procedure READ (L: **inout** LINE; VALUE: **out** INTEGER);

procedure READ (L: **inout** LINE; VALUE: **out** REAL;
                GOOD: **out** BOOLEAN);
procedure READ (L: **inout** LINE; VALUE: **out** REAL);

procedure READ (L: **inout** LINE; VALUE: **out** STRING;
                GOOD: **out** BOOLEAN);
procedure READ (L: **inout** LINE; VALUE: **out** STRING);

procedure READ (L: **inout** LINE; VALUE: **out** TIME;
                GOOD: **out** BOOLEAN);
procedure READ (L: **inout** LINE; VALUE: **out** TIME);

-- Output routines for standard types:
procedure WRITELINE (F: **out** TEXT; L: **in** LINE);

procedure WRITE (L: **inout** LINE; VALUE: **in** BIT;
            JUSTIFIED: **in** SIDE := RIGHT; FIELD: **in** WIDTH := 0);
procedure WRITE (L: **inout** LINE; VALUE: **in** BIT_VECTOR;
            JUSTIFIED: **in** SIDE := RIGHT; FIELD: **in** WIDTH := 0);
procedure WRITE (L: **inout** LINE; VALUE: **in** BOOLEAN;

```
                    JUSTIFIED: in SIDE := RIGHT; FIELD: in WIDTH := 0);
procedure WRITE (L: inout LINE; VALUE: in CHARACTER;
                    JUSTIFIED: in SIDE := RIGHT; FIELD: in WIDTH := 0);
procedure WRITE (L: inout LINE; VALUE: in INTEGER;
                    JUSTIFIED: in SIDE := RIGHT; FIELD: in WIDTH := 0);
procedure WRITE (L: inout LINE; VALUE: in REAL;
                    JUSTIFIED: in SIDE := RIGHT; FIELD: in WIDTH := 0;
                    DIGITS: in NATURAL := 0);
procedure WRITE (L: inout LINE; VALUE: in STRING;
                    JUSTIFIED: in SIDE := RIGHT; FIELD: in WIDTH := 0);
procedure WRITE (L: inout LINE; VALUE: in TIME;
                    JUSTIFIED: in SIDE := RIGHT; FIELD: in WIDTH := 0;
                    UNIT: in TIME := ns);

-- File position predicates:
function ENDLINE (L: in LINE) return BOOLEAN;
-- function ENDFILE (F: in TEXT) return BOOLEAN;
end TEXTIO;
```

❑

APPENDIX B *Syntax Reference*

This appendix presents the complete syntax of the VHDL language.[1]

B.1 Conventions

The following conventions are used in describing this syntax.

1. The syntax rules are organized in an alphabetical order by their left-hand nonterminal name.

2. Reserved words are written in **boldface**.

3. A name in *italics* prefixed to a nonterminal name represents the semantic meaning associated with that nonterminal name.

1. Reprinted here from the IEEE Std VHDL LRM 1076-1987 by permission from IEEE.

4. The vertical bar symbol (|) separates alternative items unless it appears immediately after an opening brace in which case it stands for itself.

5. Square brackets ([. . .]) denote optional items.

6. Curly braces identify ({ . . . }) an item that is repeated zero or more times.

7. The starting nonterminal name is "design_file".

8. The terminal names used in this grammar appear in upper case.

B.2   The Syntax

abstract_literal ::= decimal_literal | based_literal

access_type_definition ::= **access** subtype_indication

actual_designator ::=
      expression
      | *signal*_name
      | *variable*_name
      | **open**

actual_parameter_part := *parameter*_association_list

actual_part ::= actual_designator | function_name (actual_designator)

adding_operator ::= + | – | &

aggregate ::= (element_association { , element_association })

alias_declaration ::= **alias** identifier : subtype_indication **is** name ;

allocator ::= **new** subtype_indication | **new** qualified_expression

architecture_body ::=
      architecture identifier **of** *entity*_name **is**
            architecture_declarative_part
      begin
            architecture_statement_part
      end [*architecture*_simple_name] ;

architecture_declarative_part ::= { block_declarative_item } architecture_statement_part ::= { concurrent_statement }

array_type_definition ::=
        unconstrained_array_definition I constrained_array_definition

assertion_statement ::=
        assert condition
                [**report** expression]
                [**severity** expression] ;

association_element ::= [formal_part =>] actual_part

association_list ::= association_element { , association_element }

attribute_declaration ::= **attribute** identifier : type_mark ;

attribute_designator ::= *attribute*_simple_name

attribute_name ::= prefix ' attribute_designator [(*static*_expression)]

attribute_specification ::=
        attribute attribute_designator **of** entity_specification **is** expression ;

base ::= integer

base_specifier ::= B I O I X

base_unit_declaration ::= identifier ;

based_integer ::= extended_digit { [UNDERLINE] extended_digit }

based_literal ::= base # based_integer [. based_integer] # [exponent]

basic_character ::= basic_graphic_character I FORMAT_EFFECTOR

basic_graphic_character :=
        UPPER_CASE_LETTER
        I DIGIT
        I SPECIAL_CHARACTER
        I SPACE_CHARACTER

binding_indication ::=
        entity_aspect [generic_map_aspect] [port_map_aspect]

bit_string_literal ::= base_specifier " bit_value "

bit_value ::= extended_digit { [UNDERLINE] extended_digit }

block_configuration ::=
        for block_specification
                { use_clause }
                { configuration_item }
        end for;

block_declarative_item ::=
        subprogram_declaration
        I subprogram_body
        I type_declaration
        I subtype_declaration
        I constant_declaration
        I signal_declaration
        I file_declaration
        I alias_declaration
        I component_declaration
        I attribute_declaration
        I attribute_specification
        I configuration_specification
        I disconnection_specification
        I use_clause

block_declarative_part ::= { block_declarative_item }

block_header ::=
        [generic_clause [generic_map_aspect ;]]
        [port_clause [port_map_aspect ;]]

block_specification ::=
        *architecture*_name
        I *block_statement*_label
        I *generate_statement*_label [(index_specification)]

block_statement ::=
        *block*_label :
                block [(*guard*_expression)]
                        block_header
                        block_declarative_part
                begin
                        block_statement_part
                end block [*block*_label] ;

block_statement_part ::= { concurrent_statement }

```
case_statement ::=
      case expression is
            case_statement_alternative
            { case_statement_alternative }
      end case ;

case_statement_alternative ::= when choices => sequence_of_statements

character_literal ::= ' graphic_character '

choice ::=
      simple_expression
      I discrete_range
      I element_simple_name
      I others

choices ::= choice { I choice }

component_configuration ::=
      for component_specification
            [ use binding_indication ; ]
            [ block_configuration ]
      end for;

component_declaration ::=
      component identifier
            [ local_generic_clause ]
            [ local_port_clause ]
      end component ;

component_instantiation_statement ::=
      instantiation_label :
            component_name [ generic_map_aspect ] [ port_map_aspect ] ;

component_specification ::= instantiation_list : component_name

composite_type_definition ::= array_type_definition I record_type_definition

concurrent_assertion_statement ::= [ label : ] assertion_statement

concurrent_procedure_call ::= [ label : ] procedure_call_statement

concurrent_signal_assignment_statement ::=
      [ label : ] conditional_signal_assignment
      I [ label : ] selected_signal_assignment
```

concurrent_statement ::=
    block_statement
    I process_statement
    I concurrent_procedure_call
    I concurrent_assertion_statement
    I concurrent_signal_assignment_statement
    I component_instantiation_statement
    I generate_statement

condition ::= *boolean*_expression

condition_clause ::= **until** condition

conditional_signal_assignment ::= target <= options conditional_waveforms ;

conditional_waveforms ::= { waveform **when** condition **else** } waveform

configuration_declaration ::=
    configuration identifier **of** *entity*_name **is**
            configuration_declarative_part
            block_configuration
    end [*configuration*_simple_name] ;

configuration_declarative_item ::= use_clause I attribute_specification

configuration_declarative_part ::= { configuration_declarative_item }

configuration_item ::= block_configuration I component_configuration

configuration_specification ::=
    for component_specification **use** binding_indication ;

constant_declaration ::=
    constant identifier_list : subtype_indication [:= expression] ;

constrained_array_definition ::=
    array index_constraint **of** *element*_subtype_indication

constraint ::= range_constraint I index_constraint

context_clause ::= { context_item }

context_item ::= library_clause I use_clause

decimal_literal ::= integer [. integer] [exponent]

declaration ::=
     type_declaration
     I subtype_declaration
     I object_declaration
     I file_declaration
     I interface_declaration
     I alias_declaration
     I attribute_declaration
     I component_declaration
     I entity_declaration
     I configuration_declaration
     I subprogram_declaration
     I package_declaration

design_file ::= design_unit { design_unit }

design_unit ::= context_clause library_unit

designator ::= identifier I operator_symbol

direction ::= **to** I **downto**

disconnection_specification ::=
     disconnect guarded_signal_specification **after** *time*_expression ;

discrete_range ::= *discrete*_subtype_indication I range

element_association ::= [choices =>] expression

element_declaration ::= identifier_list : element_subtype_definition ;

element_subtype_definition ::= subtype_indication

entity_aspect ::=
     entity *entity*_name [(*architecture*_identifier)]
     I **configuration** *configuration*_name
     I **open**

entity_class ::=
     entity I **architecture** I **configuration** I **procedure**
     I **function** I **package** I **type** I **subtype** I **constant** I **signal**
     I **variable** I **component** I **label**

entity_declaration ::=
     entity identifier **is**
          entity_header

```
            entity_declarative_part
      [ begin
            entity_statement_part ]
      end [ entity_simple_name ] ;
```

entity_declarative_item ::=
      subprogram_declaration
      | subprogram_body
      | type_declaration
      | subtype_declaration
      | constant_declaration
      | signal_declaration
      | file_declaration
      | alias_declaration
      | attribute_declaration
      | attribute_specification
      | disconnection_specification
      | use_clause

entity_declarative_part ::= { entity_declarative_item }

entity_designator ::= simple_name | operator_symbol

entity_header ::= [formal_generic_clause] [formal_port_clause]

entity_name_list ::=
      entity_designator { , entity_designator }
      | others
      | all

entity_specification ::= entity_name_list : entity_class

entity_statement ::=
      concurrent_assertion_statement
      | passive_concurrent_procedure_call
      | passive_process_statement

entity_statement_part ::= { entity_statement }

enumeration_literal ::= identifier | character_literal

enumeration_type_definition ::= (enumeration_literal { , enumeration_literal })

exit_statement ::= exit [loop_label] [when condition] ;

exponent ::= E [+] integer | E – integer

expression ::=
       relation { **and** relation }
       I relation { **or** relation }
       I relation { **xor** relation }
       I relation [**nand** relation]
       I relation [**nor** relation]

extended_digit ::= DIGIT I letter

factor ::=
       primary [∗∗ primary]
       I **abs** primary
       I **not** primary

file_declaration ::=
       file identifier : subtype_indication **is** [mode] file_logical_name ;

file_logical_name ::= *string_*expression

file_type_definition ::= **file of** type_mark

floating_type_definition ::= range_constraint

formal_designator ::= *generic_*name I *port_*name I *parameter_*name

formal_parameter_list ::= *parameter_*interface_list

formal_part ::= formal_designator I *function_*name (formal_designator)

full_type_declaration ::= **type** identifier **is** type_definition ;

function_call ::= *function_*name [(actual_parameter_part)]

generate_statement ::=
       *generate_*label :
              generation_scheme **generate**
                     { concurrent_statement }
              end generate [*generate_*label] ;

generation_scheme ::=
       for *generate_*parameter_specification
       I **if** condition

generic_clause ::= **generic** (generic_list) ;

generic_list ::= *generic_*interface_list

generic_map_aspect ::= **generic map** (*generic*_association_list)

graphic_character ::=
    basic_graphic_character
    I LOWER_CASE_LETTER
    I OTHER_SPECIAL_CHARACTER

guarded_signal_specification ::= *guarded*_signal_list : type_mark

identifier ::= letter { [UNDERLINE] letter_or_digit }

identifier_list ::= identifier { , identifier }

if_statement ::=
    if condition **then**
        sequence_of_statements
    { **elsif** condition **then**
        sequence_of_statements }
    [**else**
        sequence_of_statements]
    end if ;

incomplete_type_declaration ::= **type** identifier ;

index_constraint ::= (discrete_range { , discrete_range })

index_specification ::= discrete_range I *static*_expression

index_subtype_definition ::= type_mark **range** <>

indexed_name ::= prefix (expression { , expression })

instantiation_list ::=
    *instantiation*_label { , *instantiation*_label }
    I **others**
    I **all**

integer ::= DIGIT { [UNDERLINE] DIGIT }

integer_type_definition ::= range_constraint

interface_constant_declaration ::=
    [**constant**] identifier_list : [**in**] subtype_indication
    [:= *static*_expression]

interface_declaration ::=
      interface_constant_declaration
      I interface_signal_declaration
      I interface_variable_declaration

interface_element ::= interface_declaration

interface_list ::= interface_element { ; interface_element }

interface_signal_declaration ::=
      [**signal**] identifier_list : [mode] subtype_indication [**bus**]
      [:= *static*_expression]

interface_variable_declaration ::=
      [**variable**] identifier_list : [mode] subtype_indication
      [:= *static*_expression]

iteration_scheme ::=
      while condition
      I **for** *loop*_parameter_specification

label ::= identifier

letter ::= UPPER_CASE_LETTER I LOWER_CASE_LETTER

letter_or_digit ::= letter I digit

library_clause ::= **library** logical_name_list ;

library_unit ::= primary_unit I secondary_unit

literal ::=
      numeric_literal
      I enumeration_literal
      I string_literal
      I bit_string_literal
      I **null**

logical_name ::= identifier

logical_name_list ::= logical_name { , logical_name }

logical_operator ::= **and** I **or** I **nand** I **nor** I **xor**

loop_statement ::=
      [*loop*_label :]

[iteration_scheme] **loop**
      sequence_of_statements
end loop [*loop*_label] ;

miscellaneous_operator ::= ** | **abs** | **not**

mode ::= **in** | **out** | **inout** | **buffer** | **linkage**

multiplying_operator ::= * | / | **mod** | **rem**

name ::=
      simple_name
      | operator_symbol
      | selected_name
      | indexed_name
      | slice_name
      | attribute_name

next_statement ::= **next** [*loop*_label] [**when** condition] ;

null_statement ::= **null** ;

numeric_literal ::= abstract_literal | physical_literal

object_declaration ::=
      constant_declaration
      | signal_declaration
      | variable_declaration

operator_symbol ::= string_literal

options ::= [**guarded**] [**transport**]

package_body ::=
      package body *package*_simple_name **is**
         package_body_declarative_part
      end [*package*_simple_name] ;

package_body_declarative_item ::=
      subprogram_declaration
      | subprogram_body
      | type_declaration
      | subtype_declaration
      | constant_declaration
      | file_declaration

| alias_declaration
| use_clause

package_body_declarative_part ::= { package_body_declarative_item }

package_declaration ::=
    package identifier **is**
        package_declarative_part
    end [*package*_simple_name] ;

package_declarative_item ::=
    subprogram_declaration
    | type_declaration
    | subtype_declaration
    | constant_declaration
    | signal_declaration
    | file_declaration
    | alias_declaration
    | component_declaration
    | attribute_declaration
    | attribute_specification
    | disconnection_specification
    | use_clause

package_declarative_part ::= { package_declarative_item }

parameter_specification ::= identifier **in** discrete_range

physical_literal ::= [abstract_literal] *unit*_name

physical_type_definition ::=
    range_constraint
      units
        base_unit_declaration
        { secondary_unit_declaration }
      end units

port_clause ::= **port** (port_list) ;

port_list ::= *port*_interface_list

port_map_aspect ::= **port map** (*port*_association_list)

prefix ::= name | function_call

primary ::=
      name
      I literal
      I aggregate
      I function_call
      I qualified_expression
      I type_conversion
      I allocator
      I (expression)

primary_unit ::=
      entity_declaration
      I configuration_declaration
      I package_declaration

procedure_call_statement ::= *procedure*_name [(actual_parameter_part)] ;

process_declarative_item ::=
      subprogram_declaration
      I subprogram_body
      I type_declaration
      I subtype_declaration
      I constant_declaration
      I variable_declaration
      I file_declaration
      I alias_declaration
      I attribute_declaration
      I attribute_specification
      I use_clause

process_declarative_part ::= { process_declarative_item }

process_statement ::=
      [*process*_label :]
            process [(sensitivity_list)]
                  process_declarative_part
            begin
                  process_statement_part
            end process [*process*_label] ;

process_statement_part ::= { sequential_statement }

qualified_expression ::=
      type_mark ' (expression)
      I type_mark ' aggregate

range ::=
        *range*_attribute_name
        I simple_expression direction simple_expression

range_constraint ::= **range** range

record_type_definition ::=
        record
                element_declaration
                { element_declaration }
        end record

relation ::= simple_expression [relational_operator simple_expression]

relational_operator ::= = I /= I < I <= I > I >=

return_statement ::= **return** [expression] ;

scalar_type_definition ::=
        enumeration_type_definition
        I integer_type_definition
        I floating_type_definition
        I physical_type_definition

secondary_unit ::= architecture_body I package_body

secondary_unit_declaration ::= identifier = physical_literal ;

selected_name ::= prefix . suffix

selected_signal_assignment ::=
        with expression **select**
                target <= options selected_waveforms ;

selected_waveforms ::= { waveform **when** choices , } waveform **when** choices

sensitivity_clause ::= **on** sensitivity_list

sensitivity_list ::= *signal*_name { , *signal*_name }

sequence_of_statements ::= { sequential_statement }

sequential_statement ::=
        wait_statement
        I assertion_statement
        I signal_assignment_statement

          I variable_assignment_statement
          I procedure_call_statement
          I if_statement
          I case_statement
          I loop_statement
          I next_statement
          I exit_statement
          I return_statement
          I null_statement

sign ::= + I –

signal_assignment_statement ::= target <= [**transport**] waveform ;

signal_declaration ::=
      signal identifier_list : subtype_indication [signal_kind] [:= expression] ;

signal_kind ::= **register** I **bus**

signal_list ::=
      *signal*_name { , *signal*_name }
      I **others**
      I **all**

simple_expression ::= [sign] term { adding_operator term }

simple_name ::= identifier

slice_name ::= prefix (discrete_range)

string_literal ::= " { graphic_character } "

subprogram_body ::=
      subprogram_specification **is**
            subprogram_declarative_part
      begin
            subprogram_statement_part
      end [designator] ;

subprogram_declaration ::= subprogram_specification ;

subprogram_declarative_item ::=
      subprogram_declaration
      I subprogram_body
      I type_declaration
      I subtype_declaration

```
                I constant_declaration
                I variable_declaration
                I file_declaration
                I alias_declaration
                I attribute_declaration
                I attribute_specification
                I use_clause
```

subprogram_declarative_part ::= { subprogram_declarative_item }

subprogram_specification ::=
      procedure designator [(formal_parameter_list)]
      I **function** designator [(formal_parameter_list)] **return** type_mark

subprogram_statement_part ::= { sequential_statement }

subtype_declaration ::= **subtype** identifier **is** subtype_indication ;

subtype_indication ::= [*resolution_function*_name] type_mark [constraint]

suffix ::=
      simple_name
      I character_literal
      I operator_symbol
      I **all**

target ::= name I aggregate

term ::= factor { multiplying_operator factor }

timeout_clause := **for** *time*_expression

type_conversion ::= type_mark (expression)

type_declaration ::= full_type_declaration I incomplete_type_declaration

type_definition ::=
      scalar_type_definition
      I composite_type_definition
      I access_type_definition
      I file_type_definition

type_mark ::= *type*_name I *subtype*_name

unconstrained_array_definition ::=
    array (index_subtype_definition { , index_subtype_definition })
    of *element*_subtype_indication

use_clause ::= **use** selected_name { , selected_name } ;

variable_assignment_statement ::= target := expression ;

variable_declaration ::=
    variable identifier_list : subtype_indication [:= expression] ;

wait_statement ::=
    wait [sensitivity_clause] [condition_clause] [timeout_clause] ;

waveform ::= waveform_element { , waveform_element }

waveform_element ::=
    *value*_expression [**after** *time*_expression]
    | **null** [**after** *time*_expression]

❏

APPENDIX C *A Package Example*

This appendix describes the complete ATT_PACKAGE package that has been referred to in Chaps. 11 and 12. The package is provided more as an illustration of what goes into a package rather than trying to present a single comprehensive package.

C.1 *The Package ATT_PACKAGE*

The ATT_PACKAGE contains the definition of a new 4-value type called MVL and its associated overloaded logical operator definitions. Here is the VHDL source code listing for this package.

```
package ATT_PACKAGE is
    type MVL is ('U', '0', '1', 'Z');
    type MVL_VECTOR is array (NATURAL range <>) of MVL;

    type MVL_1D_TABLE is array (MVL) of MVL;
    type MVL_2D_TABLE is array (MVL, MVL) of MVL;
```

```
-- Truth tables for logical operators:
constant TABLE_AND: MVL_2D_TABLE :=
    --   U    0    1    Z
    ((  'U', '0', 'U', 'U'),    -- U
     (  '0', '0', '0', '0'),    -- 0
     (  'U', '0', '1', 'U'),    -- 1
     (  'U', '0', 'U', 'U'));   -- Z
constant TABLE_OR: MVL_2D_TABLE :=
    --   U    0    1    Z
    ((  'U', 'U', '1', 'U'),    -- U
     (  'U', '0', '1', 'U'),    -- 0
     (  '1', '1', '1', '1'),    -- 1
     (  'U', 'U', '1', 'U'));   -- Z
constant TABLE_NAND: MVL_2D_TABLE :=
    --   U    0    1    Z
    ((  'U', '1', 'U', 'U'),    -- U
     (  '1', '1', '1', '1'),    -- 0
     (  'U', '1', '0', 'U'),    -- 1
     (  'U', '1', 'U', 'U'));   -- Z
constant TABLE_NOR: MVL_2D_TABLE :=
    --   U    0    1    Z
    ((  'U', 'U', '0', 'U'),    -- U
     (  'U', '1', '0', 'U'),    -- 0
     (  '0', '0', '0', '0'),    -- 1
     (  'U', 'U', '0', 'U'));   -- Z
constant TABLE_XOR: MVL_2D_TABLE :=
    --   U    0    1    Z
    ((  'U', 'U', 'U', 'U'),    -- U
     (  'U', '0', '1', 'U'),    -- 0
     (  'U', '1', '0', 'U'),    -- 1
     (  'U', 'U', 'U', 'U'));   -- Z
constant TABLE_NOT: MVL_1D_TABLE :=
    --   U    0    1    Z
    (   'U', '1', '0', 'U');
constant TABLE_BUF: MVL_1D_TABLE :=
    --   U    0    1    Z
    (   'U', '0', '1', 'U');

-- Truth tables for resolution functions:
constant TABLE_TAND: MVL_2D_TABLE :=
    --   U    0    1    Z
    ((  'U', '0', 'U', 'U'),    -- U
     (  '0', '0', '0', '0'),    -- 0
     (  'U', '0', '1', '1'),    -- 1
     (  'U', '0', '1', 'Z'));   -- Z
constant TABLE_TOR: MVL_2D_TABLE :=
    --   U    0    1    Z
```

```
((   'U',  'U',  '1',  'U'),      -- U
 (   'U',  '0',  '1',  '0'),      -- 0
 (   '1',  '1',  '1',  '1'),      -- 1
 (   'U',  '0',  '1',  'Z'));     -- Z
```

-- Overloaded logical operator declarations on MVL type:
function "and"   (L, R: MVL) **return** MVL;
function "or"   (L, R: MVL) **return** MVL;
function "nand"   (L, R: MVL) **return** MVL;
function "nor"   (L, R: MVL) **return** MVL;
function "xor"   (L, R: MVL) **return** MVL;
function "not"   (L: MVL) **return** MVL;

-- Overloaded logical operator declarations on MVL_VECTOR type:
function "and"   (L, R: MVL_VECTOR) **return** MVL_VECTOR;
function "or"   (L, R: MVL_VECTOR) **return** MVL_VECTOR;
function "nand"   (L, R: MVL_VECTOR) **return** MVL_VECTOR;
function "nor"   (L, R: MVL_VECTOR) **return** MVL_VECTOR;
function "xor"   (L, R: MVL_VECTOR) **return** MVL_VECTOR;
function "not"   (L: MVL_VECTOR) **return** MVL_VECTOR;

-- Common utilities:
function MAX   (T1, T2: TIME) **return** TIME;
function INT2MVL (OPD, NO_BITS: INTEGER)
    return MVL_VECTOR;
function MVL2INT (OPD: MVL_VECTOR) **return** INTEGER;

-- Overloaded arithmetic operators on MVL_VECTOR:
function "+"   (L, R: MVL_VECTOR) **return** MVL_VECTOR;
function "*"   (L, R: MVL_VECTOR) **return** MVL_VECTOR;

-- Clock functions:
function ES_RISING   (**signal** CLOCK_NAME: MVL)
    return BOOLEAN;
function ES_FALLING   (**signal** CLOCK_NAME: MVL)
    return BOOLEAN;

-- Bus resolution functions:
function WIRED_AND (SIG_DRIVERS: MVL_VECTOR)
    return MVL;
function WIRED_OR (SIG_DRIVERS: MVL_VECTOR)
    return MVL;
end ATT_PACKAGE;

package body ATT_PACKAGE **is**
    -- Function definitions for overloaded operators with MVL types:

```
function "and" (L, R: MVL) return MVL is
begin
    return TABLE_AND(L, R);
end "and";
function "or" (L, R: MVL) return MVL is
begin
    return TABLE_OR(L, R);
end "or";
function "nand" (L, R: MVL) return MVL is
begin
    return TABLE_NAND(L, R);
end "nand";
function "nor" (L, R: MVL) return MVL is
begin
    return TABLE_NOR(L, R);
end "nor";
function "xor" (L, R: MVL) return MVL is
begin
    return TABLE_XOR(L, R);
end "xor";
function "not" (L: MVL) return MVL is
begin
    return TABLE_NOT(L);
end "not";

-- Function definitions for MVL_VECTOR types:
function "and" (L, R: MVL_VECTOR) return MVL_VECTOR is
    variable RESULT: MVL_VECTOR(L'LENGTH-1 downto 0);
begin
    assert L'LENGTH = R'LENGTH;
    for K in RESULT'RANGE loop
        RESULT(K) := TABLE_AND (L(K), R(K));
    end loop;
    return RESULT;
end "and";
function "or" (L, R: MVL_VECTOR) return MVL_VECTOR is
    variable RESULT: MVL_VECTOR(L'LENGTH-1 downto 0);
begin
    assert L'LENGTH = R'LENGTH;
    for K in RESULT'RANGE loop
        RESULT(K) := TABLE_OR (L(K), R(K));
    end loop;
    return RESULT;
end "or";
function "nand" (L, R: MVL_VECTOR) return MVL_VECTOR is
    variable RESULT: MVL_VECTOR(L'LENGTH-1 downto 0);
begin
```

```
      assert L'LENGTH = R'LENGTH;
      for K in RESULT'RANGE loop
          RESULT(K) := TABLE_NAND (L(K), R(K));
      end loop;
      return RESULT;
  end "nand";
  function "nor" (L, R: MVL_VECTOR) return MVL_VECTOR is
      variable RESULT: MVL_VECTOR(L'LENGTH-1 downto 0);
  begin
      assert L'LENGTH = R'LENGTH;
      for K in RESULT'RANGE loop
          RESULT(K) := TABLE_NOR (L(K), R(K));
      end loop;
      return RESULT;
  end "nor";
  function "xor" (L, R: MVL_VECTOR) return MVL_VECTOR is
      variable RESULT: MVL_VECTOR(L'LENGTH-1 downto 0);
  begin
      assert L'LENGTH = R'LENGTH;
      for K in RESULT'RANGE loop
          RESULT(K) := TABLE_XOR (L(K), R(K));
      end loop;
      return RESULT;
  end "xor";
  function "not" (L: MVL_VECTOR) return MVL_VECTOR is
      variable RESULT: MVL_VECTOR(L'LENGTH-1 downto 0);
  begin
      for K in RESULT'RANGE loop
          RESULT(K) := TABLE_NOT (L(K));
      end loop;
      return RESULT;
  end "not";

  -- Common utilities:
  function MAX      (T1, T2: TIME) return TIME is
  begin
      if (T1 > T2) then
          return T1;
      else
          return T2;
      end if;
  end MAX;
  function INT2MVL (OPD, NO_BITS: INTEGER)
          return MVL_VECTOR is
      variable M1: INTEGER;
      variable RET: MVL_VECTOR (NO_BITS-1 downto 0)
                  := (others => '0');
```

```
begin
    assert OPD >= 0;
    M1 := OPD;
    for J in RET'REVERSE_RANGE loop
        if (M1 mod 2) = 1 then
            RET(J) := '1';
        else
            RET(J) := '0';
        end if;
        M1 := M1 / 2;
    end loop;
    return RET;
end INT2MVL;
function MVL2INT (OPD: MVL_VECTOR) return INTEGER is
    -- Leftmost is LSB.
    variable TEMP, J: INTEGER;
begin
    assert OPD'LENGTH < 32;
    TEMP := 0;
    J := OPD'LENGTH - 1;
    for M3 in OPD'RANGE loop
        if OPD(M3) = '1' then
            TEMP := TEMP + 2 ** J;
        end if;
        J := J - 1;
    end loop;
    return TEMP;
end MVL2INT;

-- Overloaded arithmetic operators on MVL_VECTOR:
function "+"       (L, R: MVL_VECTOR) return MVL_VECTOR is
    -- Assume 0 is LSB; unsigned numbers.
    variable SUM: MVL_VECTOR (L'LENGTH-1 downto 0);
    variable CARRY: MVL := '0';
begin
    assert L'LENGTH = R'LENGTH;
    for J in SUM'REVERSE_RANGE loop
        SUM(J) := L(J) xor R(J) xor CARRY;
        CARRY := (L(J) and R(J)) or (L(J) and CARRY) or
                 (R(J) and CARRY);
    end loop;
    return SUM;
end "+";
function "*"       (L, R: MVL_VECTOR) return MVL_VECTOR is
    -- Unsigned numbers being multiplied; result < 32 bits.
    variable T1, T2, R_SIZE: INTEGER;
begin
```

```
        assert L'LENGTH < 32 and R'LENGTH < 32;
        T1 := MVL2INT (L);
        T2 := MVL2INT (R);
        R_SIZE = L'LENGTH + R'LENGTH;
        if (R_SIZE > 31) then
            R_SIZE := 31;
        end if;
        return INT2MVL (T1 * T2, R_SIZE);
end "*";


-- Clock functions:
function ES_RISING      (signal CLOCK_NAME: MVL)
        return BOOLEAN is
begin
    return (CLOCK_NAME = '1') and (CLOCK_NAME'EVENT);
end ES_RISING;
function ES_FALLING     (signal CLOCK_NAME: MVL)
        return BOOLEAN is
begin
    return (CLOCK_NAME = '0') and (CLOCK_NAME'EVENT);
end ES_FALLING;


-- Bus resolution functions:
function WIRED_AND (SIG_DRIVERS: MVL_VECTOR)
        return MVL is
    constant MEMORY: MVL := 'Z';
    variable RESOLVE_VALUE: MVL;
    variable FIRST: BOOLEAN := TRUE;
begin
    if SIG_DRIVERS'LENGTH = 0 then
        return MEMORY;
    else
        for I in SIG_DRIVERS'RANGE loop
            if (FIRST = TRUE) then
                RESOLVE_VALUE := SIG_DRIVERS(I);
                FIRST := FALSE;
            else
                RESOLVE_VALUE := TABLE_TAND
                        (RESOLVE_VALUE, SIG_DRIVERS(I));
            end if;
        end loop;
        return RESOLVE_VALUE;
    end if;
end WIRED_AND;
function WIRED_OR (SIG_DRIVERS: MVL_VECTOR)
        return MVL is
    constant MEMORY: MVL := 'Z';
```

```
            variable RESOLVE_VALUE: MVL;
            variable FIRST: BOOLEAN := TRUE;
        begin
            if SIG_DRIVERS'LENGTH = 0 then
                return MEMORY;
            else
                for K in SIG_DRIVERS'RANGE loop
                    if (FIRST = TRUE) then
                        RESOLVE_VALUE := SIG_DRIVERS(K);
                        FIRST := FALSE;
                    else
                        RESOLVE_VALUE := TABLE_TOR
                                (RESOLVE_VALUE, SIG_DRIVERS(K));
                    end if;
                end loop;
                return RESOLVE_VALUE;
            end if;
        end WIRED_OR;
    end ATT_PACKAGE;
```

❏

Bibliography

Following is a list of suggested readings and books on the language. The list is not intended to be comprehensive.

1. Armstrong, J. R., *Chip-level Modeling with VHDL*, Englewood Cliffs, NJ: Prentice Hall, 1988.
2. Armstrong, J.R. et al., *The VHDL validation suite*, Proc. 27th Design Automation Conference, June 1990, pp. 2-7.
3. Barton, D., *A first course in VHDL*, VLSI Systems Design, January 1988.
4. Bhasker, J., *Process-Graph Analyzer: A front-end tool for VHDL behavioral synthesis*, Software Practice and Experience, vol. 18, no. 5, May 1988.
5. Bhasker, J., *An algorithm for microcode compaction of VHDL behavioral descriptions*, Proc. 20th Microprogramming Workshop, December 1987.
6. Coelho, D., *The VHDL handbook*, Boston: Kluwer Academic, 1988.
7. Coelho, D., *VHDL: A call for standards*, Proc. 25th Design Automation Conference, June 1988.
8. Farrow, R., and A. Stanculescu, *A VHDL compiler based on attribute grammar methodology*, SIGPLAN 1989.
9. Gilman, A.S., *Logic Modeling in WAVES*, IEEE Design & Test of Computers, June 1990, pp. 49-55.
10. Hands, J.P., *What is VHDL?* Computer-Aided Design, vol. 22, no. 4, May 1990.
11. Hines, J., *Where VHDL fits within the CAD environment*, Proc. 24th Design Automation Conference, 1987.

12. *IEEE Standard VHDL Language Reference Manual, Std 1076-1987*, IEEE, NY, 1988.

13. *IEEE Standard 1076 VHDL Tutorial*, CLSI, Maryland, March 1989.

14. Kim, K., and J. Trout, *Automatic insertion of BIST hardware using VHDL*, Proc. 25th Design Automation Conference, 1988.

15. Leung, *ASIC system design with VHDL*, Boston: Kluwer Academic, 1989.

16. Lipsett, R., et. al., *VHDL: Hardware description and design*, Boston: Kluwer Academic, 1989.

17. Moughzail, M., et. al., *Experience with the VHDL environment*, Proc. 25th Design Automation Conference, 1988.

18. Perry, D., *VHDL*, New York: McGraw Hill, 1991.

19. *Military Standard 454*, 1988 US Government Printing Office.

20. Saunders, L., *The IBM VHDL design system*, Proc. 24th Design Automation Conference, 1987.

21. Schoen, J.M., *Performance and fault modeling with VHDL*, Englewood Cliffs, NJ: Prentice Hall, 1992.

22. Ward, P.C., and J. Armstrong, *Behavioral fault simulation in VHDL*, Proc. 27th Design Automation Conference, June 1990, pp. 587-593.

❑

Index

❑